# ROUTLEDGE LIBRARY EDITIONS: JORDAN

Volume 4

# POLITICS AND THE MILITARY IN JORDAN

# POLITICS AND THE MILITARY IN JORDAN

A Study of the Arab Legion
1921–1957

P. J. VATIKIOTIS

LONDON AND NEW YORK

First published in 1967 by Frank Cass and Company Limited

This edition first published in 2017
by Routledge
2 Park Square, Milton Park, Abingdon, Oxon OX14 4RN

and by Routledge
711 Third Avenue, New York, NY 10017

*Routledge is an imprint of the Taylor & Francis Group, an informa business*

© 1967 P. J. Vatikiotis

All rights reserved. No part of this book may be reprinted or reproduced or utilised in any form or by any electronic, mechanical, or other means, now known or hereafter invented, including photocopying and recording, or in any information storage or retrieval system, without permission in writing from the publishers.

*Trademark notice*: Product or corporate names may be trademarks or registered trademarks, and are used only for identification and explanation without intent to infringe.

*British Library Cataloguing in Publication Data*
A catalogue record for this book is available from the British Library

ISBN: 978-1-138-62955-4 (Set)
ISBN: 978-1-315-20177-1 (Set) (ebk)
ISBN: 978-1-138-70645-3 (Volume 4) (hbk)
ISBN: 978-1-138-70647-7 (Volume 4) (pbk)
ISBN: 978-1-315-20178-8 (Volume 4) (ebk)

**Publisher's Note**
The publisher has gone to great lengths to ensure the quality of this reprint but points out that some imperfections in the original copies may be apparent.

**Disclaimer**
The publisher has made every effort to trace copyright holders and would welcome correspondence from those they have been unable to trace.

# POLITICS AND THE MILITARY IN JORDAN

A STUDY OF THE ARAB LEGION
1921–1957

P. J. VATIKIOTIS

FRANK CASS & CO. LTD.
1967

First published in 1967 by
FRANK CASS AND COMPANY LIMITED
67 Great Russell Street, London WC1

Copyright © 1967 P. J. Vatikiotis

Printed in Great Britain by
Billing & Sons Limited, Guildford and London

TO
THE BRITISH OFFICERS WHO TRAINED
AND COMMANDED THE LEGION
UNTIL 1956
AND TO THEIR ARAB SUCCESSORS

# Contents

PREFACE ix

CHRONOLOGY xi

*Chapter I*
INTRODUCTION 1
  1. Some Relevant Data for the Study of the Military 8
  2. A Brief Note on Sources 13
  3. Some General Preliminary Formulations 15

## PART I

*Chapter II*
HISTORICAL BACKGROUND OF THE FIRST ADMINISTRATION IN TRANSJORDAN: THE EMIRATE 1923–1928 33

*Chapter III*
THE PRESENT POLITICAL SYSTEM. A BRIEF SURVEY 46
  1. The Mandate Period 1921–1946 47
  2. The Independent Kingdom, Phase I, 1946–1948 49
  3. The Independent Kingdom, Phase II, 1948–1956 51

## PART II

*Chapter IV*
THE BEGINNINGS AND EVOLUTION OF THE LEGION 1921–1948 57

*Chapter V*
THE RAPID EXPANSION OF THE LEGION 1948–1956 75

## PART III

*Chapter VI*
POLITICS AND THE LEGION 1948–1957 97

| | |
|---|---:|
| CONCLUSION | 137 |
| EPILOGUE | 155 |
| APPENDIX | 165 |
| INDEX | 167 |
| MAP OF JORDAN AND ITS BOUNDARIES | 18–19 |

# *Preface*

THIS monograph grew out of a study initially undertaken for a wider collaborative inquiry into the political role of the military with several colleagues in American universities. Professor John P. Lovell of the Department of Government, Indiana University, co-ordinated what was purely individual research on the military in a number of countries in Africa, East Asia, South and South-east Asia, and the Middle East. The particular research interest of this group is partially reflected in this monograph in my formulations about the military in Jordan and in Part III dealing with politics and the military.

As a study in civil-military relations, this is only an intensive examination of one case in the setting of Jordan. As such, therefore, it does not seek to generalise about these relations everywhere. Instead, the study attempts to gauge these relations by the performance of the military in Jordan in the period 1921–1957. Even though to the extent that it can be determined, the social background of army officers is described and discussed, the emphasis in this study, however, is on the performance of these officers in certain political situations.

Briefly, this is an inquiry consisting of three parts. In addition to a general introduction which tries to set the context of the study, the first part of the inquiry is a general consideration of the peculiar historical conditions from which a state emerged in Jordan, and the role of the Arab Legion in its creation and consolidation. The second part describes the beginnings of the Arab Legion, its evolution and development from 1921 to 1957. Illustrative material on the organisation, structure, and composition of the Legion during the period of its greatest and most rapid expansion (1948–1956) is also presented here. Finally, the performance and involvement of the Legion in the politically turbulent period (1954–1957) is discussed in some detail. Here an attempt is made to assess the role of the Legion in maintaining the integrity of the regime in Jordan at a time when the integration of west and east Jordan was at its most problematic and dangerous stage.

For information about the rapid expansion of the Legion in the period 1948–1956, I am grateful for the assistance of several British officers who had served with the Legion, among them Major-General Lunt, Brigadier Peter Young, Brigadier Elliott, Colonel Walden, Colonel Vaines, Lieut.-Colonel Blackden, Major Horne and Major

Freeman. I have also had the benefit of the views and wise counsel of Sir Alec Kirkbride, especially on the early days of the Transjordan Principality and the long reign of the late King Abdullah. Sir Alec and Brigadier Young read the first draft of the monograph in its entirety and offered valuable comments and criticism for its improvement. So did Professor Morris Janowitz of Chicago University. I owe, however, a special debt of gratitude to Lieut.-General Sir John Glubb for his extensive comments and criticisms which helped me to avoid many errors.

My colleagues Professors Bernard Lewis and Ernest Gellner read the manuscript and made many suggestions for its improvement. Professor Gellner in particular made extensive comments about the crucial problem of establishing a viable central authority in areas, or countries, where the prevailing ethos is that of a tribal society. Another of my colleagues, Lieut.-Colonel H. Moyse-Bartlett, Secretary of the School of Oriental and African Studies, brought to my attention technical military literature relevant to my study, and helped me to secure it.

While I gratefully acknowledge my debt to all the persons mentioned above and many others I have not named, I remain solely responsible for any errors of fact, and for the views expressed in this study.

P. J. V.

December 1966

# Chronology of Events
## 1920–1957

| | |
|---|---|
| 11 November 1920 | Abdullah arrives at Maan from the Hejaz |
| 2 March 1921 | Abdullah enters Amman and sets up his first "private" government |
| 28 March 1921 | Churchill–Abdullah talks in Jerusalem which led to the formation of the Principality of Transjordan under Amir Abdullah |
| 21 April 1921 | First administration of the Principality headed by Rashīd Ṭaliʿ as Administrative Secretary; Arab Legion founded |
| May 1921 | Incident of the Kūra rebellion |
| March 1922 | New government and administration headed by Rikābī Pasha, an ex-officer and political leader in the short-lived Arab Government of Faysal in Damascus |
| July 1922 | British mandate over Transjordan declared |
| 25 March 1923 | British–Transjordanian Agreement providing for an autonomous administration under Abdullah |
| April 1923 | First Advisory Council (administration) and Legislative Assembly formed |
| March 1924 | Annexation of Maan and Aqaba and their incorporation into the new Principality after their cession by King Husayn of the Hejaz |
| November 1925 | Frontier agreements with Nejd and Hejaz |
| 1926 | Kirkbride appointed Financial Adviser to Transjordan government; Transjordan Frontier Force (TJFF) formed by an Order of the British High Commissioner in Jerusalem; Legion strength cut down |
| 20 February 1928 | A new agreement between Transjordan and Britain signed in Jerusalem which provided for further autonomy of the Principality |
| 16 April 1928 | First Organic Law of Transjordan |

| | |
|---|---|
| July 1928 | First National Congress and the formation of political parties |
| 2 April 1929 | Elections for the first Legislative Council; Formation of an Executive Council (government) |
| November 1930 | Desert Patrol Force organised under the command of Major John Bagot Glubb |
| 1931 | Second Legislative Council elected |
| 21 March 1933 | Diplomatic relations with Saudi Arabia established |
| June 1934 | Amendment of the February 1928 Anglo-Transjordanian Agreement |
| October 1934 | Elections for Third Legislative Council |
| 1936–1937 | Arab Rebellion in Palestine began; Britain approves formation of a Reserve Force to strengthen Arab Legion; Mechanised Desert Force formed |
| 5 August 1939 | Executive Council formally became a Council of Ministers |
| March 1939 | General F. Peake retired as Commander of the Arab Legion and was succeeded by Glubb. Brigadier Norman Lash succeeded Glubb as O.C., Desert Force, and became Deputy Commander, Arab Legion |
| May–June 1941 | Participation of Arab Legion units in HABFORCE against Rashid Ali government in Baghdad, and in campaign against the Vichy forces in Syria |
| November 1941 | New Anglo-Transjordanian Agreement concluded in Jerusalem, removing previous limitations upon strengthening of the Arab Legion |
| June 1942 | Elections for Fifth Legislative Council |
| 1945 | Desert Force strengthened from one to three regiments under a division headquarters; Azraq Base Training Camp formed; Purchase of vehicles and other transport from the United States of America |
| 22 March 1946 | Proclamation of independent Kingdom of Jordan after the conclusion of a new Anglo–Jordanian Agreement |

| | |
|---|---|
| February 1947 | New Constitution to replace 1928 Organic Law; King Abdullah Supreme Commander of the Arab Legion; General Glubb designated Chief of the General Staff, Arab Legion |
| April 1947 | New Electoral Law |
| 20 October 1947 | Elections for First National Assembly |
| 15 March 1948 | New Anglo-Jordanian Treaty: limited British military presence in the country to airfields at Mafraq and Amman; Reappearance of political parties |
| 14 May 1948 | On the eve of the Arab–Israeli War in Palestine, Arab Legion units mass in Jordan Valley at Shuna near Jericho; Opening of military road Jericho–Bettīn–Ramalla–Bab el–Wad–Jerusalem; speeded up construction of another Jericho–Beit Sahur–Bethlehem |
| 15 May 1948 | Arab Legion units cross the river Jordan via Allenby Bridge |
| 11 June 1948 | First truce of Palestine War. Legion in control of Old City in Jerusalem |
| 9 July 1948 | Resumption of hostilities |
| 18 July 1948 | Second truce |
| February 1949 | Jordanian Armistice Delegation for Rhodes: Col. Ahmad Sudqi al–Jundi—Head of Delegation Col. Muhammad al–Maʿāyiṭa Major Rādī Hindāwi Captain Ali Abu Nuwār Two legal advisers |
| March 1949 | Military government in Central Palestine controlled by Arab Legion replaced by a civilian administration |
| 3 April 1949 | Jordan–Israel armistice signed |
| November–December 1948 | Palestine Congress in Amman and Jericho Congress. Palestinian leaders accept incorporation into the Kingdom of Jordan, and express their allegiance to King Abdullah |
| May 1949 | First Jordanian cabinet with three Palestinians in it |

| | |
|---|---|
| April 1950 | First elections after the joining of the two banks, with representatives from the Palestine sector |
| 24 April 1950 | Unification of the two banks officially approved by Parliament |
| 20 July 1951 | King Abdullah assassinated while entering Aqsā Mosque in Jerusalem for Friday prayers. Succeeded to the throne by his son Crown Prince Talal |
| January 1952 | New constitution superseding one of 1947 |
| February 1952 | Arab Baath Party, led by Abdullah al-Rīmāwī formed |
| September 1952 | King Talal deposed on grounds of mental illness |
| April 1953 | King Husayn ascends the throne |
| 13 November 1953 | Israeli army attacks Qibya village |
| 28 March 1954 | Israeli army attacks Nahālīn village |
| May 1954 | Attempt to form a National Front Party prevented by the government |
| July 1954 | National Socialist Party founded. Its first secretary-general the late Hazzāʿ al-Majālī resigned in October, and succeeded by Sulaymān al-Nābulsī |
| April–October 1955 | Military discussions between King, Government and GHQ regarding a National Defence Plan, expansion and strengthening of the Army; Constitutional amendments strengthening the National Assembly *vis à vis* the cabinet and reducing term of office for members of the Senate (House of Notables) from eight to four years |
| October–December 1955 | Visits of Celal Bayar, President of Turkey, General Gerald Templer, British CIGS, and Field Marshal Abdel Hakīm Āmer of Egypt to Jordan |
| March 1956 | Dismissal of General Glubb; his replacement as CGS by Brigadier Rādī-ʿInnāb (now promoted to Major-General); Dismissal of Colonel Patrick Coghill as Chief of Intelligence; Dismissal of Brigadier Hutton, Chief of Operations, GHQ |

| | |
|---|---|
| May 1956 | Retirement of General 'Innāb; Ali Abū Nuwār new CGS of Jordan Army (now promoted to Major-General); Ali al-Ḥiyārī new Division Commander |
| July 1956 | Police and Darak (gendarmerie) forces removed from Army control and command. New Directorate of Public Security in charge of these two internal security forces established under Brigadier Bahjat Ṭabbāra. |
| October 1956 | Elections: National Socialist government under Sulaymān al-Nābulsī formed |
| 10–11 November 1956 | Israeli Army attack on Jordan Army positions in Qalqīliya |
| January 1957– February | Arab Collective Security Pact with Joint Military Command (Jordan–Egypt–Saudi Arabia–Syria) |
| March 1957 | Termination of Anglo-Jordanian 1948 Treaty |
| 8 April 1957 | 1 Armoured Car Regiment surrounds Amman |
| 9 April 1957 | Retirement of Ṭabbāra from post of Director General, Public Security ordered by Nabulsi government; Wide transfers of officials: General Muhammad Maʿāyiṭa appointed Director-General, Public Security; Nablus Chief of Police transferred to same post in Amman |
| 10 April 1957 | King asks for resignation of Nabulsi National Socialist government; Dr. Husayn Fakhri al-Khālidi unable to form new government; ʿAbd al-Ḥalīm Nimr (Interior and Defence Minister in dismissed Nabulsi government) also unable to form new government as a result of pressure from his party colleagues |
| 13 April 1957 | Said al-Muftī, President of the Senate, entrusted with formation of new government; Generals Ali Abū Nuwār, Ali al-Ḥiyārī, and Muhammad Maʿāyiṭa warn Muftī of Army unrest and deliver ultimatum to the effect that only the National Socialist ʿAbd |

|  |  |
|---|---|
|  | al–Halīm Nimr must form a government by 9 p.m. that evening;<br>Veiled ultimatum to King delivered at the Palace on the same day by a delegation from the National Socialist Party to form government headed by Nimr;<br>Amīra ʿĀliya Brigade ordered by its C.O., Brigadier Maʿn Abū Nuwār, to move without weapons to Wādī al–Batm, some 40 miles east of Zarqāʿ;<br>Clash between units and troops of 1 Armoured Car Regiment and Artillery Regiment in the Brigade leading to some casualties. |
| 14 April 1957 | After taking refuge in the home of the President of the Senate, ʿAli Abū Nuwār leaves for Syria;<br>King rejects resignations of Ḥiyārī and Maʿāyiṭa, and appoints Ḥiyārī Deputy CGS |
| 17 April 1957 | Ali Ḥiyārī appointed Army CGS |
| 18 April 1957 | Military Commission of Inquiry appointed under the chairmanship of Brigadier ʿIzzat Ḥasan to investigate events of 9–13 April; Eleven officers in Division HQ suspended for one month and placed under house arrest |
| 19 April 1957 | On pretext of a frontier meeting with the Syrian Army CGS Ḥiyārī absconds to Syria and telephones his resignation from his post as Army CGS;<br>Other officers, including General Maʿāyiṭa, fled to Syria;<br>General Ḥābis al–Majālī appointed new CGS |
| 25 April 1957 | After prolonged and often violent party activity against the régime (since April 1954), the government orders all political parties dissolved and bans their activities in the country |
| May–July 1957 | British evacuation of Mafraq and Aqaba |

CHAPTER I

# Introduction

A NUMBER of formulations about civil-military relations in the state have been in existence for a very long time. One of these relates to the possible role of the military in a situation of political instability—the provision of national leaders, sometimes saviours, in times of extreme national crisis. Another relates to the role of the army in the quelling of domestic political disturbances and in the defence of national frontiers against external aggression by the organised and disciplined use of force. Such military activity constitutes the ultimate sanction and coercive measure at the disposal of the legitimately constituted authority in the state.

These formulations are relevant to the study of the military in a polity where the functions and jurisdiction of its component institutions are legally and constitutionally allocated and specified. Under these conditions, a disturbance of the accepted norm in civil-military relations is considered deviant, an anomaly, and a reflection of serious trouble in the system. But in polities where these conditions do not obtain, it is somewhat unrealistic to study civil-military relations with the same assumptions. Much of what is said by Westerners about the role of the military, specifically its political involvement, in under-developed countries derives from the initial conception of the military as strictly an arm of the state, possessing specific functions and duties. We do not readily conceive of conspiracies among its ranks, because we do not expect it to govern, but only to serve government.[1] This fundamental attitude immediately gives rise to a number of other assumptions: for instance, a young man chooses the army for a career because he is primarily motivated by, among other things, service to his nation and state—to his country. He joins, that is, a professional organisation—the officer corps—of which he is presumably proud. He is above all

---

[1] I am not unaware of the political activities of the military in most advanced states in seeking the implementation of military policies by the state that are favourable to their organisation or institution: appropriations, advanced weapons, etc. But this is politics of a different kind and at a different level, and within the accepted institutional processes of a system, not necessarily aimed at overthrowing the existing regime, or political system.

loyal to his commander, to his regiment, and to his sovereign, whether that sovereign is institutionally and legitimately vested in a monarchy or a republic. The matter of serving "King and Country", "God and Fatherland", rests upon there being a prolonged socialisation (e.g., education, communal activity) of individuals and groups which inculcates in the members of the political community the veneration of these national and patriotic symbols. This process itself must, moreover, be expressed in workable institutions.[2]

One hardly expects such symbols of loyalty and structures for the institutional expression of allegiance to be developed—or even to exist—in societies, or countries, where the idea of a nation-state is so recent; or in regions where many sovereign states have emerged, or were deliberately created, in geographical contiguity to one another, amidst what their inhabitants consider to be one *umma* (their spiritual notion of the nation determined by the universalist tradition of Islam); where the tribal members of this "nation" find it difficult by custom and tradition to recognise legal boundaries that restrict their free movement; and where until recently the principle of legitimacy and the basis of loyalty were based upon a religious identity and determined by membership in a religious community. For many centuries the ideological commitment of this religious community carried with it the assumption of a universal political realm. The commitment was rigid and ambitious, whereas its political dominion was never realised. Nevertheless, it withstood the pressure and rejected the idea of the nation-state until barely seventy-five years ago. When the nation-state as the organisational unit of a sovereign political order finally came to these societies less than fifty years ago, it was largely the result of a combination of circumstances and the outcome of a series of events upon neither of which the native general public had great influence or control. Nor did they appear to have a choice in the matter of their new political order. Two European Great Powers—Britain and France—practically imposed a new political order in the area known as the Fertile Crescent, consisting of quasi-autonomous and mandated territories.

The break-up of the Ottoman Empire in 1918 represented the destruction of the last great Muslim imperial order. It also marked the rejection by Muslim leaders of that time of a rigid Islamic ideology with universalist political claims. A small group of educated Arabs throughout the Arab provinces of this empire which constituted the Fertile Crescent had, since the 1870s and more actively

---

[2] See Samuel P. Huntington *The Soldier and The State* (New York, 1964), ch. 1. See also on this matter Alfred de Vigny, *The Military Condition* (*Servitude et grandeur militaires*, 1835), translated by Marguerite Barnett (London, 1964).

since the turn of the century, begun a revival of an Arab sentiment of identity distinct from the Ottoman one and sought to achieve autonomy within that great empire via decentralisation. At the instigation of Britain in the Great War and with her financial support an Arab Revolt was raised by the Sharif Husayn of Mecca—a religious-dynastic leader—against their ruler-caliph in Istanbul. Some Arab officers serving in the Ottoman armies joined this revolt. With the imminent destruction of the Empire at the hands of the Allies, and with the encouragement of wartime British promises of an Arab kingdom, initial Arab aspirations for autonomy were quickly transformed to demands for independence in an Arab dynastic state.

The subsequent fragmentation at the end of the war of the greater Arab state (desired and expected by the leaders of the Arab Revolt, 1916–1918) was dictated by the interests of the Great Powers. It produced such states as Iraq, Greater Lebanon, Syria, Transjordan. Except in Lebanon perhaps, there were in these states no mature developed political institutions to cope with the problems of independence. The people living in them had been subjects of the Ottoman Sultan, who was represented in the various areas by governors and other officials appointed from Istanbul. The administrative machinery of government was supervised by high Turkish, as well as Arab, Ottoman officials assisted by many local Arabs in its service. When a parliament came into being in Istanbul in 1908, Arab representatives from such provinces as the Hejaz, Syria, and Iraq were elected to it. At the same time political groups and parties with Arab separatist and nationalist aspirations were then of recent origin and secretly organised to avoid detection and persecution by the Ottoman authorities. Originally, these aimed at securing further political rights for the Arabs from the Ottoman Padishah.

In the territory which came to be known after the First World War as Transjordan political inexperience was coupled to a tribal society which comprised both settled and nomadic beduin tribes. Ever since the destruction of Mamluk power in Egypt and Syria by the Ottoman Turks in 1517, this area remained the unruly domain of warring tribes. It was only with the greatest of difficulty that the Ottoman authorities were able, from time to time, to extend their influence and impose their control upon this area south of Syria and east of Palestine. Raiding between tribes, and the raiding by tribes of settled communities of cultivators in villages and small towns, were common occurrences. The regions in the north-west and all lands lying west of Kerak and Ma'an in the south were frequent victims of beduin raids. So were the government garrisons established by the Turkish authorities in the nineteenth century when they sought to extend their control southwards in order to protect the pilgrimage route to Mecca. The tribesman—both settled and nomadic—was rarely willing to pay taxes. Rather the beduin taxed the cultivator in the form of blackmail payment in return for leaving him unmolested. The willingness of the beduin to pay tax symbolised and meant submission to the representative of central power. This did occur occasionally. It usually followed a punitive military expedition by Ottoman forces against a particular tribe or group. But tribal defeat and temporary submission to central authority were usually accompanied by a government subsidy to the tribal chief, who in turn promised to keep his tribe in check for a while. Thus, while the effective pacification of the tribes in Transjordan by the Ottoman authorities was never really achieved, relations between these groups continued to be expressed in tribal customary law and practice, not in any elaborate codified legal arrangements.[3]

Under these conditions it is essential to realise that political control over tribal society could be achieved by the dual use of force and conciliation. The Ottomans had employed both approaches, but without total or continued success. The latter technique took the form of financial concessions (subsidies to tribal chiefs, and often outright bribes) by the government, and special privileges with regard to land and administration. Where Ottoman power and administration were able to establish themselves certain tribal groups tended to settle down to agricultural pursuits and to become sedentary communities in villages or towns. After the establishment of the Amir Abdullah in Amman in 1921, the same pattern with regard to the tribal issue was followed. But, as will be shown, with greater success. Side by side with force, the Amir in Amman bestowed upon tribal chiefs honorific titles and appointed some of them to positions in his incipient central government. Within less than a decade after his founding of the Principality, the more restless and truculent tribes in the south and east had been pacified. Most of them settled as part of a larger state entity. All these developments took place in Jordan, and to a great extent, if not primarily, through the efforts of the Arab Legion, assisted in the early years (1921–1930) by the Royal Air Force (RAF). Where the Ottomans had previously failed, Amir Abdullah and his Arab Legion, with British help, succeeded.[4]

---

[3] For some illustrative details of this tribal problem, see the section below on the Historical Background of the First Political System. See also F. G. Peake, *History and Tribes of Jordan* (Miami, Florida, 1958), esp. pp. 84–97 and 105–109.
[4] In 1935 there were an estimated 200,000 beduins in the Transjordan area. As a result of the government's efforts to evolve an agricultural and land settlement

While Jordan has been an independent sovereign state only since 1946, its army dates back in one form or another to 1921. The army, that is, preceded the emergence of a sovereign independent state in Jordan. In fact, one could argue in this case that the army created the state.[5] More significant still, the army was a vehicle and an instrument for the pacification and integration of a predominantly tribal society into a state to whose central authority the tribes became responsive and to whose administrative control they became subjected. The army has transformed nomadic and semi-nomadic tribesmen into disciplined soldiers and officers responsive to rational command and capable of sustained organised life. If restraint, both social and individual, is a mark of civilisation, then the army civilised the tribesman towards a measure of modernity by diverting his sense of tribal collectivity and *esprit de corps* into a sense of loyalty and a feeling of allegiance for a paramount chief—the monarch. From an occasional raider of other tribes or of settled agricultural communities for pillage and plunder, the tribesman has been transformed in the Legion into an expert professional in the organised and disciplined use of force for purposes determined and ordered by a central government. Instead of serving the Banu Sakhr, the Huweitat, the Majali, the Maʿāyiṭa, the Tarawina, or the Shamayila, the Mutair, Shammar, Ruwwala, or Aneiza tribes, he now serves the King and his government in Amman.

Although there are differences in the organisation and structure as well as operational history of the Legion between its early years and

---

policy, the nomadic groups among these gradually dwindled. Many remained semi-nomadic, but inclined more and more towards agricultural economy. Yet the problem of demarcating frontiers in the desert with neighbouring states, especially Saudi Arabia, in the 1920s and 1930s led inevitably to a restriction upon the beduin's traditional freedom of movement, i.e. his free migration across frontiers, which he had enjoyed in the past. See Eliahu Epstein, "The Bedouin of Trans-Jordan: their Social and Economic Problems", *Journal of the Royal Central Asian Society*, vol. 25 (April 1938), pp. 228–236. For later developments see Naval Intelligence Division, *Palestine and Trans-Jordan*, Geographical Handbook Series (December 1943). Generally, on the tribes of Transjordan, see F. G. Peake, *op. cit.*

[5] The embryonic Ministry of Defence of what was to become the State of Israel issued in 1948 immediately prior to the outbreak of hostilities between Israeli forces and the armies of the Arab states in May of that year a handbook on these Arab armies. This apparently was meant to acquaint the Israeli soldier with the imminent enemy. In the section on Jordan the handbook states clearly: "In Jordan there is an army which owns a state." See Agra (pseudonym), *The Armies of the Arab States in the context of their environment* (in Hebrew), Tel Aviv, 1948. (I am indebted to my colleague Professor Bernard Lewis for drawing my attention to this reference, as I do not read Hebrew. See also "The Armed Forces of Transjordan", *Maarakhot* (January 1948), pp. 87–133).

in the 1950s, the clear distinction in terms of its political role in the country must be emphasised. The evolution of the Legion from a police and gendarmerie force to a sophisticated army can, as was suggested above, be traced through distinct stages in its growth. From a "praetorian guard"[6] of a prince-ruler in the very early days (roughly 1921–1925) the Legion has developed since that time into an army of some importance to both Jordan and the neighbouring Arab states. The garrison state east of the river Jordan, maintained by the Legionnaires, who were trained and commanded by British officers, was enlarged when the Legion secured in 1948 a portion of Central Palestine. When this new territory west of the river Jordan was annexed and officially incorporated into the expanded Hashemite Kingdom of Jordan in April 1950, it posed new problems for both the government and the army. While this event was soon followed by a generally turbulent political period (1950–1956) for the country, it hastened the expansion and accelerated the transformation of the Legion itself from a *corps d'élite* to a substantial military institution. The intricate technical requirements for the logistical and administrative support organisations of a modern army entailed new departures in the recruitment and training methods for the Legion, not dissimilar to the deliberate measures taken by the civilian government in integrating a new population and society from the West Bank into the Kingdom's political life and establishment.

In its earlier history the function of the Legion was mainly to extend and impose the authority of Amman, i.e. of Prince Abdullah, over a fractious society. It also had to contend with tribal raids and inter-tribal conflict. Having done this its role was to maintain order and effective security. With the expansion of the kingdom's territory and the infusion of a new population, the political role of the Legion acquired new dimensions: namely, to prevent any successful challenge to the authority of its Commander-in-Chief, King Abdullah, and, after him, that of his grandson. In short, it now had the major task of protecting the dynasty, its regime and establishment from internal and external threats. But, for the first time also, this joining of Palestinians to Transjordanians exposed the Legion itself to new and dangerous political currents. The process of expansion itself, which became essential for the creation of a larger, more self-sufficient military institution carried similar dangers.

This process, however, cannot be investigated generally over the

---

[6] By "praetorian guard" I do not mean a palace guard in the literal sense. Rather the term I use here refers to the instrumentality of the Legion, especially in the first decade of its existence, at least, in extending and establishing the authority of Prince Abdullah over the country.

last forty-five years of the history of Transjordan and Jordan without distinguishing different stages in the development of the Legion. Thus one can study the Arab Legion as primarily an internal security police and desert patrol force in the period 1921–1940. Then, during the Second World War, the Legion presents itself as a military force consisting of a number of garrison units helping to guard British installations and communications in the Middle East. In the Palestine War in 1948 the Arab Legion appeared mainly as a *corps d'élite* fighting force. It consisted then of some five operational regiments, but lacked fully developed or elaborate technical and supporting services. Nor was it backed up by a force of reservists recruited from a system of national conscription. Most interesting and relevant for the purposes of this study is therefore the description of the transformation of the Legion from this state into an efficient military force during its period of greatest expansion from 1948 to 1956. From a body of eight to ten thousand men the Legion grew by 1956 into an establishment of some 25,000 officers and men. This included three Brigade Groups, a Division Headquarters, an Artillery Corps, Signal Corps, and Engineer Corps, together with an incipient Air Arm in the process of becoming a Royal Air Force.[7]

While it may be argued that many states in the Fertile Crescent were artificial creations of the European Powers who came to control the area at the end of World War I, Transjordan was perhaps the most artificial of them all. This beginning is now most interesting in itself as regards the Legion, for the maintenance of the State of Jordan is very much an accomplishment of the Legion. It is even more interesting today when related to the political changes that have accompanied the integration of that part of Palestine secured by the Legion in 1948. Although most of the integration so far has been undertaken in the civilian institutions of government, in the economic, financial, educational and social fields of state and national endeavour, some of it is being done in and through the Jordan Army. To have to depend now upon native—and largely ex-Palestinian—tradesmen for the manning of technical services in the military when once the Legion did so totally upon the British Armed Forces in the area is in itself an impressive and significant change. To have to

---

[7] By 1953 each of the three Brigade groups comprised three regiments, or a total of nine. Of these 1, 2, 3, 7, and 9 Regiments were beduin; 4, 5, 6, and 8 non-beduin, i.e. a ratio of 5:4 in favour of beduin. In March 1956 the strength of the Legion was one Division and one Armoured Brigade, or roughly ten fighting regiments. There were sixty-nine British officers in the Legion at that time, many of them seconded from the British army, and others on contract. After the dismissal of General Glubb only twenty-five of these had remained by May 1956 in technical and advisory positions. These too were eventually replaced.

depend, since March 1956, on a completely Arab GHQ, staff and line officers and NCOs for training, education and administration of the army is an equally revolutionary development in the Legion.

Given however the limited industrial base at best which a country like Jordan can ever have, it is difficult to say whether or not it can in the future continue to maintain such an army. It is also difficult to assert, given this limitation, that such an army can ever be a self-sufficient military institution beyond its basic garrison character. One of course finds no difficulty in preparing an impressively long list of small—and not so small—states in Asia and Africa that maintain sizeable armed forces without possessing the necessary national industrial base. This inadequacy is usually met with foreign technical assistance and military aid. It should not therefore concern us here and prevent us from an initial examination of civil-military relations in Jordan in so far as these can be observed from a study of the Legion.

## 1. SOME RELEVANT DATA FOR THE STUDY OF THE MILITARY

The area covered by the Hashemite Kingdom of Jordan is given as approximately 37,000 square miles. (Approximately, because of certain undemarcated desert areas in the east.) The West Bank, or that portion of Palestine incorporated into Jordan in 1948, occupies 2,165 square miles of this area. The remaining 34,000–35,000 square miles constitute the wide desert and highlands east of the river Jordan, or what used to be Transjordan and what is now referred to as the East Bank, or East Jordan.

As rainfall and cultivation are concentrated in the north-west corner of the country, seven-eighths of the population, estimated in 1963 at 1,860,443, live in less than one-eighth of the land area. This population complex extends from Amman north-westwards to the Balqa' and 'Ajlun districts, and includes the West Bank to the west of these. Of the remainder of the population, four-fifths live in sparsely settled town regions (Madaba, Kerak, Ma'an); one-fifth lives in the desert. Among the latter, pure nomads are now few; the vast majority consists of semi-nomads who leave their cultivated land only for the winter, returning in the spring for the harvest. Of these there are probably no more than 50,000–70,000 today.

Villagers number roughly half a million, living in about 1,200 villages and hamlets, 800 of which are in the West Bank. These people cultivate the lands immediately surrounding their villages and are economically almost completely dependent upon agriculture. Another

350,000 Jordanians constitute the so-called urban population in both banks of the country. The remainder live in town centres that do not quite exhibit purely urban characteristics, for in the smaller towns a substantial proportion of the inhabitants are engaged in agriculture. Until it lost much of its farmland to Israel, a town like Qalqiliya in the West Bank, for instance, resembled an "agrotown" in southern Italy. But it is always difficult to define precisely modes of living in Jordan.[8]

If one stretched a point, one could suggest that some 750,000 Jordanians, or roughly under half of the population, live in towns and cities of over 5,000 inhabitants. Most of these are concentrated in the Balqa' and 'Ajlun districts in East Jordan and in Jerusalem–Ramallah, Nablus–Jenin–Tulkarem, and Hebron in West Jordan. In this sense, whereas the country's area is largely desert and the overall population density about twenty to the square mile, this density in the north-western population centre of five to six thousand square miles is about 800 to the square mile. Statistically then today about 43 per cent of Jordan's population is urban; 52 per cent is rural; and 5 per cent is tent-living nomadic and semi-nomadic. The most fully urban districts are Amman and Jerusalem.

It is socially and economically significant that the state more than trebled its population in 1948 with the annexation of Arab Palestine. From an original population of approximately 400,000, clearly divided between nomads and semi-nomads of the desert on the one hand and primarily settled rural (hardly any urban) inhabitants on the other, Jordan in 1948 acquired an additional 1·1 million people. Of these roughly half a million were refugees; about 450,000 were actual residents of the West Bank that was secured by the Arab Legion in the Palestine War; and some 100,000 were Arabs from other parts of Palestine who, because of the course of the hostilities or as a result of Israeli military action, had somehow managed to move into the West Bank area controlled by the Legion, but not as completely destitute refugees.

Even the Jordan Census is not clear on how one defines a refugee. The published Census for 1961 states: "Not all Palestinian refugees are resident in camps . . ."[9] Furthermore, no data were collected on

---

[8] "The line dividing the urban from the rural sedentary population is not a clear one in Jordan. . . " See the Hashemite Kingdom of Jordan Department of Statistics, *First Census of Population and Housing* (18 November 1961), vol. 3, Final Tables (August 1964), p. xvi. Another difficulty in definitions recognised by the Census is the fact that nomadism and village life merge among the semi-nomads, "and the larger villages and smaller towns show characteristics of both rural and urban life" (*ibid.*, p. ix).

[9] See *Census for 1961, op. cit.*, p. xvi and n. 1, and p. x.

refugee status for that Census. "The inhabitants of Palestinian refugee camps are a distinct category, but cannot be presented as such because of a commitment by the department not to reveal the numbers reported."[10] Yet Palestinian refugee camps lying outside towns are included in the rural population calculations, whereas for urban localities of over 10,000 inhabitants nearby areas inhabited by Palestinian refugees were excluded from the census. Thus if 30 per cent of Palestine refugees live in UNRWA camps, these are not included in the Census. But if, say, about 350,000 Palestinian refugees went to live on border villages (on the frontier with Israel, that is) along with an indigenous rural population of 120,000, these are included in the Census.

Apart from the difficult problem of the refugees, there was the infusion into the commercial, professional and political stream of society of over 100,000 skilled and educated Palestinians. Before this, the East Jordanian settled population was relatively homogeneous in ethnic and religious terms. Most of them were the descendants of tribes that had emigrated from the east and the overwhelming majority was Sunni Muslim Arab. Although the Palestinian population added in 1948 was predominantly Muslim, it still increased the number of Christians in the country to over 110,000.

Then, under the mandate, that part of Palestine which was annexed by Jordan was agriculturally dependent upon the plains to the north which now lie is Israel. Moreover, villagers on the Israeli frontier whose agricultural lands—or a large proportion of these— were placed in Israeli territory, or split in the middle between Israel and Jordan by the armistice agreements, lost their source of livelihood. This condition has been not only a source of bitterness ever since, but also the cause of infiltration by these villagers to grab when they can what they consider to be rightfully theirs.[11]

For purposes of this study it suffices to note that in the period 1950–1957 the largest item in Jordan's budget was that of the Arab Legion, i.e. defence and security. The Legion spent more than all the other government departments combined, the figure rising, for example, from £4,898,000 in 1951 (total budget expenditure for that year was £9,763,000) to £12,272,000 in 1957 (total budget expenditure for that year was £23,181,000).[12] A British annual subsidy and loans

---

[10] *Ibid.*
[11] See on this question, N.C., "Jordan's Frontier Villages, the scene of border tension", *The World Today*, vol. 9 (1953), No. 11, pp. 467–475.
[12] The budget announced for the period 1 April–31 December 1966 estimates a total expenditure of approximately £51 million, almost equally divided between departmental and development appropriation. Of the former, roughly half was

covered practically the total figure of this item. Thus, if in 1956 the total budget was roughly £23 million, £12·5 million of this represented the British subsidy. Of the latter, just over £9 million went to the army, £2 million (in approximate round figures) went to the Development Board, and about £1 million was used to cover the budget deficit. In contrast the Regular Ministries' total budget was £7·7 million, and this was financed wholly by taxes (direct and indirect), fees, and other internal revenue. Income tax in this case provided about half of the direct tax revenue, while customs duties produced about 60 per cent of the indirect taxation revenue. In addition to all this the United Nations Relief and Works Agency provided about £6 million for relief and rehabilitation of Palestine Refugees. The American Point IV Programme was at the time also providing about £3 million in grants for development projects.

One of the political bones of contention between the National Socialist opposition in 1954–1955 and also when they came to power under Sulayman al-Nabulsi in October 1956 was the mode of payment of this subsidy. At the beginning of each financial year the Legion prepared estimates which were then presented to London through the British Embassy in Amman. Once these had been approved the money would be made available in London to be drawn upon by the Liaison Officer of the Arab Legion. Under certain circumstances, Britain could query overspending or unusual situations in this account after a Jordanian audit had been made.

It is therefore politically important to consider that when the question of the abrogation or revision of the Anglo-Jordanian 1948 Treaty arose in 1956–1957, it was not so much the existence of the subsidy as such that mattered to the politicians as it was the way it was paid out. After all, it is inconceivable that even the most rabid Arab nationalist, anti-British members of the Nabulsi government in 1956–1957 would have wished to forgo over half of the country's source of revenue. They rather spoke of abrogation and revision only synchronously with their chances of securing alternative sources of financial support. Especially those among them who spoke of revising the Treaty were betraying their major political concern, to wit, the overtone of subservience implied in the mode of payment. To a great extent, the dismissal of the Nabulsi government in April 1957 was made easier when, despite its Arab nationalist commitment, it could

---

for defence and security. It was estimated that local resources would cover less than half of expenditure. The balance was to be made up from foreign aid (mainly US and Arab League), foreign financial aid and assistance (largely US and Britain), and development loans (mainly from the West, but lately increasingly from Kuwait).

not guarantee alternative sources of financial support, e.g. from Egypt, Syria, and Saudi Arabia.

Also politically significant was the fact that such a large proportion of the annual budget provided by the subsidy to the Legion constituted the largest single contributive factor to the country's total economy. To a large extent, the Jordan Army today continues to be one of the most important factors in the country's economy.

When one considers that the grand total of the economically active population in 1961–1962 was approximately 390,000—say, 500,000 today out of an estimated total of 2 million—a modern military establishment of 25,000–30,000 in 1957 (roughly 60,000 today) becomes economically meaningful. Farmers (i.e. all categories engaged in agriculture), craftsmen and unskilled labour constitute together about 65 per cent of the economically active population. Professional and technically skilled people are a mere 16,000–17,000. Workers in transport and commercial-trade activities are slightly over this, about 21,000.

The *per capita* income in 1962 was given as JD£73 ( = £73), or about 200 dollars. One wonders if this is a realistic figure, since about half a million of the population are still refugees, a third of whom continue to receive UNRWA relief. The GNP was given as JD£129,000,000. Agriculture, foreign aid, and defence and public expenditure constitute the largest sources of the national income—the three together accounting for over one-third of the GNP. Manufacturing and mining as sources of domestic productivity have risen steadily and appreciably since 1959. Wholesale and retail trade still represents the single largest source, constituting about one-fourth of the GNP.

The pattern of education is most revealing. One should bear in mind that the ex-Palestinians had been exposed—and accustomed—to a relatively higher standard of primary and secondary education under the mandate than the Transjordanians. The private local and foreign schools were also of high quality. On the other hand outside Amman, al-Salt, Irbid, Kerak and other smaller towns in East Jordan, education was limited to the village mosque school and Christian community schools, as well as to the schooling system of the Legion.

In 1962–1963 there were 1,761 schools in the country: 1,308 of these were under the supervision of the Ministry of Education; 206 were listed as "national private", i.e. maintained by private Jordanian institutions and organisations; 51 were "foreign private"; and 173 were refugee schools maintained by UNRWA. 10,631 teachers taught in these schools, of whom 4,631 were women. The total student enrolment was 322,750, one-third of whom were female. Two-thirds of this total attended government schools. The remaining one-third was almost equally distributed between private and UNRWA schools. 75 per cent of this enrolment was in primary schools; 15 per cent in preparatory schools; and 10 per cent in secondary schools.

In the same year there were only two agricultural schools with a total enrolment of 250 students, 75 per cent of whom studied at the secondary level, and the remainder at a "higher", i.e. college, level. Trade and industrial schools were more numerous (fourteen of them), in which enrolment was about nine times higher than in agricultural schools and roughly equally distributed between secondary and elementary-preparatory.

There were also seven teacher training institutions with a total enrolment of 1,144 students, among whom men exceeded women by three times. A university was founded in 1962–1963, with two basic faculties: Arts and Sciences, and Agriculture. Enrolment in 1963–1964 was 257, double that of its first year, with a marked increase in women students. There were fifteen full-time members of the teaching staff, nine of whom had Ph.D.s, and fourteen part-time, four of whom had Ph.D.s. Jordanians who undergo higher training, in the majority of cases, still go abroad for higher study (in the Arab world, mainly to Cairo and Beirut; overseas, mainly to the UK, Western Europe and the USA).

It should be noted that when Jordan annexed Arab Central Palestine in 1948, many Palestinians had already left the country and were living in a number of Arab states. Many of them sought Jordanian citizenship or nationality after the merger of the two Banks, so as not to remain stateless. Jordan was willing to grant it to them, even though they were domiciled in other Arab countries. Thus today Jordan officially enumerates over 65,000 Jordanians living abroad, mainly in Egypt, Syria, Iraq, Lebanon, Saudi Arabia, Kuwait, Germany, Brazil and the United States. Half of these (approximately 32,000) live in Kuwait. One assumes that these are ex-Palestinians in the main.

## 2. A BRIEF NOTE ON SOURCES

The best-known source in English about the Arab Legion consists of the two volumes by Lieut.-General Sir John Bagot Glubb (Pasha), Chief of the General Staff of the Legion from 1940 to 1 March 1956.[13]

---

[13] *The Story of the Arab Legion* (London, 1948; 1956); *A Soldier with the Arabs* (London, 1957). Godfrey Lias, *Glubb's Legion* (London, 1956), contains a general account. In addition to the information given by Glubb and Sir Alec

There had appeared, before Glubb's books, a small number of works, but these were confined to telling the story of the first commander of the Legion, Frederick Peake Pasha.[14] For other—and different— sources of information relevant to the Legion one must look to the memoirs and personal accounts of those who were involved in Jordan in one official capacity or another.[15] There are general books in English which deal with Transjordan and Jordan; but rather few in Arabic.[16] A few British officers have published accounts of their experiences with the Legion. These contain useful information on the regimental level, as well as valuable insights regarding the beginnings of the technical branches of the Legion since 1948.[17] The regimental logbooks kept by several British commanding officers are a mine of data on each officer, NCOs and other enlisted ranks, ranging from level of formal education, level of military and technical

---

Kirkbride (see below) on the Transjordan Frontier Force (TJFF), see L. K. Lockhart, "The Transjordan Frontier Force", *Journal of the Royal Artillery*, vol. 56 (April 1929), pp. 77–84, and J. M. Sinclair, "Trans-Jordan and the Trans-Jordan Frontier Force", *Journal of the Royal Artillery*, vol. 60 (January 1934), pp. 471–485. On the Arab Legion, see also "Transjordan Army: the Arab Legion", *Palestine Affairs*, vol. 3 (April 1948), pp. 44–45; Somerset S. De Chair, *The Golden Carpet* (London, 1944); J. B. Glubb, "Transjordan and the War", *Journal of the Royal Central Asian Society*, vol. 32 (January 1945), pp. 24–33; and Stewart Perowne, "The Arab Legion", *The Geographical Magazine*, vol. 27 (November 1954), pp. 352–358.

[14] See, for example, C. S. Jarvis, *Arab Command*, the biography of Lieut.-Colonel F. G. Peake Pasha (London, 1943). See also F. G. Peake, "Trans-Jordan", *Journal of the Royal Central Asian Society*, 26 (July 1939), pp. 375–396.

[15] For example, King Abdullah ibn al-Husayn, *mudhakkirāt al-malik 'Abdullah* (Amīn Abu al-Sha'r edition, Amman, 1965, fifth printing), and King Abdullah's earlier *al-āmāli al-siyāsiyya* (Amman, 1939); Khayr al-din al-Zarkalī, *'āmān fi 'Ammān* (Cairo, 1925); Sir Alec Kirkbride, *A Crackle of Thorns* (London, 1956); Abdullah al-Tel, *kārithat filasṭīn, mudhakkirāt Abdullah al-Tel* (Cairo 1959); Hazzā' al-Majālī, *mudhakkirātī* (Amman, 1960), and *hādha bayān lil nās, qissat muḥadathāt tembler* (Amman, n.p., n.d.).

[16] Some of these in English are cited in the notes to the monograph. The best general history in Arabic is Munib al-Māḍī and Sulaymān Mūsā, *tārīkh al-urdun fī'l-qarn al-'ishrīn* (Amman, 1959). A volume of lectures on the Jordanian economy delivered at the Arab League Institute of Higher Arab Studies by Ali al-Dajani is very useful: *muḥādarāt fī iqtiṣādiyyāt al-urdun* (Cairo, 1954). For a good and representative selection of both English and other general works on Jordan, see the bibliography in Aqil Hyder Hasan Abidi, *Jordan, a Political Study* (London, 1965).

[17] For example, Brigadier (then Lieut.-Colonel) Peter Young, *Bedouin Command* (London, 1956); Lieut.-Colonel J. Constant, R.E., "The Arab Legion Engineers", *The Royal Engineers Journal*, 70: 2 (June 1956), pp. 122–125; and contributions by other Arab Legion British officers in the *Royal United Services Institution Journal* (London).

training, to origin and tribal distribution, number of wives, periodical rating reports based on performance in service examinations, conduct and efficiency.[18]

It should be noted that among the British officers I interviewed were some who had raised their own regiments in the Legion, and others who had met the difficult task of either founding a new technical branch from scratch, as with Engineers, or of expanding, re-organising and training a whole service arm, as with Artillery. I interviewed officers who had commanded infantry, armour, artillery —including light AA—regiments and engineers. Unfortunately, I was unable to locate British officers who had been responsible for the training of Signals. Moreover, I had the opportunity of prolonged and profitable conversations on two or three occasions with Sir Alec Kirkbride, who had been intimately connected with the affairs of Jordan since 1921.

There are, of course, a large number of sources on Jordan, which I have used, dealing with the agricultural, economic and political problems of the country. These range from British Command Papers and Reports, Admiralty Handbooks, Jordan Government official publications to periodical English literature. A variety of Arabic publications I found mainly polemical. United Nations publications, especially on the refugees and economic development, are also abundant. The brief section on relevant data relies primarily upon the 1961 Census and the "Directory of Jordan" issued by the Department of General Statistics in 1964, No. 2.

### 3. SOME GENERAL PRELIMINARY FORMULATIONS

1. If internal violence, whether of an insurrectionary nature or otherwise, erupts in Jordan in the immediate future, it will not be as a result of the strains of "development", "industrialisation", and such other common strains of new states in the process of rapid change and development. Rather the incidence of violence in Jordan is clearly related to two essential factors affecting its domestic political tranquillity and stability. One is the armed truce between Jordan and its neighbour Israel. These two small countries share a frontier of some 400 miles which is garrisoned by their respective armies. When one considers the continuous infiltration and counter infiltration by villagers on either side of this border, clashes between the two forces inevitably occur. The other is the major political and

---

[18] I was permitted to examine carefully one such log-book kept by Brigadier Peter Young, the Commanding Officer of a Beduin Infantry Regiment in 1953–1956.

economic problem of the integration of both Palestine refugees and non-refugee Palestinians of the West Bank into the national-state structure. This problem of integration has led to internal violence in the past (1954-1955). Even though the deliberate policy of the government to minimise the dangers inherent in this process since 1950 has gone a long way towards removing its more explosive aspects, it could still lead to violence in the future.

Nor are these two major sources of potential violence unrelated to one another. The need to guard and permanently patrol 400 miles of frontier presents peculiar problems for the Jordanian military which, in turn, affect the argument regarding a professional, long-enlistment army versus a national conscription one. These problems also bear directly upon the conception of a National Guard and its relationship to the regular army.

Thus, what happens on the Jordan-Israel frontier can affect the political equilibrium of the state of Jordan. Reprisal raids by Israeli forces into Jordan to punish, or retaliate for, infiltrators—and currently Arab guerilla attacks mounted from Jordanian territory—can lead to serious political disturbances in Jordan. If these Israeli raids inflict extensive damage to life and property they can result in popular political agitation against the regime. The political demonstration against the regime is directed against the inability of the state to give Arabs on the frontier adequate protection against Israeli raids. This, in turn, often carries the political charge that the state is not interested in restoring the forfeited rights of its Palestinian subjects. So much for civilian political opposition to the regime under these conditions. If also defending units of the Jordan Army suffer serious casualties at the hands of the Israeli attackers—casualties which could be attributed to lack of military preparedness, a lax command, or to the negligence of regime political leaders—the loyalty of officers can waver, and thus lead to conspiracies in the army. (See further on this in the Epilogue.)

I am obviously suggesting that these two interrelated problems facing Jordan monopolise, for the time being, the capacity for generating violence. On the other hand, I am not excluding the possibility that the more ordinary, or common, strains of development (even if this takes place on a limited scale) will not also be contributive factors to the eruption of violence.

2. Until the end of 1961 Jordan was a garrison state in terms of the Lasswell hypothesis,[19] in so far as the monarchy expected to have to use more rather than less force for the mainenance of its

[19] See his "The Garrison State Hypothesis To-day", in Samuel P. Huntington, editor, *Changing Patterns of Military Politics* (New York 1965), pp. 51-70.

rule. Jordan, though, has not been, and is not today, a nation-in-arms in so far as not all civilians are required to do military service.[20] With the exception of villagers living on the border with Israel, the requirement of National Guard service, for example, for all males between the ages of 20 and 40 (actually one month's active training each year) has not appreciably affected townsmen. In fact, as we shall see later in this study, many townsmen, and particularly their leaders in west Jordan, vehemently opposed the creation of the National Guard in 1949-50 for political reasons. Yet, in one sense, the long border with Israel and the expectation of conflict have placed Jordan, in terms of military readiness, in the garrison state category *vis-à-vis* the Israeli nation-in-arms.

3. One of the approaches proposed by Janowitz in the comparative analysis of the role of the military in new nations, namely, the examination of the common "societal context of the military" in these new nations, needs qualification when used for study in Jordan.[21] The qualification will be particularly necessary when dealing with propositions about social structure and military organisation. The social basis of recruitment into the army is not as uniform in Jordan as in other non-Western states. While a large proportion of the Arab Legion has been recruited from the rural areas (the lower middle and lower classes), it continues to retain a powerful core of beduin ground forces, recruited from both settled, semi-nomadic, and nomadic tribes. The military education of the officer, moreover, did not until 1956 produce a "cultural lag" between the military and society at large. That is, the army did not appear as the leader of modernisation, whereas society remained traditional. And while there may be "social cohesion" among officers as a result of their "ability . . . to intervene in domestic politics and produce stable leadership . . ." this may not be a safe assumption to make about the Arab Legion given its tribal ground force core.[22] Possibly the question of the social and political integration of the two Banks already referred to is parallel, though not quite similar, to national integration problems facing other Arab states, viz. Iraq. In this connection, both civilian legislative and administrative measures as well as changes within the army to deal with this crucial matter will be noted.

4. Until very recently, the officer corps of the Legion was not an

[20] See David C. Rapoport, "A Comparative Theory of Military and Political Types", *ibid.*, pp. 71-100.
[21] See his *The Military in the Political Development of New Nations* (Chicago, 1964), pp. 23-30.
[22] *Ibid.*, pp. 28-29.

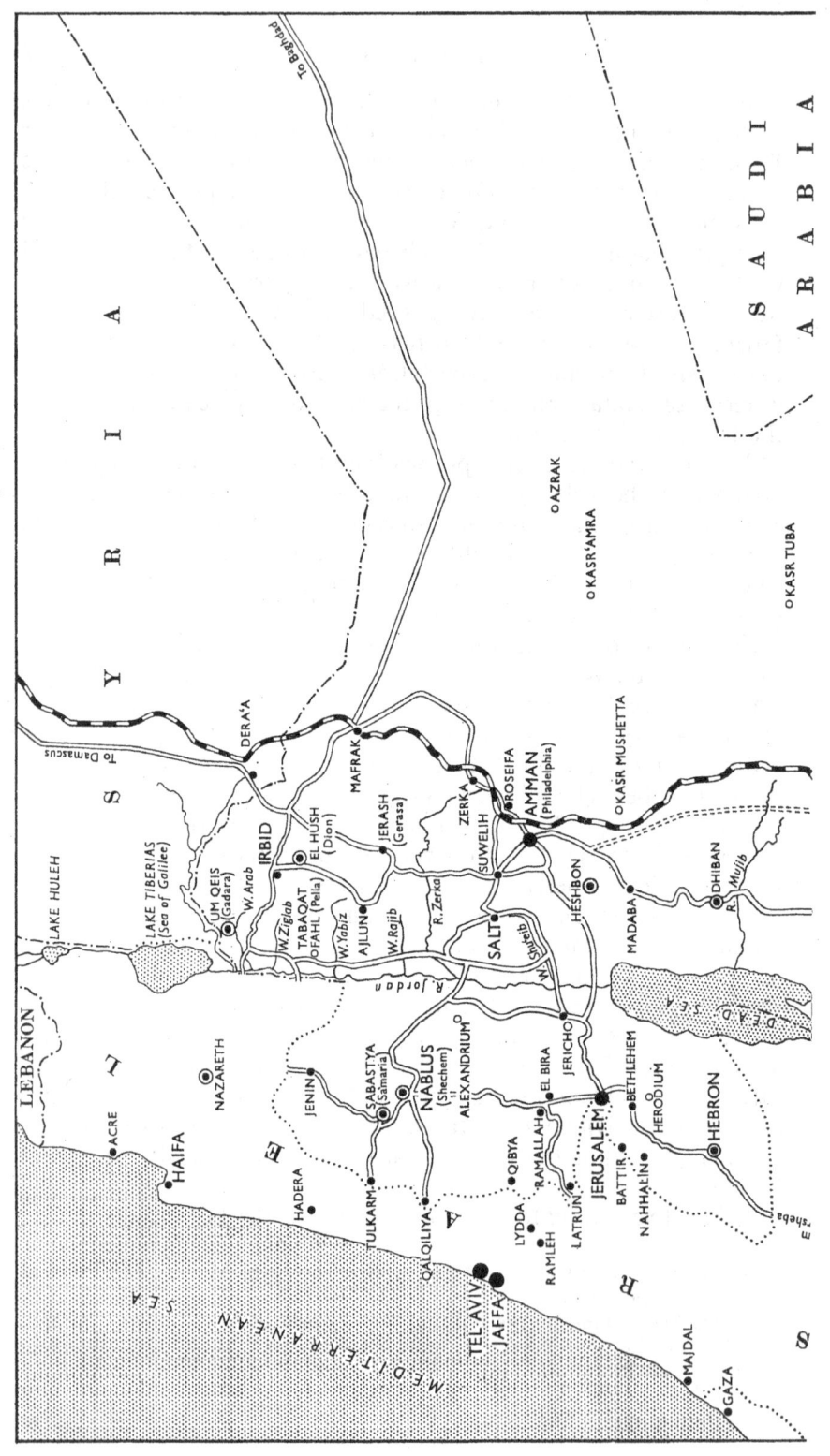

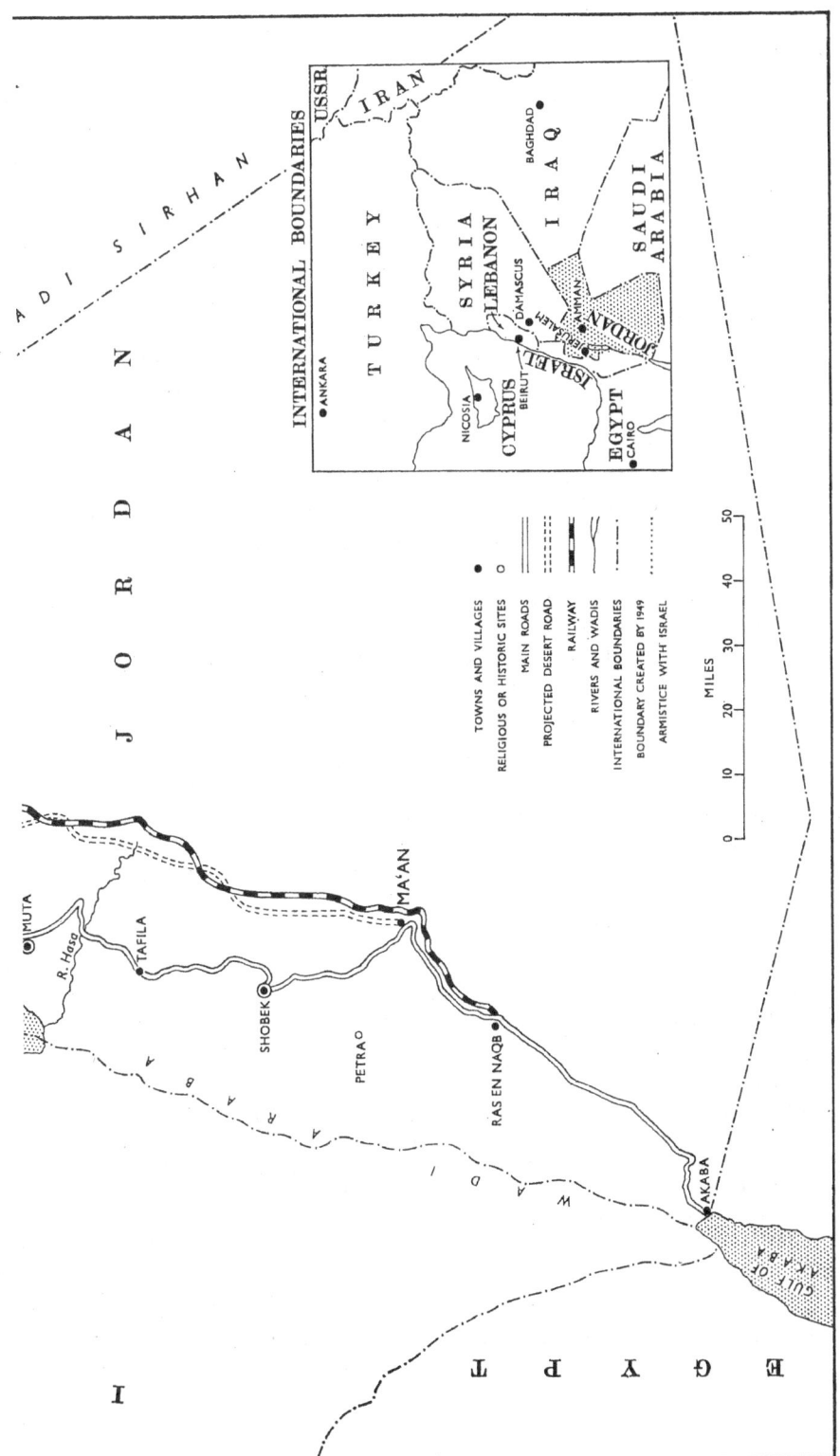

exclusive body. It did not constitute a class within the army distinct from the enlisted ranks. There was no special educational qualification for officership at a direct professional level. Rather all Legion officers were selected from NCO ranks for special training in the Cadet School which was really properly organised only as late as 1950. Moreover, only in the last two or three years has Jordan established an institution comparable to a Military Academy.[23] Consequently it is difficult to speak of the "military mind" of Legion officers, at least until 1956, or even today, in terms of a professional ethic which derives from, or inheres in, the nature of the military function. In an army that continues to be 30–40 per cent beduin or tribal, what one can speak about with certainty is the traditional-occupational ethos of the beduin as a warrior. This is perhaps his basic value and perspective in terms of which he views his membership in the military institution. Until 1956, however, it would be inaccurate to assume that the beduin in the Legion viewed the state as the basic unit of political organisation. The relation of the military to the state in this context was sustained by the primacy of the monarch-chief, not of the nation-state. The beduin, in a sense, came to the Legion with an anti-individualistic ethic, made possible by the primacy of collective security and responsibility in the tribe, clan and family; so that his sense of tribal corporateness carried over to his army life and career.

The uneasy relationship in this connection will be noted between tribal and non-tribal (*hadarī*)[24] officers and men in the Legion, which was characterised not so much by an overt enmity or friction, as by scorn. Yet, because of his tribal background, the beduin officer and soldier, for instance, appeared until 1956 readily capable of loyalty

---

[23] See below, the section on the Legion Training Centre. Huntington clearly states in *op. cit.*, 18: "The difference between the officer and enlisted vocations precludes any general progression from one to the other." This was not the case in the pre-1956 Legion. In fact, officers who had no previous record as enlisted men, particularly of NCO rank, were, with the exception of medical officers, unknown.

[24] While the term *hadarī* is loosely and popularly applied to townsmen and city-dwellers, it may be used to refer to the distinction between nomadic and semi-nomadic tribes (beduin) on one hand, and all categories of a settled population on the other, i.e. including villagers and peasants (*ḥadar*). In Jordan, however, especially since the pacification of the tribes in the 1930s, tribesmen and settled villagers (*fellaḥīn*) have been closer in ethos and custom to one another than, say, the villagers are to city-dwellers. In this sense one could use the dichotomy *tribal-hadarī* in the Legion to refer to both beduin and peasant personnel from villages on the one hand, and city-dwellers and townsmen on the other. The 1964 *Statistical Guide to Jordan*, No. 2, uses *ḥadar* to refer to urban population as opposed to rural.

to the military ideal of professional competence and obedience to the command hierarchy. What is interesting and complicating at the same time here is that pre-service values were not transient at all. Rather they continued to influence the tribal officer's or soldier's values and norms of conduct in the service. To this extent, they remained divisive influences, as is manifested in the petty intrigues in units and regiments between tribesmen and non-tribesmen, or between one tribal group and another. Political and ideological considerations, on the other hand, do not appear to affect the beduin's attachment or loyalty to the Legion's military ethic or ideal until 1956. One may be safe in making this assertion for conditions obtaining today also. One must also remember that the factors which would normally tend to erode the tribal ethic are not so strongly manifest in Jordan, e.g. rapid industrialisation, urbanisation, etc. Here there is a slight paradox. In one sense, the beduin does not have a *professional* military ethic, because he identifies with the values of the warrior. This in itself colours his whole life and personality and does not necessarily imply a professional activity which he assumes at a given date. In another sense, the tribesman in the Legion was, until 1956–1957 at least, militarily more professional exactly because he was less political. Following the life of a warrior was not something conditional upon this or that political need. Furthermore, this life was in the Legion subjected to modern military training and discipline.

The professional military ethic has been eroded to some extent with the expansion of the Legion in the period 1950–1956, and especially by the Arabisation of its command since then, and also by the influx of more townsmen particularly from among Palestine refugees and Palestinians generally into the technical services.[25] All British officers interviewed agreed to the following significant factors of change (these officers were *not* against Arabisation):

*a.* Politicisation, or the infiltration of political influence, occurred largely in the administrative network of officers and NCOs. Even though the Adjutant to a British CO of an infantry regiment was often a beduin, the Quartermaster (responsible for pay, clothing and rations) was usually a townsman (captain rank), the Signals officer

---

[25] General Glubb suggests a division among townsmen between the well-to-do on the one hand, the poorer masses on the other. Among the latter one finds the skilled, semi-skilled and unskilled workers, such as mechanics, tradesmen, small shopkeepers and clerks, who, in joining the Legion, did not present the same problems as the few recruits who either ended up as top NCOs or officers and who came from the more influential—and richer—families in towns and cities.

and ranks were townsmen, and company orderly room clerks and HQ clerks were all townsmen. These personnel were in frequent touch with the *Qiyada* (GHQ) Amman, as well as with their counterparts in other units. Whereas the Adjutant was concerned with routine orders for the regiment, the second-in-command of the unit was invariably the officer in charge of training. In Armoured Cars it appears that the second-in-command was not necessarily the automatic successor to the British CO. Succession in command rather fell upon the senior company CO in the unit. Such company commanders were perhaps favoured for their operational experience. A somewhat similar pattern was to be followed in Artillery units also. On the whole, administrative officers and other ranks, as well as signallers and QM personnel, had usually attained a higher level of formal education than, say, the line command officers—usually the equivalent of some stage of high school—and therefore had greater opportunity for inter-service affiliations, as well as some outside the service.

*b*. Officers in Artillery, Signals and Engineers did "talk politics" more passionately and sophisticatedly in their messes than officers in other branches of the Legion. But, since promotion and other advancement recognition were still under British officer control and strictly dependent upon training, performance and examination, the political interest of officers was for long related to (if not confined to) matters of bureaucratic status: security of employment, pay rises and promotion, and generally the degree of prestige in the community.

*c*. The very few instances of attempted direct political involvement by Legion officers involved men who had a military career development that was the exception rather than the rule in the Legion of that time. The defection of Colonel Abdullah al-Tel in 1949, and the abortive coup led by General Ali Abu Nuwar in April 1957, constitute the two cases in point. Thus al-Tel came from Irbid, a relatively populous town in Transjordan, and had had a high school education. He had been a Customs officer on the Transjordan–Palestine border before joining the Legion. He was subsequently selected by the late King Abdullah, for no other apparent reason than that he took a liking to him, to serve as his personal courier with the Israelis in 1947 and 1948 when he was seeking the negotiation of a peaceful settlement with them. From a clerk in GHQ to a company commander at the outbreak of Arab–Israeli hostilities in 1948, and a CO of 6 Infantry Regiment deployed in the Old City of Jerusalem soon thereafter, al-Tel was appointed Governor of Arab Jerusalem. In this post he had access to civilian political leaders, or one could say to aspirants to political power, most of whom at that time were alienated from the Jordanian throne and inimical to its occupant.

From there it was an easy step for al-Tel to seek wider political contacts with, and support from, the Syrian and Egyptian authorities for a proposed movement against the regime in Jordan. It will be shown, however, that he did not have any extensive inter-service connections within the Legion. This largely contributed to the failure of his plans.

Ali Abu Nuwar came from al-Salt, another leading town in Transjordan near Jericho. He was a high school graduate who had also trained in Sandhurst and Camberley, England, served as military attaché in the Paris Jordanian Embassy, and later became ADC to the young King Husayn. His inter-service connections were wider in 1956–1957 than those of al-Tel in 1948–1949, for by that time Abu Nuwar had become Chief of the General Staff of the Legion. Moreover, there had been by then more Arab officers of his age group (34–38) with Sandhurst training in the administrative and staff hierarchy of the Legion than in the late 1940s. Abu Nuwar's failure though, as will be shown, was not simply due to the *ḥadari-beduin* division in a 25,000 man army which comprised some 1,500 officers, but more so to his inability to rally enough fellow conspirators to any clear national political aim, or vision. In March–April 1956 it looked as if Abu Nuwar and his officer friends had no idea about how to use to advantage the political initiative they had acquired immediately following the dismissal of General Glubb. Abu Nuwar's machinations appealed largely—on the surface at least—to the bureaucratic perspective and attitudes of fellow officers with similar aspirations for advancement. He neither manifested a heroic image nor was he known among fellow officers for exceptional managerial skill in the control of the instruments of violence. Moreover, social cohesion between officers of his background and those among the beduin in command of mechanised infantry units (five of these were beduin) were lacking.

To this natural lack of affinity between beduin officers and the townsman officers whom Ali Abu Nuwar represented there was added the fact that the armoured car regiments were beduin. The mobility and tactical advantage in deployment which these regiments possessed proved to be crucial. Also the fantastically sudden promotion of Abu Nuwar from Lieutenant-Colonel to General, after Glubb's dismissal, did not work in his favour, for this had left deep resentment among other officers. Promotions of his favourites when Ali Abu Nuwar became Chief of Staff further deepened resentment.

It is important to note here that the Arab Legion differed from the armies of certain other Arab states in another important respect that is quite relevant to the frequency and success or failure of political conspiracies in the military. Most significantly, there was until 1957 no military academy or staff college in Amman. In the absence of these two institutions, officer cabals were not easily possible. In this, of course, Jordan differed from the Syrian military, from whose officer corps emerged, for example, a pro-Baath cabal in 1954–1958. Prominent in this Syrian cabal were members of the 1947 and 1948 Homs Military Academy graduating classes. Jordan also differed from Iraq in this respect where, in the 1936, 1941, and 1958 coups, cabals of staff and other officers consisted exclusively of graduates of the Baghdad Military Academy, joined by very few air force officers. Finally, Jordan differed from Egypt, where many of the eleven Free Officers constituting the Revolutionary Command Council in 1952 and their few associates in the armed forces had been contemporaries in either the Military Academy or the Staff College. In Jordan, however, Cadet School, to which NCOs and other ranks from the Legion were sent, in no way resembled the environment and peculiar experience of a military academy.[26] Also, when Legion officers were sent off to Sandhurst or Camberley, their number in any given year was usually small—two to three at a time.

Moreover, entrants to military academy in the Arab countries mentioned above usually share a relatively common educational experience. They have normally completed secondary or high school or its equivalent. Some of them may have transferred from university. This was—with very rare exceptions—not the case with entrants to the Legion Cadet School. The overwhelming majority of cadets were not entrants from secondary school. Until 1956 none of them had entered the school from university.[27]

Nor was the social class origin of cadets and officers a factor present in Jordan to the extent and degree that it was present in other Arab states. Whereas one might safely assume that before 1936 in Egypt and Iraq a large proportion of officers came from the upper middle and upper classes (the use of European terminology here is dangerous), i.e. sons of landowners, notables, high civil servants, in Jordan this was hardly the case—again with very few exceptions. The

---

[26] On conspiracies beginning in military academies and staff colleges, see the interesting information in D. A. Rustow, "Harbiye", *Encyclopedia of Islam* (new edition: hereafter *EI²*), vol. 3, 1966, pp. 203–204. The Committee of Union and Progress (CUP) for instance began as a secret organisation in Staff College at Istanbul in the 1890s. Also, students in the Staff College and Military Academy of Turkey played an important role in the military coup of 1960. It is, moreover, interesting to note that when after 1900 the proportion of staff trained Arab officers in the Ottoman Army went up from 6 to 14 per cent, secret Arab societies led by these officers began to appear.

[27] See section on Training below.

recently opened Military Academy could change this pattern significantly.

5. It can be said, to borrow the Janowitz formulation,[28] that a certain division of labour—internal skill structure—began to emerge in the Legion since 1948. Until then, the Legion was largely a highly trained, completely mobile—General Glubb described it as an "army on wheels"—*ground* force that maintained effective organisational control of all instruments of coercion in Jordan. It controlled, for example, the police and was in general responsible for both internal and external security. It did not have to maintain itself any logistical, technical and other support services, for these were provided by the British military in the area. With the need to improvise and soon to provide all these services a nucleus of military managers and technologists came into existence; and this is now rapidly expanding, if one considers the expansion of the Air Force since 1951. What is significant about these two new groups—or skill categories in the Legion—is that they consist mainly of townsmen, and, in the technical branches particularly, of Palestine refugees and West Bankers generally. The beduin apparently is by nature of his cultural predilections averse to the acquisition of technical skills in the Legion, even though I have ascertained in the course of my interviews that he is fond of driving vehicles. In this sense, the beduin officer and NCO prefer to remain largely in the skill category of the heroic warrior—the leader in combat. As such, they also identify with the monarch-chief whom they view also as a warrior.[29] Thus, until 1956, the military technologist was scorned by the beduin warrior. Moreover, technology is not rampant in a country where industrialisation has not occurred on any significant scale.

Only the College of Arts and that of Agriculture are actually functioning in the new university at the time of this writing. Technical and trade schools are still very few; schools of engineering do not exist. The technological development of society at large must consequently be limited. Until 1956, technological development was an internal need of the Legion. Even if the military technologist had wished it, he would not have had the opportunity to incorporate his technical and scientific skills in society at large.

While in 1956 there were very few officers—perhaps about

---

[28] See *op. cit.*, pp. 40–49.
[29] With Sandhurst training behind him, King Husayn in his frequent addresses to army units insists upon calling himself a soldier. The founder of the first Field Engineers' unit in 1948 reported that beduin line officers and NCOs in the Infantry units immediately assumed upon seeing Field Engineers that they were there to dig their trenches and foxholes!

twenty altogether—with staff experience in comparison with, say, Iraq or Egypt, where the number of such officers is indeed high, there were, on the other hand, in Jordan a proportionately high percentage of officers with useful and encouraging, if not completely successful, operational experience. This experience in the Arab–Israeli war, for example, was not one of military defeat for the Legion officer as it was, say, in the case of the Syrian or Egyptian officer.

The number of staff officers for all branches and services in the Legion has risen appreciably since 1953. If two a year have been going to Camberley since that time, there are at least twenty-six such professionally trained officers today. One must add to these the Engineers who go to the School of Military Engineers in Chatham, Kent, and to the Young Officers' courses, since some of these are often used in staff posts. The number of officers roughly qualified for staff positions and duties may have risen by 75–100 since that time.

6. The Legion until 1956 (and to a large extent now) was an army in which all officers followed prescribed careers; in fact, they underwent similar career training. We shall see that the Legion Training Centre, Amman, which was also responsible for the Cadet School, the Education Branch with its elaborate system of schools in the Legion, and patterns of recruitment of beduin and other boys from the villages, all aimed at giving Legion personnel a uniform training leading to a prescribed career. There were thus no direct commissions to holders of high school diplomas or university degrees wishing to enlist in the Legion, with the exception of the rare instances mentioned earlier. The exception naturally was medical officers. Whereas Egypt has met many of its requirements for technical services in her armed forces via direct commissions for graduate engineers and other technically trained personnel liable to national military service,[30] Jordan has trained its own within the military establishment. In fact, until 1956 the Legion did not welcome graduates into direct commissions.

7. Whereas the military in Jordan had been recruited until 1948 mainly from the rural communities and beduin tribes, in its period of rapid expansion and until 1956 it had to recruit increasingly from lower middle and lower class town groups to meet the needs of its new technical branches. Tradesmen and skilled craftsmen were recruited for Signals and for Engineers especially. Many of these

---

[30] The current policy of Egypt is to select 5 per cent of all graduates from higher institutions of learning in the country each year. From an average of 10,000 graduates this gives Egypt 500 new subalterns every year. 50–100 of these could easily be graduates of scientific and technical curricula.

were Palestine refugees and Palestinians from the West Bank. They soon came to man almost exclusively the Legion's maintenance workshops, for example. Many of them had been technicians employed by the Palestine Mandate in such public services and utilities as railways, ports, posts and telegraphs, land survey and registry.

For a long time, therefore, there had been no emphasis on nationwide selection in recruitment, although by force of circumstances and need this is developing now. Until recently, however, recruits came mainly from two sources: the peasant villagers and the tribes. In the case of the latter, many came from *outside* Jordan, particularly Saudi Arabia, Iraq, and north-eastern Syria. Nor had educational achievement been a criterion for selection in recruitment. The Legion took in beduin boys, for example, at age ten, schooled them until seventeen, and enlisted them automatically after that (see section on the Training Centre). All of these, incidentally, held the Legion—the *Jeish*—in very high esteem, to the point that for many years the Legion was inbred in its recruitment policy consisting of children of Legionnaires from one generation to the next. To this extent one could consider the Legion until 1949 a *corps d'élite*.

Generally, one can say that the Legion preferred its own internal educational system of making recruits literate and teaching them limited skills necessary for the performance of their military duties and functions to civilian education. (*a*) This way it avoided a clash of values and perspectives between beduin and village peasants on one hand—or even more generally the Legion-educated Legionnaire —and those who came in with a comparatively high level of civilian education on the other. (*b*) In the absence of any strong sense of patriotism or national identity in those days, this system provided a feeling of cohesion among Legionnaires. (*c*) It avoided any serious clash of outlook or attitudes between those coming from the desert and rural areas (the hinterlands) and those few from more urban or metropolitan centres. Yet until 1950 there were no metropolitan centres of any size in Jordan to speak of. Even Jerusalem and Amman today are not quite metropolitan centres in the true sense of the term. The possible dichotomy today may be one between East Bankers generally (including tribesmen) and the more sophisticated, alienated (because of their 1948–1949 experience in Palestine) West Bankers.

Regarding the ability of the military in Jordan to act as an *effective* political force, one must say, on the basis of this study at least, that the Legion so far cannot do so. Tribal, familial primary attachments and loyalties and the *hadarī-beduin* dichotomy have yet to be thoroughly superseded by any universal attachments or perspectives of the officer corps as a professional body, whether to a professional ethic, a sense of public responsibility or a feeling of corporateness. Although the old nexus of army loyalty to the monarch-chief (which was coloured by both religious and tribal premises of allegiance and legitimacy) may now be undergoing a transformation to a loyalty towards a nation-state entity, the 30–40 per cent tribal element in the *Jeish* makes a facile generalisation still difficult and hazardous. Greater expertise among the administrative managers and technically skilled officers in the Legion—now greater in number—may further speed up the development of a national consciousness in the Legion. On the other hand, it could foster allegiance to an alternative conception of the national interest than the one represented and upheld currently by the present regime and its political order.

Again, though the problem of the "nationalisation" of the Legion is a difficult one. The transformation of the Jordan Army from an originally private *corps d'élite* of a monarch which maintained a dynastic state into a national army (for which recruitment is nationwide and approaches conscription) is linked to the successful integration of the two communities in Jordan—the Palestinians and the Transjordanians. It is not unfair, on the basis of the evidence that was available to me, to state that until 1956 General Glubb believed that he could maintain the Legion as a *corps d'élite* and resisted the inevitable influx into the technical branches of personnel that had perforce of needed skills to be recruited from among Palestinians. In his tight control of recruitment policy, promotions to the lowest enlisted ranks, and the final choice of candidates for further training after examination results, Glubb Pasha was trying to maintain a politically safe cohesion within the Legion. As CGS, he was responsible for the organisation of an effective force to defend the country's frontiers against possible Israeli attack. He had therefore to ensure the existence at all times of a highly trained professional force that would fight loyally. The unprecedented expansion of the Legion, however, in the years 1951–1956, and its need for greater self-sufficiency in services that could not possibly be manned by the traditional recruit for the Legion, began to erode—although as it turned out unsuccessfully and only temporarily—this cohesion of the Legion.

Yet the most interesting aspect of the identification of the Legion in the minds of Jordanians as a national, i.e. an Arab, army since the 1951–1956 period has resulted mainly from the actions of the monarch. First, there were his adroit measures for the tolerably smooth political and administrative integration of the two communities in Jordan. The expansion of the governing establishment to include a large proportion of able Palestinians has minimised the infiltration of disruptive ideas held by the discontented and alienated among them into the army officer corps, particularly now that the *Jeish* comprises so many more administrative and technical personnel who are Palestinians. On the other hand, the monarch has been careful to retain the traditional tribal element as the preponderant one in the operational ground forces units, namely, infantry and armoured car regiments. In doing this, the monarch has managed to continue to identify himself with the traditional forces in the Legion, while at the same time he has led the process of a viable integration of the various elements in the country that is so essential to political stability. He has also managed to associate with his rule the leaders of earlier dissident forces by enlisting their services in the state. Thus he has tied their interests with those of his regime.

Most commentators on Jordan have emphasised the courage displayed by its young monarch in times of crisis—and his luck. They have not, however, considered his political instinct, intuition and shrewdness in attracting a composite political élite to his service. Whereas his grandfather was a ruler of great, though controversial, vision in the context of the wider arena of politics among Arab states, King Husayn has successfully limited this vision to the identification of exactly the forces within his state to which he must respond.

The expanded political establishment, moreover, and the gradual identification of its role in a more integrated nation-state entity, increases its capacity to impose its civilian control over the military. In consciously trying to retain the expanded and nationally more inclusive military as a Royal Army, the King on the other hand encourages its development into a highly professional institution, further insulated from civilian political influences. And this, in turn, depends upon continued foreign aid. Helping this development is the fact that conditions which could erode and transform the tribal sectors of Jordanian society are not, as was noted earlier, massively present in the country. To this extent the tribesman—as well as the village peasant—continues to identify himself with the military institution and its functions. The tribesman especially continues to maintain his traditional role of warrior which is not being rapidly superseded by available alternatives for him in civilian life.

So long as the operational units of the ground forces remain predominantly beduin and peasant, it is not very likely that political conspiracies among officers from the town and city in the technical branches will succeed.

There is one major source of possible conflict and political upheaval that may involve—indeed, affect—the army. That is the new Palestine Liberation Organisation (PLO) which was launched in the spring of 1965 under Arab League auspices and largely financed by Egypt. The training of commando units, consisting of Palestinians—especially Palestinians in Jordan—first to infiltrate and attack Israeli positions across the Arab borders, and later to shoulder the major task of "liberating" Palestine via an armed attack, is based on the premise that only Palestinians can, in the long run, best do this. Such activity, however, can undermine the precarious truce currently prevailing between Israel and Jordan and bring Israeli retaliation against the regular Jordan Army. The political implications of this situation are very grave for the stability of Jordan. And King Husayn first expressed his concern and recently his outright condemnation of the Organisation's military and political activities in Jordan in no uncertain terms. At the same time, the King appears to be trying to commit further the new generation of leaders among his ex-Palestinian subjects to the service of the state. In January 1966, for instance, it was rumoured that he was considering the future possibility of a Palestinian as Prime Minister. If this came to pass it would not mark a radical departure from the country's political conventions.[31] It was also rumoured that he was considering the possibility of a military service law that would encompass all citizens, but quickly abandoned the idea. While a national conscription law could conceivably undermine the divisive effect and appeal of the PLO, it might, on the other hand, affect adversely the efficiency and the loyalty of the regular army.[32]

---

[31] Both Tawfiq Pasha Abu'l Huda and the late Samir Rifāʻi Pasha, several times Prime Ministers of Jordan over the last thirty years, came originally from Palestine.

[32] For further comments on the political implications of the PLO for the State of Jordan, see below.

# PART I

CHAPTER II

# Historical Background of the First Administration in Transjordan: The Emirate, 1923–1928

A FAIRLY detailed presentation of the political evolution of Jordan is necessary to emphasise vividly the phenomenon of the present state of Jordan. It also helps to focus the vital relationship between the role of the Legion and the evolution of this state from such an improbable beginning—from a chaotic background.

Before its creation and designation as the Emirate of Trans-Jordan in 1923, the geographical area comprising the principality east of the river Jordan, north to the Yarmuk river, south to Aqaba, and east to the undemarcated deserts, had no fixed name. The most common appellation was "the lands east of the Jordan" (*sharqī al-urdun*). The chief reason for this vagueness was that this territory in its entirety had never been a separate, or independent, political entity. Even the Christian Arab kingdom of the Ghassanids, who as vassals of the Byzantine Roman emperors came to garrison this area in the sixth century, did not completely control it. Even though a beduin tribe, they eventually gravitated from the south to the northwestern and northern cultivated highlands on the border of Syria. Moreover, their capital, which was essentially a military camp, shifted from place to place according to the needs of war and security.

In short, its geographical location had always exposed the area from ancient times to a succession of conquerors who occupied it, or portions of it, primarily in order to protect and secure trade and other routes. Hebrews, Assyrians, Chaldeans, Persians, Nabateans, Arabs from the south, Greeks, Romans, Byzantines, Muslim Arabs, Crusaders, Ottoman Turks, and Britons did this successively. It did however experience a brief period of prosperity under the Romans, who irrigated and cultivated some of its lands, built temples, amphitheatres, and palaces. It rarely again knew such prosperity, and the area soon lapsed into a long period of desolation and reverted into a vast preserve of nomadic tribes.

The Ottomans who ruled over Transjordan for some 400 years considered it no more than an area lying astride the pilgrimage route from Syria to Mecca—both a west–east and a north-south highway. They therefore paid the tribes roaming its vast expanses in order not to attack the caravans or molest travellers. They also built some forts and water reservoirs across it to serve and secure the safety of these caravans. They did not however set up any government or administrative apparatus for the area. Meantime, inter-tribal warfare and tribal raids against the settled villages huddled in the odd river valleys or around oases caused the decline of agriculture; and with terror came depopulation and general desolation.

While the efforts of the Turks to establish law and order were both intermittent and only occasionally successful, the settled farming communities of the 'Ajlun district in the north-west, for example, had to protect themselves somehow from the tribes. Six hundred years of Roman rule, a tolerant Arab and later Mamluk government had helped the originally tribal population of this district to settle in farming villages and towns. The defeat of the Mamluks in the sixteenth century left this area unprotected against tribal attacks. Its chiefs therefore devised a system of local districts (*nahiya*) charged with the defence against the raiding beduin. Further south, however, settled life was not as secure. Consequently, villages and small town communities between say al-Salt in the Balqa' district and Ma'an were sparse.

At this time also a vast migration of tribes from the interior of Arabia took place. Two major, and ever since rival, tribes, namely the 'Adwan and Banu Sakhr, entered Transjordan. Their rivalry and frequent wars dominated events in that area until the nineteenth century. Inevitably, settlement and cultivation under these circumstances remained difficult and hazardous.

Throughout the seventeenth and eighteenth centuries the Turks could protect the pilgrimage road to Mecca and other routes of communication only by subsidising the tribal shaykhs. This however did not always guarantee the passivity of the beduin, for he could still act wantonly and violently against travellers and settled communities.

The Turks faced similar difficulties in checking the raids of the Wahhabis from Arabia at the beginning of the nineteenth century. It was then that the Sultan requested the aid of his vassal Muhammad Ali Pasha in Egypt, who sent a punitive expedition led by his son against the Wahhabis. Egyptian subjugation of Arabia was later followed by their conquest of Syria in the 1830s. So long as Egypt controlled the area between Syria and Arabia, security conditions appeared better than before. But by 1839–1840, when Egyptian troops had to be withdrawn from all these areas, the Transjordan territory reverted to chaotic tribal rule. Life in the settled districts in the west and north-west, such as 'Ajlun, became precarious again. At this point, in the mid-nineteenth century, the Turks made a concerted effort to restore order. They sent out administrative officers, governors (*qaimaqam*), accompanied by small garrison forces, to various districts in the area.

Incipient Ottoman administrative organisation was first introduced into that part of Transjordan immediately east of the river Jordan and therefore close to the vilayets of Syria in 1851. First, this section of the territory was divided into three administrative units: 'Ajlun, with its seat of Irbid town, was attached to the *sanjaq*, or district, of Hauran in Syria; al-Balqa', with its seat of al-Salt town, was annexed to the vilayet of Nablus in Palestine, and later to the province of Kerak to the south; Kerak was made a governorate (*mutaṣarrifiyya*) under the vilayet of Damascus. Aqaba was attached to Egypt until 1892 and, after 1906, turned over to the Hejaz administration. A military garrison was stationed at al-Salt; a government house, school, and courthouse were maintained in Kerak. The latter came to being only after a garrison of three infantry regiments (a total of 600 men) and a cavalry regiment (200 men) had been stationed in Kerak. This force helped impose security over the district, thus enabling its population to engage in agriculture.

The presence of a garrison in that area, however, led to tribal uprisings in 1905. Nevertheless, this new and direct Ottoman administration which followed the introduction of the telegraph in the area and the construction of the Hejaz Railway improved conditions generally. The railway, for instance, had reached Transjordan early in this century. The Damascus–Darʻa'–Amman section was opened in 1903, and a branch line was extended from Darʻa' to Haifa on the Palestine coast. The Amman–Maʻan line southwards was completed the following year. By 1906 the line had been extended further south to Mudawwara, and by 1908 it had reached Madina in the Hejaz.

Improved communications and control thus strengthened direct Ottoman administration in these areas of Transjordan. A serious effort at taxation was initiated, covering land and other immovable property, produce, cattle and camels, a profit tax on merchants and craftsmen, as well as rates for public services. A special tax on non-Muslims in lieu of military conscription came also into effect. A few three-year elementary schools appeared, and four government preparatory schools were opened in Kerak, al-Salt, Irbid, and Maʻan.

Usually the native educational system consisted of (a) village and town mosque schools (*kuttāb*), and (b) Christian church, or community, schools, especially those operated by the Greek Orthodox Patriarchate in Jerusalem.

While more direct Ottoman administration over this territory had some salutary effects, it also elicited grievances and opposition from the local, or native, population. Relative success in the collection of taxes had prompted the Turkish authorities in 1910 to introduce further administrative schemes in the Kerak district. There was already much discontent among the local population against heavy taxation. But when the Turkish governor proceeded in 1910 to attempt the disarming of the tribes and to carry out a census for military service and a land registration scheme, the Keraki tribes led by their paramount *shaykh* (chief) Qadr al-Majālī rose in open rebellion. This had to be suppressed by military force.

The rebels claimed that the Ottoman government (a) had suspended financial subventions to the tribal *shaykhs*, (b) had refused to appoint the paramount *shaykh* of the province, Qadr al-Majali, to its administrative council, (c) had imposed oppressive taxes, and (d) had introduced military conscription, while at the same time it had proceeded to disarm the population.

Such open rebellion against the government did not in any way represent an *Arab* challenge of Turkish authority. Rather the tribesmen were reacting against growing administrative control in their area, which implied above everything else taxation and possible military conscription. It cannot be assumed that such forceful expression of local grievances against the Turkish authorities reflected the rising enmity at that time between say the more sophisticated Arabs of Syria and the Turks. It would be a mistake therefore to associate this local rebellion with the wider political developments among the Arabs at that time and soon thereafter in the First World War. The latter reflected themselves in the demands made by Arabs for a measure of decentralisation and local autonomy within the Ottoman Empire.

Until Faysal's Arab forces entered Aqaba in July 1917, the operations of the Arab Revolt had been confined to the Arabian Peninsula. To push northwards and westwards in order to co-ordinate military operations with the British campaign against Syria soon rendered the Transjordan territory a crucial area in the war, and the centre of operations for Faysal's northern armies. By that time, also, the Turks had virtually deforested the whole area for badly needed fuel for their Hejaz Railway.

Despite Faysal's appeal to the tribes to join him, and his father's

(Sharif Husayn's) proclamation[1] of the religious nature of the Arab struggle against the Turks, the local population, especially in Kerak and Maʿan, did not respond. Repressive measures by the Turkish military against their leaders had been temporarily effective. In addition to arresting some of them (Qadr al-Majālī, for example) for complicity in Faysal's revolt, the Turks exiled some of the Christian leaders of Kerak. In both Maʿan and Kerak the local population were reluctant to make common cause with the Arab Revolt because they feared both Ottoman Turkish reprisals and the beduin tribes further south who were already fighting on the side of Faysal (Huweiṭāt, for instance).

Upon Turkey's defeat in October 1918, Transjordan became part of Occupied Enemy Territory (O.E.T.) with British, Australian, and Indian troops present in the area until December 1919. During that time Transjordan became part of Faysal's Syrian Arab State with its government seat in Damascus. The latter appointed military governors to the three recognised provinces in the territory.[2] Transjordan also sent representatives to the Syrian Congress in Damascus in June 1919. With the aid of local notables Faysal proceeded to disband the army of the revolution and organise a new one. Yet these and other measures by the Faysal government to strengthen its position *vis-à-vis* growing French pressure in Syria did not evoke widely favourable response in Transjordan. In al-Salṭ, for example, the locals rebelled against the new conscription law passed by the Damascus government in December 1919 as well as against new taxes levied to support the required military forces. There were some clashes between them and the gendarmerie. Elsewhere, in Tafilah and Kerak, conscription produced meagre results.

When the independence of geographical Syria, comprising Syria, Lebanon, Palestine, and Transjordan, was proclaimed by the Syrian Congress in March 1920 it appeared initially that Faysal would be able to reorganise his kingdom on a more permanent basis. But as a result of the San Remo Conference in April which stipulated for a French mandate in Syria and Lebanon and a British one in Palestine, Transjordan and Iraq, this arrangement proved short-lived indeed. The French ousted Faysal from Syria in July 1920, but did

[1] See text of the proclamation in Munīb al-Māḍī and Sulaymān Mūsā, *Tārīkh al-urdun fī al-qarn alʿishrīn* (The History of Jordan in the Twentieth Century), (Amman, 1959), p. 54. See also text of this proclamation in English in C. Ernest Dawn, "Ideological Influences in the Arab Revolt", in *The World of Islam*, Studies in Honour of Philip K. Hitti, edited by James Kritzek and R. Bayly Winder (London, 1959), pp. 233-254.
[2] For the administrative divisions at this time and local officers, see Māḍī and Mūsā, pp. 85-87.

not touch the Transjordan area which had been assigned for a British mandate.

Now a combination of circumstances threw the area in a state of flux and inadvertent development. Despite Allenby's original O.E.T. order assigning Transjordan to Faysal's military jurisdiction, some British authority remained in al-Salṭ, Jerash, and Kerak represented by British resident officers who also served as political agents. Moreover, the British were so preoccupied with setting up a civil administration west of the Jordan that they gave only sporadic thought to Transjordan. Moreover, there was no thought at this time of forming an independent, or other Arab state east of the river Jordan.

Faysal, on the other hand, did not retreat to Transjordan to consolidate his rule there. By August 1920 he was on his way to Europe and to England. Whether he hoped for British aid to restore him to his Syrian throne, or whether the British had already apprised him of their intended plans for his establishment in Iraq, was not clear at that time. Sir Herbert Samuel, British High Commissioner in Palestine, was meantime about to initiate a semblance of government in Transjordan. Aware of tribal differences and local peculiarities, Samuel proceeded to deal with the Transjordan situation accordingly, and asked local leaders in such towns as Irbid and al-Salṭ to form local administrations.

To some extent British strategic considerations influenced Samuel's early course of action in Transjordan. The territory lay between the Red Sea and the oilfields in Iraq; it also sat astride the overland routes to the Persian Gulf; it was not a bad buffer zone between the raiding nomads from the east and the settled Mediterranean littoral. But most probably considerations of local policy were paramount in his mind. Sir Alec Kirkbride was of the opinion that Transjordan at that time was viewed as an area designated for exclusively Arab development over which British wartime promises to the Jews for a National Home would not apply.[3] But if British officials assumed that a fully Arab Transjordan would compensate for the loss of the Faysal Syrian kingdom to the French, events showed this assumption to be erroneous. Yet the net effect of Faysal's departure for Europe, and the scattering of his political lieutenants and collaborators from Syria, was that of leaving the field clear in Transjordan for a British initiative from Jerusalem. This was only disrupted by the sudden arrival of Abdullah in Ma'an in November 1920.

[3] See his *A Crackle of Thorns: Experiences in the Middle East* (London, 1956), pp. 19–20.

On 21 August 1920, Samuel declared to the assembled notables and tribal leaders in al-Salṭ that the United Kingdom did not wish to incorporate Transjordan into the Palestine administration, despite its mandate responsibilities for the area. Instead, he announced his plan to establish separate, autonomous administrations for the various centres of Transjordan with the help and advice of a few British officers to be attached to them, especially in judicial and financial matters. He further promised that there would be no conscription for Transjordanians and that free trade with Palestine would be the rule. Significantly however Samuel did not suggest the establishment of a single central government for the whole territory. Instead he outlined three major local governments in each of Kerak, al-Salṭ and Irbid, with local advisory councils assisted by a British resident.[4] Soon however some tribes refused to co-operate under such a scheme, especially in the Irbid district, and sought to form their own independent government in order to assert their autonomy.

The period 1920–21 therefore was marked by strong parochialism, tribal conflict and widespread factionalism. In one sense, the British merely fell in with the exigencies of a situation they had not created, even though their early attempts at institutionalising these divisive conditions tended more wittingly than unwittingly to strengthen and perpetuate it. In September 1920, for instance, a "Moabite Arab Government" was established in Kerak under the Majālis' (the paramount shaykhs) tribal leadership which replaced all previous officials with local ones.[5]

Some resentment against these arrangements initiated by British officials in Palestine and apprehension over their outcome was expressed by the more sophisticated members of the 'Ajlun district community.[6] It is doubtful, however, if these isolated efforts would have greatly affected the political evolution of Transjordan. Continuing tribal unrest and separatist tendencies among local governments would have nullified isolated demands for a unified Arab state under an Arab prince.

Briefly, none of these local governments was able to impose its authority or command the allegiance of its inhabitants. In Kerak, for instance, government rested on the personal authority of its

[4] See the treaty agreement between the British and the 'Ajlun District in Māḍī and Mūsā, pp. 106–109, for an illustration of these early British initiatives at administrative organisation.
[5] See a humorous description of this government by H. St. John Philby, "Trans-Jordan", *Journal of the Royal Central Asian Society*, vol. II (1924), part iv, pp. 296–312.
[6] See a petition presented to the British Political Officer, Major F. R. Somerset, by Arab shaykhs entitled *maṭālib al-ahlīn* in Māḍī and Mūsā, pp. 106–109, note 2.

governor appointed by Faysal's government which was not institutionally supported. It was incapable of ending the armed clash between the Maʻāyiṭa and al-Dhumaybat tribes, for example. Similarly, the al-Salṭ government was unable to extend its authority beyond al-Salṭ itself and its surrounding villages. ʻAjlun with its greater population presented a spectacle of open inter-tribal conflict for influence. There was open opposition to the government and civil disobedience from the start. Independent village governments sprang up, such as the one in Kura, while the tribes hung on to their traditional independence. The resulting chaos afforded tribesmen the opportunity to impose their control over their immediate surroundings, to terrorise cultivators and their villages. Inability on the part of these local authorities to levy and collect taxes soon led them to bankruptcy. One must add another danger at this time: whereas security forces at the disposal of these local governments were meagre and unorganised, the tribesmen and the rest of the population were well armed.

Such local governments, especially in Kerak, were soon reporting their inability to collect taxes: the population would not pay them in and the government had no means of coercing them to do so. The few badly organised security forces at their disposal were infrequently paid and often remained unpaid. They could not cope with dissident tribes who took to attacking the railway and telegraph lines. Auda Abu Taya, for instance, the leader of the Huweitat in the south, and one of the first to join forces with Faysal in 1917, claimed an undisputed leadership for himself over that area. In the Hauran area on the Syrian border, moreover, haphazard organisation and the lack of a response by the population to Faysal's conscription law rendered them impotent in the face of French punitive measures against them.

So that in the brief Faysal interlude of September 1918–August 1920 there was no public order or security in Transjordan. The local authorities set up were haphazard with a shabby civil service and unpaid mutinous security forces. Tax collection could not reach beyond the settled population in towns and villages, since tribesmen refused to pay any taxes. The latter reverted to their traditional behaviour. Any influence the Faysali state hoped to exert in the territory depended either on the personality of the local governors, or on the relations between the tribal chiefs and Faysal or his men on the spot, or upon the feeling of a few enlightened Arab nationalists about the necessity to support these embryonic administrative units against dissident elements and foreign, i.e. British, influence and control.

HISTORICAL BACKGROUND OF THE FIRST ADMINISTRATION 41

The chaotic conditions prevailing during this interlude were described by Frederick G. Peake, first commander of the security forces and the Arab Legion raised by Amir Abdullah in 1921-1923, many years later as follows:

"Several months before the arrival of Amir Abdullah [March 1921], the Palestine government decided to send a few British officers to Transjordan to try to help the local governments—if they could rightly be dignified with such a name—which had been formed in Irbid, Amman, and Kerak. In Es Salt the governor sent by the old Damascus government was still in residence, but had no power. . . . There were still a few police in the towns, remnants of those who had served the Turkish and Damascus [i.e. Faysal's] governments. They had received little pay for many months, and their uniforms were worn out; their officers had fared no better. They had no authority at all."[7]

It was at this juncture that Abdullah appeared in Ma'an in the south, an area which was still under the jurisdiction of Husayn's Hejaz kingdom. Amman, until then a relatively insignificant town, had in the meantime become the centre of Syrian Arab nationalists who had fled French repression.[8] Abdullah's motives for coming to Transjordan have been the subject of controversy ever since. According to his own declaration, he had come to Ma'an to raise a force for the liberation of Syria from the French and its restitution to the Arab kingdom of his brother Faysal.[9] It was of course unlikely that Abdullah could have ousted the French from Syria, and he quite definitely must have realised this from the outset. He was however encouraged about his prospects when local politicians in Amman had requested his father, King Husayn of the Hejaz, to

[7] See his *History of Jordan and its Tribes* (Miami, Florida, 1958), p. 106.
[8] Transjordan then was under the jurisdiction of the Arab Military Administration set up by Faysal in Damascus as per the October 1918 O.E.T. order issued by General Allenby. This Administration was headed by General Riḍā Pasha al-Rikabi as Military Governor-General. The Balqa' district (the area comprising al-Salṭ and Amman) was administered by the local military governor, Ja'far Pasha al-'Askari, an Iraqi officer, in his capacity as Officer Commanding the Arab armies there. Amman, moreover, was at that time the headquarters of 2 Division of the Arab army under the command of another Iraqi officer, Rashid al-Midfa'i.
[9] See text in his proclamation to "All Our Syrian Brothers" from Ma'an in Māḍī and Mūsā, *op. cit.*, pp. 133-136, in which he appealed to such rallying elements as "religious faith, freedom, and manliness". This is reproduced in King Abdullah's Memoirs, *mudhakkirāt al-malik 'abdullāh* (Amman, 1965), pp. 153-155.

despatch one of his sons to organise a movement against the French in Syria. It should be noted moreover that throughout this period Faysal and his entourage were too preoccupied with matters of foreign policy in Europe and England (thinking perhaps that their negotiations would resolve the Arab Question as a whole) to pay too much attention to developments in Transjordan.

There is perhaps some truth in the explanation that Abdullah had been angered by the British offer of the Iraqi throne to his brother Faysal. He claimed at one time that Iraqi leaders had promised that throne to him during the Syrian Congress in Damascus a year earlier. He therefore considered this a double-cross, both on the part of the British and of his brother. Whether, as was alleged, Abdullah believed that the Transjordan territory was in a rebellious mood and ready to move against the French only if a leader arrived to rally them is difficult to determine. But he was the only son of King Husayn at loose ends after the war. His brother Ali was Crown Prince of the Hejaz and Governor of Madina. Faysal was in Europe, accompanied by another brother Zayd, and by now it was clear he would be settled in Iraq. Abdullah was then left with nothing. His determination, though, was undaunted.

It took Abdullah twenty-seven days by train to reach Maan from Mecca, stopping every so often on the way for the crew to chop down fuel for the steam engine. When he arrived there on 11 November 1920, he declared himself Regent for his brother Faysal, and proposed to make Ma'an (still in Hejaz territory) the temporary headquarters of the Syrian Government. From there he issued his call for everyone to join his *jihad*, or Holy War, two weeks later. But very few members of the old Syrian Congress responded. Old Arab officers made their co-operation with Abdullah conditional upon payment of their salary arrears and a guarantee of their pensions by King Husayn of the Hejaz. The tribes, on the other hand, expected Abdullah to pay them sizeable sums for any services they were willing to offer, as Faysal had done previously during the Arab Revolt. Some Syrian politicians came forward with competing plans for the organisation of propaganda services against the French in Syria which called for the expenditure of relatively vast funds. Before long Abdullah realised that the enthusiasm of all these groups was heavily conditioned by financial considerations. At that point he also recognised that there was no alternative open to him but to come to terms with the French, and to depend upon British aid for the attainment of his own ends. He soon discarded his role of "Saviour of Arab Syria".[10]

[10] See Abdullah, *Al-āmālī al-siyāsiyya* (Amman, 1939).

By December the French in Syria were protesting strenuously to the British about Abdullah's sudden and, in their view, inopportune arrival in Transjordan. On the other hand, his brother Faysal was forcefully trying to dissuade him from annoying the French, arguing that such policy would adversely affect his negotiations in Europe on the whole Arab question. (Or was Faysal already assured of his Iraqi throne?) The Saltis with their parochialism and newly formed local administration were urging him not to proceed north of Ma'an. The British on their part publicly denounced his movement and his intentions. Privately they were convinced he would not dare proceed north.[11]

Abdullah, however, was not to be discouraged. He sent Sharif 'Alī al-Hārithī to Amman as his personal representative to establish contact with the nationalists there and to prepare for his entry into the town. Meantime, the Iraqi rebellion against British occupation forces had erupted in 1920 and this soon led to a British review of their overall Arab policy. Moreover, as mentioned earlier, the British authorities in Jerusalem believed at the time that Abdullah would not dare enter Amman. Nevertheless Abdullah and his entourage left Ma'an on 29 February 1921 with great panoply and ceremony, arriving in Amman on 2 March.

One must note that even at this late date Abdullah still believed in the feasibility of raising a united Arab force. He thus attacked, in his farewell speech at Ma'an, the rampant parochialism and factionalism of the day. Moreover, his arrival faced the British in Jerusalem with a *fait accompli*, and they wisely perhaps did not interfere with the initial steps he took in Amman to impose his authority over the various factions and localities. Immediately thereafter, during the rest of March, Abdullah was invited to meet Churchill, then Colonial Secretary, in Jerusalem. The result of their talks on 29 March was the first agreement between the British and Abdullah which permitted him to establish a government in Transjordan.

According to the Churchill–Abdullah agreement, this government was to have an independent administration under Amir Abdullah. But it agreed, in turn, to take the advice of a British representative resident in Amman. Britain, on the other hand, undertook to extend

---

[11] This private British conviction in Jerusalem was vividly illustrated recently to this writer by Sir Alec Kirkbride. The latter, who was on the spot and had to deal with the train passage of Abdullah north, found himself without *any* instructions from Jerusalem which could have guided him in dealing with this extraordinary situation. The courier he dispatched to Jerusalem for instructions did not return until after Sir Alec himself had decided to meet Prince Abdullah on his way. The instructions which arrived for Sir Alec *after* the event read: "We do not believe Abdullah will proceed north"!

to this administration financial aid, especially for the purpose of organising a security force capable of maintaining law and order. The working of this agreement, however, was to be tried for a period of six months in the first instance, during which Abdullah was to receive from Britain a financial subsidy of £5,000 per month. A stipulation in the agreement that Britain would work towards the improvement of relations between Abdullah and the French authorities in Syria meant in effect the abandonment by Abdullah of his original call for the liberation of Arab Syria.

Abdullah then appointed a government on 11 April 1921, and on 27 April an Organic Law of the Executive was published. Al-Salṭ, Irbid, and Kerak became the first three official provinces of the Principality and the first budget was introduced. This marked the end of not only Abdullah's Syrian Scheme, but also of the schemes of refugee Arab nationalists, and the virtual beginning of the State of Jordan.

Whereas Churchill's attempt in the autumn of 1921 to reach a more general and final settlement of the question of Anglo-Arab relations with King Husayn of the Hejaz failed, Lawrence's mission to the area was not a complete loss. The latter found Abdullah in Amman in September–October 1921 faced with serious financial and political difficulties. The original £5,000 a month subsidy agreed upon earlier that spring was not only insufficient to meet the expenses of raising a respectable security force, it was also far too inadequate to meet the Amir's policy of influencing—through the distribution of material largesse—intransigent tribal leaders and ensuring their political acquiescence to his plans, not to speak of winning their allegiance or loyalty. Moreover, the six months trial period had elapsed. Abdullah on his part was therefore anxious to enter upon a more lasting—and financially more substantial—agreement with Britain. For this he was willing to ignore his father's obdurate dismissal of the British offer of a treaty. Moreover, his brother was already settling down in Iraq as the crowned head of a new state. All this led to a new arrangement with the British. The previous arrangement of a part-time British representative in Amman (Abramson) was superseded at the end of 1921 (at the recommendation of T. E. Lawrence) with the arrival of H. St. J. Philby as the new Resident and Adviser in Amman.

This new arrangement in effect recognised the principle of an independent administration in Transjordan, separate from that of Palestine though still under the general supervision of the High Commissioner. An annual British subsidy of £150,000 was authorised to be paid through the British Resident. This and other relevant arrangements were later formalised in the Anglo-Transjordan Agreement signed in London in April 1923. Even though with this Agreement Britain formally recognised the autonomy of the Emirate, a formal political system was not fully devised until 1928.[12]

[12] For a survey of this early period, see H. St. J. Philby, "Trans-Jordan", *Journal of the Royal Central Asian Society*, vol. II (1924), part iv, pp. 296–312.

CHAPTER III

# The Present Political System
# A Brief Survey

It is clear that the Principality was not simply a British creation, but in great measure an accomplishment of consummate political skill on the part of Abdullah. Obviously, in pursuing his goal he appreciated the two most important means to his end, namely, the relationship of dependence with Britain (especially when the latter was a major source of financial support) and the instrumentality of a well-trained, disciplined security force. By spring 1923, not only had Abdullah achieved British recognition for an autonomous administration in Transjordan, but as will be shown in Part II below, he had acquired the means to raise and organise a security force. This was to be trained, disciplined, commanded, equipped and financed by British officers and British money. It was soon to develop into what came to be known as the Arab Legion. Through the activities of this Legion and his own diplomatic efforts, Abdullah was, within less than a decade after his establishment in Amman, well on the way to imposing his authority over a fractious, tribal society.[1]

Abdullah also proved no mean match for the Independence party (*istiqlāl*) Arab nationalist politicians (mainly Syrians and Palestinians) who had hoped for a unified Arab state comprising Iraq, Syria, Palestine and Transjordan under Faysal. Those who did not accept his new scheme found themselves in 1924–1925 unwelcome in the country. The exile of many of their leaders from the country was precipitated as will be noted in Part II by the attacks by armed bands of Arab rebels operating from Transjordan on the Syrian border in August 1924. Moreover, Frederick G. Peake, the first commander of the Arab Legion just formed in April 1923, had in that year too

[1] Abdullah's keen appreciation of the role of a British financed, equipped and trained security force is reflected in this statement by Frederick G. Peake, first commander of this force: "One of the first acts of the Amir on his return [from London, that is, in 1923] was to amalgamate the Reserve Force and the Police [see Part II], and to call it the Arab Legion. The present writer was appointed to command the Legion, and became responsible to the Amir for public security." *Op. cit.*, pp. 107–108.

purged the new security force of all officers known to be members of, or sympathisers with, the Independence party. The Nationality Law of 1928 further made it impossible for any of these to acquire Transjordan nationality, for the Law stipulated that only those permanently resident in Transjordan in 1924 could be considered nationals of the Principality.

It is important now to trace briefly the evolution of the political system and characterise its development. Its evolution can best be observed in three distinct phases of the country's political history, namely the period of the British mandate 1923–1946, the period of independence during which Central Palestine was annexed and King Abdullah was assassinated, and the period of its rapid expansion after the Palestine war until 1956. Only the last period should interest us in detail, for two important reasons. First, in this period the problems of the integration of Palestine into Transjordan emerge clearly and manifest themselves in the difficult and troublesome political life of the country. Second, in this period occurred the greatest and most rapid expansion of the Legion. Moreover, the latter played perhaps the key role in maintaining the integrity and stability of the monarchy and its regime while the integration of the East and West Banks of the country was taking place.

### 1. THE MANDATE PERIOD (1921–1946)

The first seven years of this period were taken up by the consolidation of the Principality, founded 1921 to 1923, and with the attainment of autonomy. This was accomplished when Britain recognised the Principality in the Anglo-Transjordanian Agreement of 1923. In addition to the opposition Abdullah faced from the Arab Independence party (*Istiqlāl*) in 1921–1924, he had to contend with more serious tribal and local townsman opposition to his rule. Tribal resistance to his integrating authority was expressed in a series of local rebellions, such as the ones at Kura (1921), Kerak, Tafileh, and 'Ajlun (1921), and the 'Adwan uprising in Balqa' in 1923. With the help, as will be shown below, of the new Legion under its British commander, Frederick G. Peake, Abdullah succeeded in suppressing all of these. As for the opposition from townsmen, this rallied mainly round the *Istiqlāl* party. By defeating them politically Abdullah placated the local chiefs, especially the tribesmen. A series of frontier demarcation agreements in the east and south-east, protected successfully by the Legion with Royal Air Force support, further strengthened his position.

A second agreement with Britain in 1928 led to the creation of an identifiable, though incipient, political system with limited constitutional characteristics. A rudimentary unicameral legislature was set up by the promulgation of an Organic Law in April 1928. According to the Electoral Law of August 1928, this body was elected for three years to serve as a Legislative Council. Legislative power was vested in the Council and the Prince. Significantly indicative of the level of political consciousness in the Principality was the very low percentage of polling in the first elections held: only 3 per cent of the electorate voted.

Yet, even at this early stage in its political evolution, there was some organised opposition to the new political order. There were serious limitations on the powers of the new Legislative Council, e.g. no law passed by the Council could be implemented without the Prince's approval. The latter, in turn, had to get the concurrence of the British Resident in Amman under the mandate status. In these circumstances, the Council was no more than a debating society. Moreover, disagreement between the Prince (i.e. Abdullah as ruler), and the Council did not imply political deadlock. There was no need for such disagreement to be resolved since the Prince could resort to rule by ordinance or decree.

A series of five National Congresses (1923–1933) were held by opposition leaders to demand the limitation of the Prince's power as a necessary step towards a truly constitutional system. So long, however, as the Prince was supported by the British relationship—a major source of his legitimacy and authority—and so long as he controlled the Legion, these opposition efforts bore little fruit, although Abdullah permitted the organisation of political parties in this period. But all of these were at least agreed upon the separate statehood of Transjordan; they also comprised mainly notables, tribal and other leaders, and reflected the interests of propertied groups in the country. Their leaders and members were no longer interested in Pan-Arab schemes, or in the overthrow of Abdullah. What they sought was a measure of greater power *vis-à-vis* the Prince, and a further measure of independence via negotiations between the Prince and the British mandate authorities. Nonetheless, and in a limited way, these early parties and their activities mark the beginning of a semi-organised public opinion in the country, and the evolution of a separate Transjordanian national-state identity, especially when the latter was, under Abdullah's rule, developing separately from the wider Arab political question and particularly separately from Palestine.[2]

[2] On legislation generally for this period see C. R. W. Seton, ed., *Legislation of Transjordan, 1918–1930* (London, 1931). On the Organic Law of April 1928 see

Generally, with the assistance of Britain and the determined use of his Legion force, Abdullah achieved his goal of founding a state for himself. This he did unashamedly at the expense of the wider Arab cause during the First World War and in the teeth of his Pan-Arab opponents. He had won the first round.

## 2. THE INDEPENDENT KINGDOM, PHASE I, 1946–1948

In July–December 1941 an agreement was concluded between Britain and Transjordan to amend certain clauses of the 1928 Agreement. Because of the war, Britain agreed to remove the restraints placed by the 1928 Agreement upon Abdullah as regards the raising of an armed force, i.e. the expansion of the Legion. The 1941 amended Agreement permitted the Amir to do that without prior—or any—approval of the British government. This was a significant step towards the further strengthening of Abdullah's position in Transjordan which later stood him in good stead in the Palestine War.

Partly in recognition of Abdullah's active, even though minor, contribution to the war effort—particularly the supply of garrison units to guard military installations in the Middle East theatre—the British agreed to new talks for the formal ending of the Mandate and the negotiation of a treaty with an independent State of Transjordan. In response to a Transjordanian memorandum in June 1945, requesting such talks, the British Government invited Abdullah to London. His visit took place in February 1946 and in March negotiations had been completed for the termination of the Mandate and the signature of a new Treaty. The latter was ratified in June. It recognised the independence of Transjordan.

While the Transjordanians proclaimed their independent State as the Hashemite Kingdom of Jordan, the British retained the protection of their vital strategic-military interests in the country under the new Treaty. A new constitution for the kingdom was promulgated in 1947. It changed much of the legal terminology of the State's formal institutions but not the nature of rule and authority. Thus the Principality (*imāra*) became the Kingdom (*al-mamlaka*) and in place of the Organic Law (*al-qānun al-asāsī*) there was now a Constitution (*dustur*). The Legislative Assembly (*al-majlis al-tashrī'ī*)

---

Helen Miller Davis, *Constitutions, Electoral Laws, Treaties of States in the Near and Middle East* (Durham, 1947). On political parties in the 1930s see I. Chizik, "The Political Parties in Transjordania", *Journal of the Royal Central Asian Society*, vol. 22 (April 1935), pp. 96–99.

became a National Assembly (*majlis al-umma*) consisting of two Houses: a lower house designated as the Chamber of Deputies and comprising twenty members elected by a 150,000 electorate, or a quarter of the total population, and an upper house, the Chamber of Notables, comprising ten members appointed by the King for an eight-year term,

The 1946 Treaty was superseded in 1948 by a new one which eliminated the more stringent British riders regarding defence arrangements. The earlier provision permitting Britain to post armed forces throughout the kingdom was replaced by a new arrangement limiting British military facilities to two airstrips, one in Amman and the other at Mafraq, together with a small garrison in Aqaba. Jordan on the other hand was to receive, under the amended provisions of the Treaty, further military aid.

Many Jordanians have expressed the view that under the direction of Sir Alec Kirkbride, British Resident in Amman, 1939–1946, and Ambassador thereafter until 1951, the mandate relationship with Britain was at its happiest. They have argued that Sir Alec worked assiduously for the gradual relaxation of the more stringent mandate controls over the country, established an intimate working relationship with Abdullah, and thus helped Jordan develop its own experienced civilian administration and institutions.

To some extent the ability of Abdullah to revise the 1946 Treaty within less than two years of its initial negotiation was due to the revived political opposition in the country. New parties sought actively to sever further the country's relationship with Britain. And as the Arab question in Palestine was gaining momentum and coming to the forefront of Arab politics, the pressure upon the monarch mounted. On the domestic level, the opposition sought a more liberal constitution than the one promulgated in 1947. The elections of that year indicated that power continued to be concentrated in the hands of the new King, assisted by his Executive.

Partly in response to these domestic pressures and partly motivated by his own ambition, Abdullah became very active in the field of Arab nationalist politics throughout this first phase of independence. He worked on two fronts. Having secured and strengthened his position in an independent kingdom across the river Jordan, he took a renewed and intensified interest in the Palestine Question. Abdullah, in this case, tended to support such moderate groups in Palestine as the Nashashibis (a leading Muslim family in Jerusalem) and the Tuqans (a leading Muslim family in Nablus) in order to strengthen their hand against his major adversaries there, the Husaynis (the rivals of the Nashashibis, led by the Mufti of Palestine al-Hāj

Amīn al-Husaynī). On the wider Arab front, especially since the formation in Cairo of the Arab League in 1945 with Egypt looming large in the struggle for its leadership, Abdullah revived his Greater Syria and Fertile Crescent schemes. The latter were especially relevant and timely since in 1945–1946 Syria and Lebanon had just been removed from direct French rule.

It should be noted that political opposition groups and parties in Transjordan during this phase were still seeking to curtail the power of the new monarch via a more liberal constitution which guaranteed a genuine separation of powers. The Jordan Arab Party founded in 1946 stands out in this connection. Its membership, then, is meaningful for the political developments in the country ten years later. Thus Sulayman Nabulsi, Shafiq Rusheydat, Abdel Halim Nimr, Abd al-Qadir Tel, and others were, if not all members, at least identified with this group. Not only did they demand a liberalisation of the political system, but significantly opposed the new 1946 Treaty and its amended form in 1948, and called for a loyal attachment to the Arab League Covenant.[3]

## 3. THE INDEPENDENT KINGDOM, PHASE II, 1948–1956

Political developments in this period were dominated by two epochal events: the Arab–Israeli War in Palestine, and the annexation of Central Arab Palestine by Jordan. For our purposes only the political consequences of the latter event should concern us here.

Without discussing in any detail the annexation of the territory controlled by the Legion in Palestine in October–December 1948,[4] suffice it to say that a temporary arrangement to administer the area was quickly improvised, using Palestinian personnel. Mandate laws and ordinances remained in force. The most important step in

---

[3] Sulayman Nabulsi came from al-Salṭ and Amman (though originally from Nablus), Abdel Halim Nimr from al-Salṭ, Shafiq Rusheydat and Abdel Qadir Tel from Irbid. In fact all of these, with the exception of Nabulsi, had been elected deputies in the first 1947 elections after Independence. Note below in the discussion of "Politics and the Military" that Nimr from al-Salṭ was the acceptable candidate for a national coalition government during the April 1957 crisis to General Abu Nuwar, CGS of the Legion, who also came from al-Salṭ.

On Political Parties in Jordan see the detailed informative chapter in Abidi, *Jordan, A Political Study* (London, 1965), pp. 191–212; see also Māḍī and Mūsā, *op. cit.*, pp. 426–439.

[4] I shall be dealing with this question in detail in my forthcoming book *The Modern History of Jordan, 1921–1965* (London: Weidenfeld and Nicolson, Asia-Africa Series).

terms of political development was the inclusion of three Palestinians in the Jordanian Cabinet of May 1949, a year after the outbreak of the Palestine War.[5] This was a most important change pending a more permanent constitutional-legal arrangement, as the newly annexed territory comprised about 750,000 people, or over twice the population of the original kingdom east of the Jordan.

The Electoral Law was amended in order to double from twenty to forty the number of seats to be contested for the Assembly—twenty from each Bank. The number of Senators was increased to twenty, of whom the King appointed seven Palestinians. The Cabinet was expanded further to about a dozen ministers, and included five Palestinians. The first elections in the enlarged kingdom took place on 11 April 1950 and on the 20th the membership of the new Chamber was announced. The newly elected Chamber formalised the annexation of Palestine and legalised the integration of the two Banks. During the next year and a half a series of cabinet shuffles were accompanied by the emergence of a National Front Opposition party. The important thing, though, was that 750,000 Palestinians had acquired Jordanian citizenship and, the males among them of voting age, the franchise.

Despite this advance in political development, including the legalisation of an opposition party, King Abdullah and his government came under heavy criticism from various quarters, especially over budgetary matters relating to the Legion. This was not extraordinary, since over 80 per cent of the budget in 1950–1951 was allotted to security (both army and police). The opposition was obviously clamouring for the control of the purse-strings by the Chamber—a constitutional principle not operable in Jordan of the time.

Abdullah was assassinated in Jerusalem on 20 July 1951 and for a while it looked as if political development would be arrested. The assassin as well as those who conspired the murder of the monarch were predominantly Palestinian. Nevertheless, new elections were held on 29 August 1951 without serious incidents.[6] In the brief reign of Talal (until September 1952) a new constitution was promulgated in January 1952 which, with several amendments

---

[5] These were Rūḥī Abdel Hādī, an old Abdullah sympathiser, for Foreign Affairs; Khuluṣī Khayri for Commerce and Agriculture; Musa Nāṣir for Communications. The latter was to my knowledge in 1963 Headmaster of the Bir Zeit College near Jerusalem.

[6] For the changes resulting from the incorporation of the Palestinians on the West Bank as reflected in the election results, see "The Composition of the Jordanian Parliament" (Hebrew), *Hamizrah Hehadash*, vol. 3 (Winter 1952), pp. 196–197.

(major ones in 1954), is still the fundamental law of Jordan. It liberalised the political system further insofar as it made the Cabinet more responsible to the Chamber, especially in matters of the budget, votes of confidence, and dissolution. The term of the House of Notables (or Senate) was halved from eight to four years. A General Accounting Office was established for the audit of public expenditures. As for the new departures in party activity, these are discussed briefly in relation to the military and politics in the last section.

Thus having acquired 2,165 square miles of territory in 1948-1949, comprising a new population of three-quarters of a million, over half of whom were destitute refugees, the system managed to make the transition without serious trouble. The extension of the franchise went hand in hand with an amended legislative-judicial structure. The nature of the Executive, however, remained unaffected in terms of its extensive power until 1952. The first limitations upon it were placed by the new constitution of 1952 and its amended articles in 1954.

Since 1956 there has been a more liberal relationship between King, Cabinet and Legislature. There have been equal advances in the administrative integration of the two Banks. The country was reorganised into eight administrative provinces, headed by governors appointed by the Ministry of Interior. All local administrative officers in the West Bank are now predominantly Palestinians. The provinces are subdivided into districts administered by district officers. The districts in turn are organised into village local authorities. New civil service regulations make all Jordanians eligible for government employment as per certain prescribed qualifications. There has been surprisingly little, if any, parochial or other group discrimination in appointments and transfers. On the contrary, the civil service has so far worked well on an inter-regional basis. Notably, an increasing number of Palestinians staff such departments as Tourism, Development, Social Welfare, and Education. Similarly an ever-increasing number of Palestinians has come to staff the Foreign Office.

So that in a matter of a few years the integration of the two Banks proceeded fairly smoothly to produce an ever-expanding political community of new Jordanians. The Palestinians came to have an interest and a stake not only in a transformed parliament but in a functioning administration. In the former, in less than a decade, a greater measure of parliamentary control over the Executive was achieved by the new provisions of a vote of confidence and the power to impeach ministers. The latter became collectively and individually responsible, or accountable, to the Chamber for their policies. Some control over fiscal policies of the government was also introduced. But it must be noted that the monarch in Jordan is still not a mere constitutional head of state who simply reigns. His powers of summoning, proroguing, and dissolving parliament and, hence, his ability to rule by decree even if only temporarily, still afford him extensive governing powers. Yet the provision of the 1952 Constitution which requires a cabinet to resign within one week of the dissolution of parliament and make way for a caretaker government to conduct fresh elections is a big step towards a more realist constitutional system.

Despite its shortcomings one cannot but view the measures taken by the authorities since the merger of the two Banks in 1948–1949 as a bold and deliberate policy of integrating an economically less advanced (though politically perhaps more experienced) Transjordanian population with an economically and socially more advanced, though politically shattered, one. The step moreover was taken when half of the Palestinian population were destitute refugees, and the other half were perhaps ready to accept the protection and security offered by Jordan at the close of the Palestine war. When in 1958–1959 West Jordanians could have easily rejected the suggestion that Jordan was their country, it is almost certain that the vast majority today considers it as such. Moreover, a new generation has grown up since then as native-born citizens of the kingdom. It is for this and other reasons that the present Organisation for the Liberation of Palestine, for instance, has to operate from Beirut and Cairo, with some support from Peking.

# PART II

CHAPTER IV

# The Beginnings and Evolution of the Legion, 1921–1948

UNTIL August 1920 Transjordan formed part of Faysal's Arab Syrian Kingdom. British troops had been withdrawn in December 1919. Local security forces under Damascus jurisdiction were badly organised, irregularly paid, and thus unable to cope with the tribal unrest which followed the ousting by the French of Faysal and his government from Syria in the summer of 1920. Several local governments sprang up in the 'Ajlun district of northern Transjordan, while, as was noted earlier, tribal rule continued in Kerak in the south.

It was these conditions following the dissolution of the Arab kingdom in Damascus which led, in part, the British High Commissioner in Jerusalem to attempt in August–September 1920 the establishment of several local administrations in Transjordan. For this purpose he appointed several British officials to attend to the task. But the problem of public security was even more serious. The police and gendarmerie left by the Arab Syrian government appeared disorganised and inadequate. Thus the High Commissioner sent Captain F. G. Peake of the Egypt Camel Corps to investigate and report on the condition of the police and gendarmerie forces, and generally on matters related to public security.

At this time there was a *darak*, or gendarmerie, led by local Arab officers, remnants of the security forces of Faysal's short-lived Syrian administration. The commanding officer was a certain Lieut.-Colonel 'Arif Bey al-Ḥasan from al-Salṭ. In addition to the *darak*, there was a *shurṭa*, consisting of police units responsible for internal order in the towns.

As a result of his report, Peake stated once,[1] he received permission from the High Commissioner in Jerusalem to raise two small forces. One of these, one hundred men strong, was formed as a Mobile Force to guard the Amman–Palestine road. The other, only fifty strong, was formed to help the British official posted at Kerak in the south.

[1] See his "Trans-Jordan", *Journal of the Royal Central Asian Society*, vol. 26 (July 1939), pp. 375–396.

The picture, however, is not clear as to what security forces were available in Transjordan in the period October 1920–March 1921. Māḍī and Mūsā[2] report that a Captain Brunton had formed in Amman a company of one hundred men, which they refer to as the Mobile Force. Seventy-five of these troops were cavalry, and the remaining twenty-five were organised as two Maxim machine-gun sections. They report further that Captain Peake succeeded Captain Brunton as the commanding officer of this Mobile Force before the arrival of Amir Abdullah to Amman on 2 March 1921.

When Abdullah came from the Hejaz to Maʿan in southern Transjordan[3] he brought with him a "battalion" (*katība*) of troops: a force consisting of about 200 infantrymen. This he placed for training under the command of Captain Abdel Qadir al-Jundi while still in Maʿan. When he travelled north to Amman at the end of February 1921, the force accompanied Abdullah there.

Reinforced financially with the £5,000 monthly British subsidy for a trial period of six months, Abdullah set out to establish a central administration in Amman.[4] In the Transjordan of those days this meant in effect the imposition of his authority upon a fractious tribal society. And as tribal leaders had ready access to force, it was imperative that Abdullah have similar access to equal if not superior force if he were to succeed. The security forces in the area available at that time which Abdullah could have used appeared to be the following:

(1) The localised, or stationed, *darak*, referred to above, with an estimated strength of about 400 men. This was distributed between the three recognised administrative provinces as three units commanded by Arab captains: (*a*) ʿAjlun, (*b*) Balqa', (*c*) Kerak. In addition to these commanders there were about fifteen to twenty other Arab officers in the force.

(2) A battalion of Reserve Gendarmes (mainly cavalry) to aid the stationary gendarmes and police and about 150 strong. This was also staffed by old officers of the Arab Syrian Army, about fifteen of them, many of whom had served in the Ottoman armies. Its nucleus was probably the company originally formed and commanded in Amman by Captain Brunton whom Peake succeeded. This force was later disbanded and replaced with a new Reserve Mobile Force, raised and organised by Peake between the summer of 1921 and

---

[2] *Tārīkh al-urdun*, p. 154.
[3] See the section on the political system for the political history of this early period.
[4] See section on the political system for the chaotic tribal and other fragmentation of the Transjordan territory at that time.

summer of 1923. It was moreover to become the nucleus force of the new Arab Legion.

(3) A regular army battalion (*al-katība al-niẓāmiyya*) of some 200 infantry, commanded by Lieut.-Colonel Aḥmad al-Istambuli from Beirut. This was probably the old *katība* that had accompanied Abdullah from Maʻan to Amman.

(4) A camelry troop (*quwwat al-hajjāna*) of 100 men commanded by the Nejdi Ibn Ramih, which came to form the Amir's private guard in the early days.

When Abdullah formed his first administration in April 1921 he made himself Commander-in-Chief of all these forces, while he entrusted direct responsibility for their overall administration and supervision to his "minister"[5] of Public Order and Security (*mushāwir al-inḍibāṭ wa al-amn*), Colonel ʻAli Khulqi. Peake, moreover, had recently been appointed by the High Commissioner as one of Abdullah's advisers. He was appointed Inspector General of the *darak*. While he was to be responsible for the training of the gendarmerie forces, Peake at this early stage did not seem to have direct military command, or control, over any of these forces.

It is interesting to note here Abdullah's early appreciation of the important role of an effective security force in the success of his schemes in Transjordan. At first, for example, he envisaged a military force of several thousands, which he probably considered as the only safe guarantee against recalcitrant tribal chiefs and politicians opposed to his plans. Referring to the founding of the Arab Army (Arab Legion) in his memoirs, Abdullah speaks of his request of the High Commissioner in Jerusalem for a division of troops.

"When the administration of Transjordan was set up (i.e., April 1921), Rashīd bey Ṭaliʻ [the first "prime minister" in that administration] discussed with Sir Wyndham Deedes, Chief Secretary of the Palestine Government at that time, the matter of organising a military force to maintain internal security and protect the frontiers of the country. These conversations between Ṭaliʻ and Sir Wyndham Deedes took place as a consequence of our discussion of the matter with Mr. Winston Churchill [i.e., in late March 1921]. I had seen the need to form a regular military division with all the necessary arms and services common to a division in those days, such as infantry units, artillery, and cavalry.

---

[5] The executive council, or administration, which Abdullah formed in these early days was not quite a cabinet. So many Arabic terms have been used to refer to its members (e.g. *mushāwir*, *nāẓir*, etc.) that I decided to use "minister" in inverted commas to designate them in this section.

I thought it should consist of three brigades, each brigade comprising three regiments of 800 men each, [i.e., about 2,400 men in each brigade]. Each brigade should have its necessary complement of field and mountain artillery, and machine-gun units. One regiment should be cavalry, 1,500 strong, armed with small arms. [Here, it is not clear whether Abdullah is referring to a separate Cavalry Regiment, or that one of the three regiments in one of the brigades he proposed should have been cavalry.]

"But the British Government did not wish to support this scheme because of the great expense that its realisation would entail. But I agreed to the incorporation of the force that came with me from Ma'an—which consisted of regular volunteers—in the Mobile Force, a Cavalry unit that was present in Transjordan under the command of Captain Peake Bey (General Peake Pasha lately). The British, on their part, agreed that this new force should have a battery of mountain artillery, and be organised as a *darak* (i.e., gendarmerie) force in the three provinces, or districts: 'Ajlūn, Balqā', and Kerak. This, in addition to the police force.

"The reorganised force was begun by Captain Peake, in his capacity as Inspector-General of the army. He was assisted by Fuad Bey Salim. . . "[6]

In any event, the security forces, such as they were, at Abdullah's disposal soon proved ineffective. Peake had just begun the task of reorganisation and training before serious trouble in the Irbid area of 'Ajlūn broke out in May 1921. Moreover, Abdullah's first arrangement which entrusted administrative control over these forces to his "minister" of Public Order and Security also proved inadequate. A change in the structure, composition, control, and administration of the security forces was not long in coming.

In May 1921 a serious incident of tribal rebellion in Kura, near Irbid,[7] indicated clearly how weak the *darak* forces were and how inadequate this initial makeshift arrangement was. The incident reflected the unwillingness of tribal factions to be integrated into

---

[6] *Mudhakkirāt al-malik 'abullah* (Memoirs of King Abdullah) (Amman 1965), pp. 190–191. (My translation). Abdullah is most probably referring to the new Reserve Force Peake was authorised to raise (750 strong) in the summer of 1921, particularly after the existing units proved unable to cope with tribal uprisings, especially at Kura in May 1921.

[7] For details of this incident, see Māḍī and Mūsā, *op. cit.*, pp. 156–164, and Khayr al-dīn al-Zarkalī, *'āmān fī 'ammān* (Two Years in Amman) (Cairo, 1925), pp. 117–130. See also Peake, *op. cit., Journal of the Royal Central Asian Society*, vol. 26 (July 1939), pp. 375–396; H. St. J. Philby, "Trans-Jordan", *Journal of the Royal Central Asian Society*, vol. II (1924), part iv. pp. 296–312.

wider districts as a preliminary step to the imposition of authority by the incipient central government of Abdullah in Amman. The security forces in effect had failed in their punitive measures against the rebels. They lacked equipment and funds, as well as adequate training. While, as it turned out, Abdullah eventually resolved this and similar subsequent incidents of rebellion elsewhere in the territory by resorting to the politics of conciliation and amnesty for tribal leaders, he actually felt insecure and unsure of his authority without ultimate acess to an available effectively organised force.

The Kura incident had serious repercussions which affected both the future political evolution of the principality and the evolution of the Legion. It ushered in a second and significant phase in the rise and organisation of the Legion. More important was the fact that it foreshadowed the crucial role of the Legion in the consolidation of the Transjordan territory and the establishment of the principality under Amir Abdullah. On one side, the British Mandate authorities in Jerusalem, as well as their agents in Transjordan, were now convinced of the inadequacy of security forces commanded by Arab officers. They were now interested in increasing their control over such security forces, under a reorganised establishment. Abdullah, on the other side, was now ready to seek increased financial assistance from Britain to strengthen his position in a chaotic and hopelessly fragmented territory and so impose his authority and control over both tribal groups and townsmen. The British acceded to his request for further financial assistance on two conditions: (1) that Peake be placed in charge of all finances for the security forces instead of Abdullah's[8] "minister", and (2) that a reorganised Reserve Force with an authorised strength of 750 officers and men be raised and commanded by Peake. Originally, this essentially military force was intended to help the existing police and stationary gendarmerie forces in maintaining public order and security.

These conditions, however, produced a split between Abdullah and his then "Prime Minister", Rashid Bey Ṭaliʻ, who was identified with the so-called Arab Independence group of Syrian emigrés. As they were averse to expanded British control, Ṭaliʻ insisted upon an authorised strength of 1,500 for the new force. Abdullah let him resign and carried on with the agreement.

[8] According to Sir Alec Kirkbride, "details of the budget were all subject to British financial control. This meant, in effect, that the amount allocated to any one service was decided by the British authorities. The British subsidy was paid *en bloc* to the Jordanian Treasury to make good the recurrent deficit in the budget. The Treasury then paid funds over to individual departments in accordance with the approved budget."

Peake could not at first easily find recruits from Transjordan for his new force. This was in part due to the poor performance of the security forces in dealing with the first Kura incident in May 1921. He therefore resorted to Arabs who had served in the Ottoman armies, largely from Syria and Palestine. By the autumn of 1921 he had organised the following force:

3 Cavalry companies (sarāyā) commanded by Arab captains.
2 Infantry companies also commanded by Arab captains.
1 Battery of mountain artillery commanded by an Iraqi officer.
1 Machine-gun company.
1 Signal squadron.

In addition to these unit commanders, Peake got together about ten other Arab officers, mainly lieutenants, and set up base camp near the Amman railway station. Later, in the spring of 1922, he imported three or four line officers from Egypt to take charge of troop training, founded a school for training gendarmes and police, and engaged a British officer to look after administration.

By December 1921 the major function of this force became clear: to put down tribal uprisings and other incidents that disturbed the peace and challenged the authority of Amman, i.e. of the Amir. Just as important was its further function of collecting taxes for the principality's treasury. Generally the force was entrusted with the task of establishing order, peace and security throughout the territory. The successful performance of this task was largely responsible for the creation of the state.

Meantime, beginning in May 1921, the British had erected the beginnings of an air station at Merka, a village suburb of Amman. A small detachment of British troops had also been posted at Azraq. The air station particularly, together with another one built later at Mafrak, soon came to play a decisive role in the skirmishes between the security forces of Transjordan and raiding tribes that crossed the border from Arabia.

The new force under Peake found early occasions to test its strength, training and discipline against dissident groups throughout Transjordan. From December 1921 to February 1922 it was engaged in putting down tribal uprisings in Kerak and Tafilah in the south against the Amman-appointed governor. The rebel leaders were arrested, and the force spent several weeks restoring order in the area and collecting taxes. The Kura incident of the previous year was, at this time, still unsettled. The rebels there refused to come to terms with Abdullah and submit to the authority of the appointed ʿAjlūn governor in Irbid. Here again Peake had another occasion to test the efficiency and discipline of his new force. A forty-hour forced march from the south to Kura proved a successful punitive expedition against the rebels, whose leaders were quickly and easily arrested. Then, by the summer of 1922, the Mobile Force under Peake was fully engaged in repulsing Wahhabi raids from Arabia. Similar Wahhabi raids occurred again in the summer of 1923 and 1924. All had been successfully repulsed by the new Mobile Force with the aid of British planes and RAF armoured cars.

During this time the force also had to cope with the resolution of serious internal political conflict in the important al-Salṭ area of the Balqā' province. It involved not merely a struggle for power between leaders of a tribe, but also a direct challenge to the authority of the Amir Abdullah. The famous 'Adwan rebellion in the summer of 1923 also got out of hand when it acquired a political dimension directly affecting the Amir's relationship to Britain, and involved disaffected politicians of the Arab Independence group. It was not clear at the time whether the 'Adwan were seeking to extract further privileges from Amman, to secure certain rights, or plainly to overthrow its government. At the time it was believed by many Transjordanians that British agents had fomented the rebellion on instructions from the High Commissioner in Jerusalem. The Independence group in the Amman government feared that the movement was aimed directly at them. It appears, on the other hand, that the 'Adwan resented the fact that the administration of Transjordan under Abdullah was largely in the hands of outsiders (i.e. Iraqis, Syrians, Palestininans, and Lebanese). They demanded posts in the new administration for the natives, so to speak, and even coined the slogan "Transjordan for the Transjordanians". There is little doubt, however, that they resented above all else the favoured position of their traditional rivals and enemies the Banu Sakhr to the east with Abdullah. It was the Banu Sakhr, numerous and powerful, who, over the years, had pushed the 'Adwan further west into the Balqā' and the Jordan valley. In fact, the actual incident which precipitated the political crisis of September 1923 involved a disagreement between Mithqāl al-Fāyiz, chief of the Bani Sakhr, and Sulṭān Pasha al-'Adwan of the 'Adwan. The disagreement nearly led to an armed clash between the forces of the two tribes. When the government tried to intervene the 'Adwan threatened to march against the capital and remove the government by force. Abdullah tried to conciliate Sultan Pasha by inviting him to see him in Amman. Sultan Pasha arrived, but at the head of a large force armed to the teeth. All the same, he agreed to Abdullah's suggestion that the latter should tour the tribe early in September.

Meantime, 'Adwan's show of force compelled the Amir to form a new administrative council. The new government, however, advised against Abdullah's visit to the 'Adwan, since this could be interpreted as a sign of weakness on the part of Amman. Instead they determined to use force against the rebels if necessary, and Abdullah proceeded to arrest several personalities suspected of conspiring with the 'Adwan against the government. This change of policy—from conciliation to confrontation—elicited violent reaction from the 'Adwan. On 6 September they organised a march against Amman. This was met by units of the Mobile Force led by Fuad Bey Salim, deputy military commander to Peake, who was away at that time, as well as by other units of the gendarmes. A clash took place about four miles west of Amman. But this was very brief. A British armoured car that was on the scene was attacked by some of the 'Adwan forces. In returning the fire the machine-gunner of the armoured car killed one of the tribal shaykhs in the 'Adwan camp. This incident, together with the appearance of a RAF plane overhead, ended the engagement and, with it, the 'Adwan rebellion.

This incident, however, brought to the surface the latent conflict between the Arab Independence group and Abdullah, who wished to establish firmly his authority with British aid. It also foreshadowed the further role of the Reserve Mobile Force in resolving conflicts of this nature. Above all, it led to the further reorganisation of the security forces under tighter British control.

It should be noted that for the first two years of this early phase the Mobile Force commanded by Peake remained separate from the administration of Public Security and Order in the three districts, or provinces, of Transjordan. The latter remained under the jurisdiction of the gendarmerie and police officered entirely by Arabs. Soon after Abdullah had secured an agreement with Britain recognising the autonomy of his principality in April 1923, further changes in the administration of the security forces were introduced. In September 1923 this arrangement for the security forces was abolished. Instead all forces in Transjordan now were merged with the Reserve Mobile Force, were put under the command of Peake, and were given the new name *al-jaysh al-'arabi*, the Arab Army, and officially in English that of the Arab Legion. In November Abdullah appointed Peake to the rank of *Amir Liwā'*, or Brigadier General. He was now commander of the Legion, serving as an employee of the Transjordan Emirate Government.

These new arrangements confirmed not only the understanding between Abdullah and the British which matured in a series of agreements since March 1921 and culminated in the treaty of April

1923, but also indicated the defeat of the anti-British—and thus anti-Abdullah—Independence elements in Abdullah's first governments. They also reflected the change in Abdullah's plans and policies. From his earlier avowed aims to retrieve Syria from the French on behalf of his brother Faysal declared with such bravado when he came from the Hejaz to Ma'an in 1920, Abdullah had returned from London in the early spring of 1923 to declare to his Transjordanians that he intended to set up a state in Transjordan. In practical terms, he had settled for a dynastic state as the best and most realistic political gain he could attain under the circumstances. His initial success by the end of 1923 was very much due to the patient and determined use of the new security force organised, trained and commanded by Peake, and assisted in its operations by the RAF and its armoured cars. Abdullah's political opponents collapsed and his ascendancy was now secured in what one of his private secretaries, and, by 1924, political exiles, subsequently described as *al-dawla al-'abdaliyya*, the "Abdullah state".[9]

Even in this early phase, political agitation among some of the Arab officers of the new force was inevitable, particularly when Abdullah's schemes were not to everyone's liking. The use of the security force for the achievement of the Prince's aims and ambitions —in fact, to found a dynastic state—had political repercussions among its personnel. This kind of early political involvement of army officers first occurred in the 'Adwan rebellion. There is little doubt that several of them were implicated in that early movement against Abdullah, as surely as others among them were implicated in the armed incursions into Syrian territory to harass the French. To some extent their involvement in this way was due to their sympathy with the Arab nationalist views of the Independence group of politicians. Among the latter, a few viewed the demand by the 'Adwan for a representative assembly with sympathy, in the hope of curtailing the power of Abdullah. The late H. St. J. Philby, no friend of Abdullah, hinted at this apparent disloyalty of Arab officers years later as follows:

"One day the conversation turned on Trans-Jordan and the 'Adwan rebellion of 1923: Yusuf Yasin, who had been in Amman at the time, suggesting that, in the absence of Peake Pasha, the Arab Legion would have been ready to join the rebels if circumstances had been favourable. I challenged this view, which seemed to me groundless, whereupon Dr. Mahmud got on his hobby-horse, praising officers of the Legion like Fuad Salim who, while swearing

[9] See al-Zarkalī, *op. cit.*, p. 203

loyalty to the Amir 'Abdullah and the British and receiving their pay from them, spent all their time working against them and stirring up their troops to disloyalty. . . "[10]

In fact, Peake reported many years later[11] that he dismissed several Arab officers from the Legion, among them Latif Bey Salim who was killed in 1926 while engaged in anti-French hostilities in Syria.

Having settled the 'Adwan affair to his advantage and at the expense of his opponents, Abdullah coupled a conciliatory policy of placating local notables and tribal leaders with a positive government programme of strengthening his position and consolidating his power. The agreement signed with Britain, which recognised an independent administration in Transjordan under Abdullah, also assured the latter of a fixed £150,000 annual subsidy. This was of substantial advantage to the strengthening of his earlier precarious position when, as a result of his agreement with Churchill, he was to

---

[10] *Arabian Jubilee* (London, 1952), p. 142.

[11] See his "Trans-Jordan", *op. cit.* In connection with the political significance of the 'Adwan rebellion, it is interesting to note Philby's assessment of it. Speaking very soon after his resignation from his post as British Chief Resident Adviser in Amman in 1924, he said that the 'Adwan rebellion "which had the sympathy of a great part of the country, groaning as it was under a reckless tyranny", threatened to topple Abdullah. He suggested further in the same discourse that he saved Abdullah from this fate. See his "Trans-Jordan", *op. cit.*, p. 306. Moreover, in the same discourse Philby argued that he continually urged Abdullah to set up a representative assembly and forgo absolute power. Instead he stated Abdullah squandered huge sums of money, including the small British subsidy, in placating tribal chiefs with land and gifts. He further charged that the High Commissioner in Jerusalem wanted Transjordan brought back in the Palestine orbit and thus under closer control of Jerusalem. He (Philby) wanted to see a truly independent Arab state established in Transjordan. It should be noted here that Lawrence had recommended the appointment of Philby to replace the first British adviser, Abramson. Philby arrived in Amman towards the end of 1921 and resigned in January 1924. At that time he also left the British service.

These remarks by Philby indicate that his sympathies lay with the Arab Independence group. In great measure this also explains his life-long disapproval of—if not enmity towards—Abdullah and all the Hashemites. It is not certain, however, if Philby at that time at all encouraged the Independence group politicians and the 'Adwan to openly challenge Abdullah's still precarious authority. Yet, Sir Alex Kirkbride, who was in Transjordan at the time, told this writer in a lengthy interview in October 1965 that he suspected Philby's encouragement of the 'Adwan uprising.

Mādī and Mūsā, *op. cit.*, p. 233, on the other hand, allege that the British were behind the 'Adwan rebellion. "Evidence of British disapproval of the suppression of the 'Adwan rebellion," they argue, "is the fact that Colonel Latif Salim, chief of Staff of the Reserve Force was relieved of his post shortly thereafter, and replaced by Major 'Abd al-Qadir al-Jundī as of 10th December, 1923."

attempt the establishment of an administration with a £5,000 monthly subsidy for six months. Nevertheless he had to secure more revenue from taxation. His earlier efforts in this direction met with the opposition and open rebellion of various tribal groups in different parts of the country as was noted above. The strengthening of public order and tax reform, in this order of priority, became immediate aims of the Amir. One serious obstacle now remained in the face of implementing this programme successfully. It plagued Abdullah for another year.

Some of the Arab officers in the security forces, as stated earlier, belonged to or sympathised with the Independence group of politicians. They resented Abdullah's retreat from his initial purpose in coming to Transjordan, namely, to "liberate" Syria from the French and restore it to the Arab kingdom of his brother Faysal. They also disapproved of and opposed Abdullah's increasing dependence upon Britain which, in due course, had the effect of subordinating them to his authority. Since June 1921 there had been occasional raids by Arabs against French border outposts in Syria with the knowledge, if not collusion, of these officers. This appeared to be the case after the attack against General Gouraud's party in Qunayṭra near the Syrian-Transjordanian border by armed bands from Transjordan. When the French in Syria demanded the apprehension and extradition of the marauders, and Peake's Mobile Force was getting ready to seek them out, units of the *darak* in Balqā' commanded by an Arab officer, who was a known member of the Independence group, prepared to oppose Peake's force.

A similar instance of the political involvement of officers arose in July 1921. Ibrahim Hanano, a known leader of anti-French armed bands in northern Syria, escaped to Transjordan. The French requested his arrest and extradition. Several Arab officers in the Transjordan security forces proceeded to foment disturbances to protest any such action by Abdullah's government. These were mainly from the al-Salṭ area. They were arrested and dismissed from the forces in September. Similarly there was politically motivated opposition to the incorporation in 1923 of all the security forces into the Reserve Mobile Force commanded by Peake. Arab officers from the Balqā' province attempted to organise a mutiny against this merger, and closer British control over the security forces.

Thus while the French lodged repeated protests with the Jerusalem authorities to order their wards to stop the incursions of armed rebels into Syria, Abdullah was faced with a difficult dilemma. His administration was still largely dominated and run by Independence group members or sympathisers. His security forces comprised a sizeable number of Arab nationalist officers. To seek the arrest and to permit the extradition of marauders against the French in Syria was to court not only the displeasure and opposition of many members of his administration, but also, more dangerous, to risk open mutiny in his security forces. All the while, however, ever since Peake became commander of all security forces reorganised as the Arab Legion in 1923, he was consolidating the control of the country by this better-trained military organisation. With greater control over the finances of the Legion, Peake was also able by February 1924 to purge it of Arab officers known or suspected to be sympathisers with the Independence group of politicians. After their dismissal from the Legion, about ten of these officers left for the Hejaz and other parts.

In August 1924, further armed clashes occurred on the Syrian border in the Hauran area. At the same time, a second Wahhabi raid against Transjordan materialised. This was repulsed by the Legion with the substantial aid of the RAF using both planes and armoured cars. At this juncture, the British put pressure on Abdullah to put a stop, once and for all, to the anti-French activities of the Arab nationalist rebels. They demanded the dismissal from the government of those politically involved in these activities, the imposition of strict British control over all financial matters in Transjordan without conditions of any sort, and the extradition of the criminal marauders to the Syrian authorities. In need of money, and determined to found his dynastic state in Transjordan, Abdullah accepted these conditions and proceeded to oust the Independence politicians from his government. He therefore asked the more prominent leaders among them to leave the country within three days. These left for the Hejaz, and from there some of them went to Egypt. With the resolution of this difficulty, Abdullah was now ready to consolidate his power and rule further, but under stricter British control, and with wider use of the purged and reorganised Arab Legion.

Sweeping administrative reforms—sweeping that is for the Transjordan of those days—were being introduced in early 1925, as the reorganised security forces under Peake continued to deal with tribal unrest, tax collection, and generally the task of establishing law and order in a vast but sparsely populated country. While playing the important role of peacemaker, the Legion was also gradually weaning the tribes and the provincial population from the belief that government was weak and that by stirring up trouble they could extract money and other concessions from it as easily as they had done under the Turks in the past. Rather the Legion showed by the spring of 1926 that the government would and could levy and collect taxes, that it would and could build roads and enforce municipal ordinances. Thus the reforms that set up the administrative cadre of the new principality coincided with the role of the Legion in the first registration of the population ever,[12] and the introduction with British advice and supervision of financial accounting and control. The Legion, in short, had in this phase of its development (1923–1926) introduced by virtue of its disciplined use of force the tribesman, the restless beduin, and the townsman alike to the notion of restraint and to the acceptance of an order imposed by a central administrative authority.

It should be noted that in this phase the recruits for the Mobile Force and other units of the Legion were mainly, if not exclusively, village peasants and some townsmen. "My policy," Peake stated once, "was to raise a Force from the sedentary, or village, Arabs, which would gradually be able to check the Beduin and allow an Arab government to rule the country without fear or interference from the tribal chiefs."[13] Beduins stayed away from the Legion; in fact, they were inimical to it, for they saw it strengthening the hand of a central ruler. Until they accepted recruitment and began to enlist in the Legion in large numbers in the 1930s (especially in Glubb's Desert Patrol Force), beduins constituted—with their constant raiding—a major irritant to the state. In February–March 1926, for instance, tribesmen in the Wadi Musa area west of Ma'an launched a series of attacks against Legion outposts, government centres, and labourers working on a road. Perhaps they were indulging in the usual tribal uprising against a government that by then appeared to be introducing taxation and generally administrative control over the country. Although a strong Legion force supported by armoured cars went out to confront the tribesmen in Wadi Musa, the mere threat of the government to destroy their villages brought about their surrender.

Even so, by 1926 Peake had raised a force of over 1,500 officers and men in the Legion. He set up a three-member Selection Board for officers with two Arabs on it. This interviewed and re-engaged officers whose enlistment time had expired. He also opened a Central Training School staffed by Arab officers. This trained mainly NCOs.

---

[12] It is interesting to note that when the Ottoman governor of Kerak in the south was ordered by his superiors in Damascus in 1910 to disarm the tribes and carry out a census for military service and a land registration scheme, the tribes under the leadership of the paramount Sheikh Qadr al-Majali rose in open rebellion. See Peake, *History and Tribes of Jordan* (Miami, Florida, 1958), pp. 93–94.

[13] See C. S. Jarvis, *Arab Command* (London, 1943), p. 61.

Ten years later, in 1936, there were still only seven British officers in the Legion. Nevertheless, this force proved the most important instrument in the consolidation of the principality amidst political conditions characterised by a population that had known little loyalty to any settled government before that time. This, together with the eventual demarcation and successful guarding of the country's boundaries—also greatly the work of the Legion—strengthened the position of the Amir and his administration in Amman.

It appears, however, that the Legion suffered a serious setback in its early development in the next ten years (1926–1936). It is, moreover, a politically controversial period. In March 1926 the British High Commissioner in Palestine decreed the creation of a new armed force which came into existence on April 1, to be called the Trans-Jordan Frontier Force (TJFF). The ostensible role of this Imperial force was to defend the frontiers of Transjordan, especially those with Syria and Saudi Arabia. Although it is reasonable to assume that a strong force to protect the eastern frontier was justified at that time, there is disagreement among British officials who were involved regarding the motives of Lord Plumer in creating this force.[14] In addition to the Wahhabi raids from the east in 1922 and 1924, the Saudis had by this time conquered the Hejaz. On 13 October 1925 Ibn Saud took Mecca, on 5 December Madina, and on 23 December Jedda. On 8 January 1926 he was proclaimed King of the Hejaz. Abdullah's father, King Husayn, had lost his Arab kingdom. In these circumstances, it was conceivable that the Saudi conquerors of the Hejaz might have had further territorial ambitions.

Yet the actual effect of this policy was an immediate reduction of the Legion's strength from 1,600 to under 900 men. Its artillery, signals, and machine-gun units were abolished. Some of its officers and men were transferred to the new TJFF. The official explanation for the Legion's reduction in force was that of economy. Paradoxically, though, the Transjordan government was required to meet one-sixth of the cost of the new TJFF.

The TJFF was to be under the direct control of the High Commissioner in Jerusalem and above him the War Office in London. All squadron commanders, that is majors and above (except for medical officers), were to be British. Troop commanders and ranks below this were Arab captains mainly, with a few Circassians[15] and

---

[14] Especially Sir Alec Kirkbride, and later Sir John Glubb.
[15] The Circassians have been an interesting small ethnic muslim minority in Jordan, particularly in connection with the army. Ever since the tenth century

Jews. These officers, however, were not to attain command positions that gave them seniority over British personnel. They were also provided with a separate mess. Their status in the TJFF was similar to that of the Indians who held Viceroy's commissions in the Indian Army.

The bulk of TJFF recruits came from the disbanded Palestine Gendarmerie which had been formed in 1921. Enlistment in the Force was however equally open to Transjordanians. Thus, Circassians from Transjordan were well represented in the ranks of the Force. Some recruits came from the surrounding areas, such as Syria and Lebanon.

After an initial six months training period in Palestine the TJFF set up headquarters in Zerqa, with base camps in Ma'an to the south, and in Samakh in northern Palestine close to the Syrian border. In 1946 the Force was about 700 strong, including roughly twenty-five British officers. It was disbanded in 1948 when Britain relinquished the mandate over Palestine. It is alleged by those who were opposed to the formation of the TJFF that the quality of its officers was

---

they have lived on the western slopes of the Caucasus leading down to the Black Sea. With the advance of the Russians to the Caucasus, and especially their military campaigns there against another muslim ethnic group, the Chechens, the Circassian tribes were forced to move westwards into Rumelia. Here, as Muslims, they received gifts of land from the Ottoman Sultan. After the Russo-Turkish War of 1877–1878, several families from a number of Circassian tribes were settled by Sultan Abdul Hamid of Turkey in Syria and Transjordan. There they founded communities in several villages, especially in Jerash, Amman, Wadi Sir, and Swayleh of the Balqa' district.

Before the Second World War the number of Circassians in Transjordan was estimated at between eight and ten thousand. This figure is lower now.

Although organised in tribes, the Circassians were a settled people. Their early relations with the beduin in Transjordan were therefore not friendly. Sultan Abdul Hamid is said to have sent them to counterweigh the raiding beduin. In any event, by the 1880s, Circassians were already serving in the Ottoman Turkish garrison units stationed in Transjordan. Thus, the 200-strong cavalry regiment in Kerak at the disposal of its Turkish governor in 1905–1910 was Circassian in composition.

Circassians also served in the TJFF. Many of them enlisted in the Arab Legion from its inception. An élite unit of Circassians came to form King Abdullah's special guard. There are Circassian officers and men in the Jordan Army today.

The Circassian community is represented in the Jordanian parliament. A prominent Circassian, Said Pasha al-Mufti, has served as prime minister of Jordan and as President of the Upper House (*majlis al-a'yān*) of its National Assembly.

On the Circassians, as well as the other muslim ethnic minorities (Chechens and Turkomans), see Frederick G. Peake, *op. cit.*, pp. 222–224, and Naval Intelligence Division, *Palestine and Transjordan*, Geographical Handbook Series (London 1943), pp. 468–469.

unimpressive and that its recruits were not the most loyal.[16] They have also argued that the TJFF was nowhere as successful in defending Transjordan's frontiers or in maintaining order, as the Arab Legion had been up to that time (admittedly with the aid of the RAF and its armoured cars), or subsequently after the formation of the Desert Patrol as a special section of the Legion under the command of Glubb in 1930.[17]

The real blow to the Legion, however, was its reduction to an internal security force, largely confined in its role to police duties, short of any military functions. In 1927-1928 the commander of the Arab Legion was re-designated "Assistant Commanding Officer, Army, for Public Security".[18]

When the period 1928-1933 turned out to be a turbulent one for the country—intensified tribal raids, political agitation in the towns against the 1928 treaty with Britain—it became clear that the reduced Legion, confined in its functions as it was, could not cope effectively with the internal situation. In November 1930 Captain John Glubb, originally an officer of the Royal Engineers, arrived from Iraq, where he had been engaged for some years in the pacification of tribes, to serve as second-in-command to Peake. To meet the constant pressure from the tribes and the apparent inability of either a reduced Legion or the TJFF to counter it, the government set out to raise a Desert Mobile Force. The new factors which spelled a significant departure in the Legion's future development were:

(1) The new force, as a new element in the Legion, was to be purely beduin in composition, recruited from the nomadic and semi-nomadic tribes.

(2) It was to have both striking capacity over a range of long desert distances, as well as recourse to strategic re-grouping, re-supply and communications via a series of forts to be built throughout the desert and to be equipped with wireless sets.

This development ushered in a fourth phase in the evolution of

[16] To judge by the recruitment "pitch" made by one Royal Artillery officer serving with the Force in 1930 (hunting, sport, pay and allowances), one is tempted to think that the detractors of the TJFF may have been right. See Captain L. K. Lockhart, "The Transjordan Frontier Force", *The Journal of the Royal Artillery*, vol. 56 (1929-30), No. 1, pp. 77-84.
[17] On the TJFF see L. K. Lockhart, *op. cit.*, and J. M. Sinclair, *op. cit.*, For further details on the TJFF in this book, see Appendix.
[18] Abdullah deplored the formation of the TJFF, because according to him it was contrary to earlier agreements between himself and the British authorities. See *mudhakkirāt...*, p. 191. See also in this connection Philby's derisory remarks about Abdullah's contention that the Arab Legion was a better force than the TJFF in *op. cit.*, p. 202—a venomous chapter, entitled "Our Brother of Jordan", pp. 194-203.

the Legion, marked by (*a*) the direct recruitment of beduins into the force, (*b*) the acquisition of extensive ground operational experience, at least in desert warfare, (*c*) extensive practice in operations which involved the co-ordination of ground forces activity with supporting air strikes via wireless communication, and (*d*) the acquisition of intensive, though limited, expertise in the use of transport. In short, an *élite force* within the Legion was to acquire intensive *military* training.

Glubb's success in recruiting beduins and pacifying them over the next five to ten years was the result of a combination of expert diplomacy and efficient military action. To this extent Glubb was instrumental in raising and training what soon came to constitute the *striking force* of the Jordan Arab Army.

Further strengthening and militarisation of the Legion occurred as a result of the Arab Rebellion in Palestine in 1936–1939. In March–April 1936 armed bands from Syria descended upon the nearby 'Ajlun district of Transjordan. These were successfully engaged by the Legion on at least two occasions. The Legion was thus responsible for preventing such bands, and others from Palestine, from making trouble in Transjordan.

Whereas in 1930–1936 the Legion, police and gendarmerie numbered no more than 1,200 officers and men, the Palestine troubles led to the authorisation by Britain of a Reserve Combat Force in the Legion of two cavalry companies, and one regiment of mechanised beduin, the so-called "Beduin Mechanised Force", with a strength of 350. Yet, at the outbreak of the Second World War, when Glubb had succeeded Peake as Commander of the Legion, its actual combat strength was barely over 800 men out of a total force of roughly 1,600. This situation, however, did not prevail for very long. The General Officer Commanding, Middle East, requested the doubling of this strength to secure seven armed and well-trained permanent battalions (about 350 men in each), which were then used widely throughout the Middle East theatre for guard duties over installations, oil pipelines, communication centres, ports and air fields, trains and other land transport convoys.

The brief participation of Legion units in the swift campaigns in Iraq against the Rashid Ali al-Geylani regime and in the campaigns against the Vichy French in Syria and Lebanon in 1941 not only gave the Legion added operational experience, but also helped its further expansion and retraining as a military force.

Of course, all of this expansion was achieved by British financing and equipment, although several hundred vehicles (Ford trucks) were bought by Transjordan from Detroit. Towards the end of the war the Desert Force was enlarged from one regiment to three, and was organised in a brigade headquarters. It acquired a base training camp at Azraq, bought more transport, and generally experienced its most sustained training period.

When the mandate status of Transjordan was abolished in March 1946, and an independent kingdom proclaimed, the Legion entered an entirely new phase: this was the transition from a security force with limited military operational functions to a regular army, a fully-fledged military institution. We shall see that the first stages in this transition period were marked by the continued conception of the Legion as an élite force. The Palestine War brought about its inevitable expansion into a more comprehensive military institution. The rest of our discussion will concern these two stages in the transition. Furthermore, most of the illustrative data are drawn from the period of greatest expansion, 1948–1956.

CHAPTER V

# The Rapid Expansion of the Legion, 1948–1956

*Its transformation from a corps d'élite to a national military establishment*

## 1. ORGANISATIONAL STRUCTURE AND RECRUITMENT

Much of the operational history of the Legion has been recounted, albeit briefly, in the preceding sections. Its problems and difficulties under the mandate have been also outlined. By the end of the Second World War the Legion did not exceed 8,000 officers and men of all ranks. These consisted of a 3,000 strong mechanised brigade of three regiments, about 15 garrison unit groups totalling roughly 2,000 men, some 500 engineer, administrative and medical services personnel, and about 2,000 recruits in training centres. The Desert Patrol Force was about 500 strong. Altogether Transjordan's forces including its police stood at a total of about 9,000.[1]

With the exception of its "scout" role with Habforce in the quick British campaign in Iraq in May 1941 to quash the Rashid Ali al-Geylani pro-Axis regime, and the subsequent diversion in June 1941 to oust the Vichy forces from Syria and Lebanon, the Legion's ground force remained basically a collection of garrison infantry units. The Desert Mechanised Force grew to three regiments, organised in a brigade headquarters.

It must also be emphasised that between 1926 and 1940 the Legion was no more than a police and gendarmerie force—an internal security force. With the exception of two British officers in 1940, namely General John Glubb and Brigadier Norman Lash, a large proportion of the other thirty-five to forty officers were Arabs who had served under the Turks before 1918. The few new officers admitted into the Legion hardly received any military training at the company tactical level; the emphasis was on training at the platoon level for police duties. Only the exigencies of war in 1940–1941 enabled

[1] See "Transjordan's Army—the Arab Legion", *Palestine Affairs*, vol. 3, (April 1948), pp. 44–45.

the Legion to recruit young officers for actual military training, and to expand its strength of enlisted ranks. Thus in 1941 there was a total Arab Legion force of 1,300, or 1,600 including urban and rural police. It expanded quickly to 8,000 strong by 1945. The strength of the TJFF stood at about 700. While the total strength decreased to 6,000 in early 1948, the Legion nevertheless had acquired an officer strength of some 300, most of them possessing military training.

The officer pattern for the Legion was a key question throughout this period. In 1921–1922 Peake had staffed his force with ex-Ottoman Army Arab officers and warrant officers.[2] These were all in the age group of twenty to thirty. A few were appointed majors, fewer as colonels, and the rest as captains and lieutenants. In 1939–1940 these same officers were still serving in the Legion; and most of them were now in their forties. Only one new officer was admitted throughout this period (1922–1939): he is currently the Chief of the General Staff of the Jordan Army.

Thus, when General Glubb succeeded Peake in 1939, the Legion was entirely staffed by Arab officers in their forties, with ranks ranging from lieutenant to brigadier. Even though some of them had had brief military experience in the First World War, their subsequent service with the Legion was entirely in the nature of a police, or gendarmerie, force. Except for the Desert Patrol units which were motorised, all other units were either cavalry or infantry.

In 1941 officer expansion began in earnest, using the double method of (1) promoting NCOs and (2) admitting young cadets. This system of officer recruitment and training has since been followed with some variations in the Legion until 1956. In explaining the pattern of officer recruitment followed since 1941, General Glubb states:

> "It may be noted that the division of soldiers into officers and other ranks is a purely European system which grew out of the social organisation of Europe in the Feudal Age, when knights were an exclusive aristocratic class, who brought their servants to war as their retainers ... Arab and Muslim armies never had a system of officers and men because they did not have a corresponding division into social classes ...
> 
> "The system of appointing officers from high school or university direct to commissions as officers or cadets has the disadvantage that in Arab countries 'tribesmen', whether *fellaheen* (peasants) or

---

[2] Some of these will have had staff training in Turkey. See D. A. Rustow, "Harbiye", EI² = *Encyclopedia of Islam* 2nd ed., vol. 3, (1966), pp. 203–204.

beduins, have strong warrior traditions . . . whereas the city dwellers have no military traditions, particularly in Palestine.

". . . promotion from the ranks which I favoured was in strict Arab and Islamic tradition, whereas direct commissions for college boys, which the *effendi* and official classes supported, was a slavish imitation of unsuitable European methods, which Europe itself is now discarding . . .

"Thus, of the two sources for the recruitment of officers, I and Muslim and Arab tradition favoured no class distinctions, but the choice of officers from communities with fighting traditions."[3]

Faced with a Legion which in 1941 was staffed almost entirely by officers in their forties and whose experience was confined to gendarmerie duties, the problem for the army was to recruit and train officers for military units. This expansion was successfully carried out—albeit in a limited fashion—by the training and promotion of NCOs of the old Legion, i.e. the pre-1941 one. These non-commissioned officers came mainly from among beduin and settled peasant (*fellahin*) villagers, as well as a few townsmen. While the admission of town boys as cadets in that period was, in many cases, the result of political pressure, these served well in administrative jobs, especially when British officers were seconded to the Legion after the Second World War.

About the difficulty presented by the recruitment or selection of officers in small countries, General Glubb explained on the strength of his Jordanian experience:

"The cities and the educated classes were so few that officers chosen from these town dwellers were almost all members of families who also produced politicians and civil officials, or were in some way connected with such families. This has been the ruin of the Syrian army—a country with a much larger population than Jordan. In Arab countries where family loyalties are much stronger than national loyalties, this means that every such officer has some connection with a politician or political party . . .

"In so small a country as Jordan, it is most important *not* to recruit officers from important or powerful families. This applies

---

[3] Private communication to the writer, 25 June 1966. It should be noted that this view of an officer in a Muslim army may be oversimplified. The term officer (*ḍābiṭ*) acquired technical meaning of an army officer in the seventeenth century in the Jannissaries corps as against that of other soldier ranks (*nefer*). With westernisation in the nineteenth century the term ḍābiṭ became the equivalent of the European army officer. See B. Lewis, "Ḍābiṭ", *Encyclopedia of Islam*, 2nd ed., vol. II, p. 74.

as much to the sons of tribal chiefs as to those of cabinet ministers."[4]

The outbreak of hostilities between the Arab and Jewish communities in Palestine in 1947–1948 and the British declaration of their intention to relinquish their mandate over the country posed serious problems for Jordan. Foreseeing trouble and hostilities in Palestine that would involve the Legion directly, the late King Abdullah and General Glubb were now anxious to strengthen the army by rendering it an efficient fighting force as quickly as possible. This consideration perhaps alone prompted the importation of British officers in the late 1940s and early 1950s.

"The only way to make the Jordan Army efficient quickly was to import British officers, and persuade the British Government to pay a lot more money," General Glubb explained to me recently, indicating also that this was borne out by the events of the Arab-Israeli war, as well as by the particular battle for Jerusalem. Not only was this essential for the control of Central Palestine, but also for deterring future Israeli attack. Thus Legion efficiency required the infusion of two essentials from Britain: good officers and greater financial aid.[5]

The outbreak of the war in Palestine between Israel and the Arab States in May 1948 found the Legion with an overall strength of 6,000, of whom only 4,500 were operational, i.e. available for combat. Their operational organisation consisted of four mechanised, mobile regiments. These were quickly reorganised in two brigade groups, with brigade headquarters, each comprising two regiments. In addition, there were two artillery batteries of four 25 lb. guns each, and seven garrison units trained primarily as guard stationary units without any tactical operational capabilities. These were mainly rifle companies, their heaviest weapon being a Bren gun per platoon. They had no mortars, for example, or other weapons. A division headquarters was improvised and superimposed over all this as a purely tactical and administrative set-up without real operational formation or function. There were however very few officers with staff training to man it.

[4] Private communication to the writer, 25 June 1966.
[5] One can hardly argue with this position given security conditions in 1948–1949 and later. In fact, General Glubb was aware of the political difficulties that would ensue from such necessary action in the most vital interests of the country. To strengthen the country's defence forces required such measures that the opposition predictably interpreted them as part of British imperialist designs. Both the late King Abdullah and his CGS found themselves at the receiving end of widespread political vituperation and abuse.

Moreover, the formal organisation of the Legion did not until then provide a proper reserve force, despite a law passed in 1947 for the formation of such a force. Rather the Legion was a long-term enlisted regular but small military force. A National Guard was built up in the early 1950s. But there were no extensively organised, or even substantial, supporting services such as Engineers, Supply and Transport, Workshops, Medical Corps (except for unit MOs) and other technical services. Recruitment of British officers on a large scale had not begun in earnest until early 1948. It was accelerated between 1948 and 1953. Meanwhile, as mentioned earlier, the Desert Force had expanded from one to three regiments. Despite these difficulties, the total strength of the Legion was raised by 1949-1950 from 6,000 to 12,000. Over £6 million were spent on the Legion, even though the British subsidy authorised an expenditure of only £2·5 million. Britain, however, paid the balance.

It was at this juncture that expansion of the Legion involved more than simple recruitment. The British forces had evacuated Palestine in May-August 1948. It was now imperative for the Legion to create its own independent ancillary technical and other services, so that expansion did not mean simply officer recruitment and training, but, more significantly, technical training in the new branches. The period 1948-1956 was crucial in this respect. It was also important in the training and expansion of the National Guard. The latter reached a total strength of 30,000 recruited mainly from villagers, especially those living on the border. The Guardsmen were equipped by the Legion, and trained by regular Legion NCOs who were attached to village units. Usually a Legionnaire wireless operator was also attached to National Guard units to maintain communication with regular Legion units and GHQ. Very generally, the National Guard was conceived along the lines of the British Territorial Army. In practice, though, it came closer to a Landwehr model.

The National Guard was created practically on the sole initiative of General Glubb. Two considerations were uppermost in his mind. As the person immediately responsible to the government for the organisation of the defence of the country, the CGS was first concerned with the uneasy truce on the border. The resources of the Legion were extended to their limit. With rapid expansion, the building up of new units and technical services became crucial. Not all units could be committed permanently to guarding the whole length of the border. A certain portion of the Legion had to be in training. The conception of the National Guard to consist of villagers trained in defending their homes and fields against infiltration or attack from the other side was a practical answer. Essentially,

General Glubb was treating the problem of border defence and village security in the light of the conditions then obtaining. Moreover, he was familiar at first hand with the Israeli method of settlement defence. Villagers would defend themselves against attack until regular army reinforcements could arrive.

The second consideration was more psychological-political in nature, to wit, "to bring Palestinians into a larger share of the defence of their country".[6] This was a most significant step taken by the CGS to strengthen the defence of the country—especially its long frontier—against possible Israeli attack. Unfortunately, the creation of the National Guard was initially opposed by the government, who considered the arming of Palestinian villagers too risky. They feared that Palestinian National Guardsmen would use their weapons for rebellion against the regime, and that some among them might use them for crime. The politicians of the West Bank, on the other hand, opposed the formation of the National Guard in 1949–1950 because at that time they were still not reconciled to their incorporation into the enlarged Hashemite Kingdom. They feared that if the villagers were to share in the defence of Jordan they might come to accept integration more readily, especially when, as peasants and farmers, they were directly concerned with a secure livelihood. Moreover, several West Bank political leaders were members of big land-owning families who, for generations, exercised considerable influence and control over the peasants on their lands. For these, opposition to the new National Guard may have been motivated by fear of losing all influence over the peasants.

In this connection, General Glubb stated:

"In fact, however, the Arab Legion already had a close connection with frontier villages. The villagers were aware that the Arab Legion was completely dedicated to the defence of Palestine. Propaganda against the Arab Legion to the effect that the British were traitors or Jews had no effect on frontier villagers, who saw them fighting on their side . . .

". . . The same happened in the six months before the end of the British mandate—October 1947 to May 1948—during which there was extensive fighting all over Palestine, especially west of Jerusalem. The only *effendi* who fought and was killed was Abdul Qadir al-Husaini, a quite exceptional man. Huweitat (a tribe) from Jordan did most of the fighting at Bab el Wad west of Jerusalem. The rest was done by Palestine villagers and the *Jeish al-Inqadh* (Army of Liberation) from Syria—also all peasants . . ."[7]

[6] Private communication, 25 June 1966.   [7] Ibid.

It is interesting to note that, once the National Guard had become a going concern, diplomatic pressure from other Arab states was brought to bear upon the Jordanian Government to separate it from the Legion. As the Palestine Question was always considered a common Arab problem, it was suggested that an Arab military officer—in this instance, an Egyptian—be appointed to command the National Guard. The danger of political subversion lurking in such an arrangement was readily detected by the government, and the pressure for it was successfully resisted.

With this background and early history of the National Guard, the action taken by the Nabulsi government in 1956 to integrate it with the Legion may be reasonably interpreted in part as an attempt at political infiltration of the army.

The greatest difficulty encountered in organising the National Guard was financial. The Israelis, for instance, had been able to make every border settlement into an effective fortress defended by its own inhabitants, and concrete structures and barbed wire perimeters had been erected at great cost. Yet only the weapons needed to defend a settlement for a limited period of time were issued to the inhabitants, who also received enough training in their use. In this way, the Israelis were able to make a sizeable financial investment in equipping and training a highly mobile regular army with excellent interior lines. This could move rapidly throughout the country and across the whole length of the frontier in case of attack.

Jordan did not have the necessary funds to spend on a comprehensive scheme of village fortifications. Nor did it have highly developed interior lines. Nevertheless, frontier village guardsmen trained in the limited defence of their villages were considered a valuable addition to the regular Legion forces in case of attack. As for the Legion proper, it experienced in 1949–1953 a period of rapid expansion that was characterised by concentrated military training. It was also in this period that most of its technical branches and support services took real shape.

Thus by 1953, the Legion comprised 17,000–20,000 officers and men, including base units. Meantime, its educational and training facilities had expanded greatly to deal with its needs, and its technical and supporting services had been founded. Artillery, Engineers, Armour, grew from regiment to arm, branch or corps status. Over 1,000 new officers had to be trained to command a total Legion force of some 25,000 by 1956. Emphasis on staff and technical training increased. And this naturally was politically significant both for the Legion and the country.

G

# ARAB LEGION 1953–56

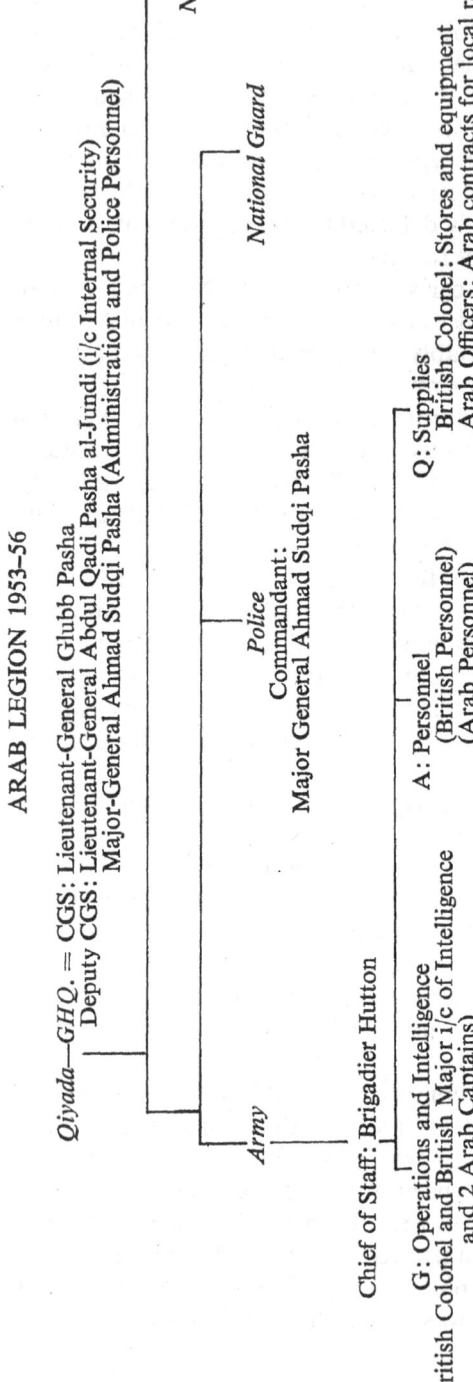
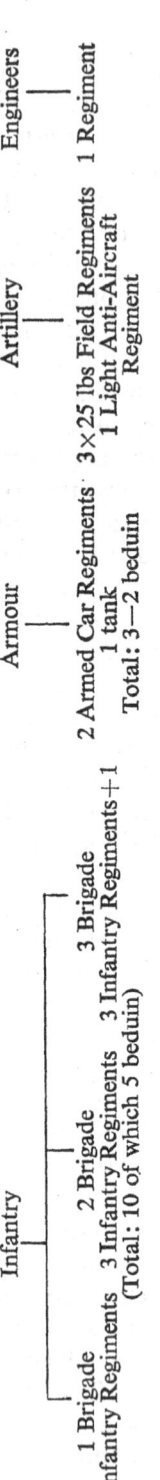

Qiyada—GHQ. = CGS: Lieutenant-General Glubb Pasha
Deputy CGS: Lieutenant-General Abdul Qadi Pasha al-Jundi (i/c Internal Security)
Major-General Ahmad Sudqi Pasha (Administration and Police Personnel)

- Army
  - Chief of Staff: Brigadier Hutton
    - G: Operations and Intelligence (British Colonel and British Major i/c of Intelligence and 2 Arab Captains)
    - A: Personnel (British Personnel) (Arab Personnel)
    - Q: Supplies
      British Colonel: Stores and equipment
      Arab Officers: Arab contracts for local rations and supplies
    - Division HQ 1 Division
      - Infantry
        - 1 Brigade: 3 Infantry Regiments
        - 2 Brigade: 3 Infantry Regiments
        - 3 Brigade: 3 Infantry Regiments +1
        - (Total: 10 of which 5 beduin)
      - Armour
        - 2 Armed Car Regiments
        - 1 tank
        - Total: 3—2 beduin
      - Artillery
        - 3 × 25 lbs Field Regiments
        - 1 Light Anti-Aircraft Regiment
      - Engineers
        - 1 Regiment
- Police
  Commandant: Major General Ahmad Sudqi Pasha
- National Guard
- Navy

Total: 18 regiments, 7 of which were beduin.

## 2. TRAINING

Although regiments carried on much of their training within the unit, an elaborate Training Centre to co-ordinate, rationalise and develop all training for the Legion was established in 1950. In 1951 a formally organised Cadet School to train subalterns (*murashshah*; pl. *murashshahin*) was opened.

The Centre was organised basically into: (1) *A School for Boys*. Recruitment for this School was from beduin and other tribal groups. Boys came in as young as ten years, and normally spent seven years in the School before they were formally inducted into the Legion. The School was referred to as the "Education Wing" of the Training Centre. (2) *A "Training Wing"* comprising "schools" or "sections" for tactics, small weapons, heavy weapons, provost marshal, administration and military justice, basic training (Boot Camp of sixteen weeks' duration), and a Police Training College.[8] All these courses were of under three months' duration (about ten weeks), and enrolled an average of twenty-four men in each at any one time, except for Boot Camp which took in lots of fifty recruits at a time.

The Centre was commanded and administered by a British officer (a colonel), with an Arab officer as second-in-command, an Arab adjutant, and an Arab QMS. Cadre officers on the staff of the Centre were all *hadarī*, i.e. townsmen, including all instructors. There were a few British warrant officers instructing drill and physical training. The Education Wing (i.e. the Boys' School) was staffed largely by ex-Palestinians, mainly from Jerusalem, Nablus and Tul Karem.

At GHQ an Education Branch for the Legion supervised and controlled both the Amman Training Centre and Education officers and NCOs in all Legion units.

All officers until 1956 came from two categories: School boys selected from the Training Centre would enter Cadet School, and regular NCOs would be sent up to Cadet School. After Cadet School they would serve as subalterns with units. The difficulty with NCOs (this difficulty did not arise with cadets selected from the Boys' School) selected for officer training was their lack of adequate formal education. This, in turn, rendered them unsuitable for higher officer ranks. These usually never rose beyond the rank of first lieutenant, and occasionally that of captain commanding an operational infantry or armoured car company. Higher grades after 1953 implied some level of staff training, which, in turn, required relatively higher educational-academic qualifications and, in the case of the Legion,

[8] It will be recalled that since 1923 all police and gendarmerie forces in Jordan had been placed under Legion control.

knowledge of English. By 1951–1953, for instance, at least two Arab officers were dispatched each year to Sandhurst and/or Camberley for further training. As Artillery, Engineers and Armour grew, more Arab officers were sent to England for appropriate training in these branches.

### 3. ENGINEERS

The origin of the Engineers is interesting because it called for ingenious improvisation. At a certain point in their early formation it must have also bordered on the comical.

The first Field Engineer Unit was hastily formed in May 1948 as Legion units were crossing the Jordan into Palestine. A sapper major seconded from the British Army borrowed a subaltern from the departing British forces in Palestine, and gathered thirty to forty men from various Legion units. None of these had Engineer training, and many of them apparently were undesirable personnel, "throw-outs" from their units. A *hadarī* Arab officer, well educated but without Engineer training, also joined. So the First Field Unit began with two British sapper officers and, it seems, an Irish sapper NCO who had deserted from the British forces in Palestine.

Equipment consisted mainly of picks, shovels and some transport. There was no regular pattern of recruitment or training at this early stage, and not enough equipment to give adequate Engineer support to an operational Brigade group already engaged in combat in Palestine. Nevertheless, the unit built some roads, laid wire defensive perimeters, and carried out demolitions.

During the first truce in the Arab–Israeli War in June 1948, the unit descended upon Beit Nabala, near Ramallah (Jerusalem sector), to "forage" in Engineer stores left behind by the British Army. There they acquired barbed wire and sandbags in sufficient quantities. The truce, moreover, gave the unit the chance to weed out the misfits and to organise their technical responsibilities for newly acquired communications, such as the remnants of the Palestine railway, in the areas the Jordan Army controlled. Two more British officers, a major and a subaltern, were engaged on contract to strengthen their sapper force. At this stage, the unit was largely occupied with setting up defence works, building roads, laying wire, anti-tank obstacles and mine fields. The latter were charted and recorded by Palestine refugees who had had surveyor experience with the mandate Survey Service. A forward base was formed south of Ramallah, and a rear base at Zerqa on the Transjordan side of the river. The latter eventually became the Engineer Base Camp of the Jordan Arab

Army. By the end of 1948, this First Field Unit was ready to begin systematic training and operations.

Eight good Legion NCOs, selected for their excellent infantry training record, were recruited into Engineers. A good Arab officer, without Engineer training, was brought in for his excellent record in regimental administrative duties. A British contract officer came in to supervise general Engineer training for both officers and men. Arab cadets were also posted to the unit as subalterns. All of these were East Bankers. The Irish "deserter" NCO was smartly replaced by a British SM (RE) who was put in charge of sapper training. Significantly, the unit recruited craftsmen and tradesmen from among the Palestine refugees (about forty of these in the first instance) rather successfully. Most of these had been civilian tradesmen with the British Army in Palestine, or with the mandate government public services. After infantry basic training, most of them became senior NCOs in Engineers. In fact,'the railway, which until 1950–1951 was the responsibility of Engineers, was run with the aid of the ex-Palestine Railway employees. Meantime, the British Army in the Suez Canal area donated, sold and lent tools and some heavy Engineer equipment and stores to the unit. From the remnants of the Palestine Survey, the unit recruited enough men to raise a Survey Section to handle cartography and mine field plotting. This Section soon came to be commanded by an ex-Palestinian, who was commissioned a lieutenant.

At the beginning of 1949, the Engineers could boast a strength of 300. The trained sapper soldiers in it were mainly Transjordanians; the tradesmen and technicians Palestinians, and the officers British and mainly non-beduin Arab. What could be politically significant is that this new and technical arm, or service, was almost 100 per cent *hadari*, i.e. townsmen.

The prestige of the unit at that time was not too high, even though by the end of 1949 Arab second lieutenants who had been sent to Chatham, Kent, for YO (Young Officers) and SME (School of Military Engineers) training were beginning to join the Engineers. Beduin and other tribesmen naturally were not attracted by Engineers, partly because this involved manual work and partly because of their traditional-occupational ethos and outlook upon the Legion as a fighting force.

Successor British COs of the Engineers until 1956 have stated that the Engineer branch continued to be mainly townsmen in composition, with some village peasants. But it comprised hardly any beduins. Tradesmen strength gradually became mixed Palestinian-Transjordanian. Officer and NCO training in YO and SME courses in

England increased. They also felt that much of the ethos and value orientation of the Engineer branch personnel was not military, but rather craftsman-bureaucratic. The tradesmen especially viewed their service in the Legion in lieu of secure civilian employment.

In July 1951 the Field Unit became known as the Independent Field Squadron with a brigade major and seven Arab officers, three of whom had been to Sandhurst and SME. A major obstacle to further expansion was the unavailability of suitable Arab officers. There was until this time no school or training unit in which new officers and men could be given extensive, or adequate, engineer training. What they did, instead, was to take Cadets and send them to the YO and SME courses in England. But under this scheme no more than two Cadets could be sent each year, or at any one time, and these had to know English. The latter requirement automatically reduced the number of qualified candidates. When, however, more field units were improvised and extensive field exercises held a training wing was set up, which later became the Engineer Training Squadron. As more senior Arab officers were sent to Chatham for Field Engineering training, it became possible to train NCOs and men within the units themselves.

The Legion, however, had been expanding rapidly since 1951 into more brigade groups. It became difficult to create, equip, and train new or additional Independent Field Squadrons to support these operational groups. So, in 1952, Engineers were allowed to reorganise (expand and train, that is) as a regiment. A base camp with training grounds, workshops, magazines and stores was developed. But this, in turn, posed serious problems with regard to equipment and personnel shortages, as well as with regard to administration. By spring 1953 a complete Division Field Engineer Regiment (including Signals) was created. Its most critical shortage was trained officers. This was, by force of circumstances, met by the use of subalterns with only a couple of years' officer experience. Systematic training on a crash programme basis was, however, put under way in both the units and the Base Camp. As new Squadrons were formed and trained they were attached to the various Brigade groups for Engineer support service.

### 4. ARTILLERY

The formal organisation of Artillery did not begin seriously until 1951. At that time it comprised one Regiment of Field Artillery (two batteries of four 25 lb. guns each and an anti-tank battery). The personnel were predominantly beduin. The officers, however, were all *hadarī*. In 1951 there was an expansion to three regiments of three, instead of two, batteries each—an organisational pattern similar to the British. A new Anti-Tank and Light AA regiment was formed. All new recruits came from the Amman Training Centre; officers from the Cadet School. In the Light AA regiment all personnel were townsmen, many of them West Bankers and a few Circassians.

Artillery training was conducted within the army's units. Gunnery instructors were all British. Officers among the latter were seconded from the British Army to serve as instructor gunners. By 1953 there were about fifteen of these, including the brigade major. In addition to these, there were a number of British warrant officers also serving as instructors. In 1952, however, an Artillery School within the arm was founded. There was apparently no set level of formal education required for admission into the School, so long as recruits, or trainees, were literate and had some knowledge of the most elementary mathematics.

## 5. INFANTRY

In a country like Jordan, infantry (which has been mobile or mechanised) is the core element in the army, crucial to the security and stability of the regime. Until 1956 there were ten infantry regiments organised in three infantry brigades. Five of these were beduin-tribal in composition. The other five consisted mainly of townsmen and villagers. Five of the infantry regiments were commanded by British officers (one of them a contract officer; all the others seconded). Of the other five infantry regiment commanders, two were Circassians and three were *hadaris*. A beduin took over 2 Infantry Regiment as CO late in 1955.

The strength of an Infantry regiment varied between 400 and 600 officers and men. Officer strength varied from 30 to 35 all grades, including Cadets. In a typical Infantry regiment there were at any one time 19 cadets, 8 second lieutenants, 4 first lieutenants, and 2 captains (all Arabs), in addition to a British CO, usually a lieutenant-colonel. All officers were promoted from the ranks by a series of examinations, except for the Cadets who came from Cadet School. Captains in 1956 had been born between 1915 and 1920; first lieutenants in the early 1920s; second lieutenants in the late 1920s and early 1930s. Most enlistments in the ranks (with the exception of long-term service NCOs) had begun in the late 1930s and throughout the 1940s. It should be noted, though, that dates of birth of officers and other ranks were not always accurate, especially among the tribal personnel.

Thus the average age of cadet-subalterns was 23–24 years. The average formal education level was about 5th elementary, or 7th elementary in army school. The *very few* non-beduin or non-tribal officers became Signal or Quartermaster Officers in the unit, since many of them spoke some English.[9] Tribal distribution in infantry units varied widely in regard to major tribes, groups, and sub-groups. Nejdis from Arabia and Shammar from the north and north-east appeared predominant. Nevertheless, major tribal groups from within Jordan, especially the south, were adequately represented. The vast majority of the personnel were married, and some had more than one wife.[10] All officers had passed various training and specialised courses such as administration, drill, signals, anti-tank, weapons, and map reading.

Among the warrant officers and top NCOs (colour sergeants and sergeants) the age distribution was higher than that among cadets and lieutenants. This was roughly about thirty years, with ten to fifteen years' Legion service. The clerical-administrative NCOs were exclusively *hadarī*, many of them from the West Bank. Many of them had some secondary education qualification, and knew both Arabic and English. All NCOs and men would, however, carry on with, or pursue, "further education" within the Legion to attain equivalent levels of more civilian schooling.

Transfers from some infantry regiments at one time to the police or gendarmerie force, and to training duty with the National Guard were used by COs to get rid of undesirable personnel. Two-thirds of the beduins who left a regiment after a five-year enlistment returned to their tribe. Those who could re-enlist did so, for inability to re-enlist for one reason or another was considered by them to be a calamity.

### 6. ARMOUR

At the same time, there was in the period 1953–1956 one armoured brigade, consisting of two armoured car regiments and a tank regiment. The car regiments were almost wholly beduin and their strength was greater than the average infantry regiment as they were always over-strength. Thus an armoured car regiment often mustered

---

[9] In the 1950s townsmen officers who ran Signals and Administration in practically all units of the Legion were viewed by COs as a significant network with mischievous political capabilities. One may note here the role of telegraphists in Young Turk conspiracies in Turkey in 1908. See Bernard Lewis, *The Emergence of Modern Turkey* (London, 1961), p. 183.

[10] It should be noted that families of troops usually lived near a unit camp, in nearby villages and towns, and in black tents.

700–800 officers and men with an officer strength that exceeded forty to forty-five all grades.

In these regiments recruits came mainly from the Amman Training Centre. Tribal distribution could vary widely as from sixty to seventy groups and sub-groups.[11] Procedures and patterns of officer promotion were similar to those in infantry regiments. The educational level of personnel amounted to the equivalent of four, maximum five, years of school. One of the two car regiments had only one townsman, a Sandhurst-trained officer with troop command. Its signals officer was also a townsman; and so were the administrative NCOs. By 1956, however, armoured car regiments were showing a higher proportion of West Bankers in their composition than did infantry. These began to come in especially as mechanics and unit maintenance personnel.

While the operational organisation of armoured car regiments in their early days consisted roughly of four car squadrons plus a headquarters squadron, later on the two regiments in the early fifties were reorganised into an Armoured Brigade Headquarters.

With five beduin infantry regiments and two armoured car regiments, the beduin-tribal element in the Legion constituted a powerful mobile ground force.

## 7. TECHNICAL SERVICES

One of the most impressive developments in the rapid expansion of the Legion in 1948–1956 was the setting up from scratch of elaborate technical support services for the army.

In 1946–1948, the Legion consisted of three motorised regiments plus two static garrison groups. Between them they had 400 miscellaneous vehicles, largely obtained from the British Army, about nine or ten 3·7 howitzers, plus the usual small arms, i.e. rifles, light machine-guns, and revolvers.

The Legion operated a small base workshop in Amman (after 1948 in Zerqa) and another smaller field workshop near the Palestine border. About 350 men were involved in these two outfits. A British officer directed the Amman base workshop; two other British officers served with the field workshop. These were assisted by about seven British NCOs.

But these workshops were capable of only very light repairs for vehicles. Heavier repairs were normally done by British army

---

[11] These rather arbitrary terms for tribal distribution are used on the basis of Peake's classification of tribal distribution in Jordan. See *History and Tribes of Jordan* (Miami, Florida, 1958), pp. 143–224.

workshops in Palestine. These also provided the Legion with all spare parts for vehicles. Civilian contractors in both Transjordan and Palestine were engaged for certain major technical repairs, such as engine overhauls. Only with the end of the British mandate in Palestine did the Legion face the major task of providing extensive and complete technical facilities and services for its units. On the other hand, the subsequent rapid expansion of the Legion engendered the further need of technical maintenance for bigger, more varied and complex weapons, and transport vehicles. The formation of such new arms as Armour, Artillery, and Engineers with weapons and technical equipment (such as Signals) more sophisticated than anything the Legion had handled until that time further emphasised this need.

By 1953 there were over 4,000 vehicles in the Legion, from motor-cars, trucks, and armoured cars to tanks, heavy weapons and other complex equipment.[12] The Base Technical Organisation (BTO) of the Legion was by then capable of maintaining and servicing this equipment, together with that of three Field Artillery regiments and one Light AA regiment. The Organisation came to comprise 2,300 officers and men, including workshops, stores, vehicle depots, Mechanics' Training School (MTS), Driving School (DS) and ancillary services or units. The 2,300 figure included students in both of these schools.

The establishment comprised thirty-five to forty officers commanded by a British colonel. There were four or five other British officers and sixteen to twenty British other ranks. Ten per cent of the BTO were Arab NCOs. The MTS and DS establishments had a 25 per cent NCO complement. Moreover, the overall composition of the BTO was 90 per cent *hadarī* (townsman) and 10 per cent beduin. Of the former 20 per cent were West Bankers, i.e. ex-Palestinians. This percentage must be higher today. In the Divisional Technical Organisation (DTO) (i.e. technical service groups attached to various units, e.g. infantry brigades, artillery, armour, engineers, etc.), 80 per cent of the personnel were townsmen and 20 per cent beduin. Again, of the former, 20 per cent came from the West Bank.

Early recruitment in 1946–1948 was by a process of selection via examination and interview. Two qualified students each year would

---

[12] It should be noted that an embryonic Air Arm was begun in 1950–1951. Its rapid growth, especially under King Husayn—an accomplished pilot himself—must have further aggravated the need for technical services of a new order and magnitude. I have left the new Royal Jordan Air Force out of the scope of my study, primarily because I have not been able to interview the British officers who have been responsible for the earliest training of this Force.

be selected to attend a three-year Automotive Engineering course in the UK. In some years as many as six such candidates were selected. The CO of the BTO actually set the examination papers in mathematics, very elementary physics and mechanics at approximately matriculation standard. He also marked the papers, which were all in English. This naturally limited the number of potential candidates or applicants. The Chief of the General Staff, namely, General Glubb, made the final selection, though not strictly on the basis of examination results. While studying in the UK these personnel carried the rank of Cadet. At the successful completion of the course they were commissioned lieutenants in the Legion to serve with the BTO. Thus, the system primarily aimed at the training of a cadre of officers for the Technical services. Yet, apart from these technically trained, or qualified, cadre, all other officers in the BTO were recruited and promoted according to the prevailing pattern in the Legion, i.e. largely from the ranks and from the Cadet School.

In 1948–1949 a more rapid expansion of the BTO set in with the enlistment of West Bankers who were tradesmen, clerk-storemen of varying skills, and some ex-TJFF personnel who had just been released from that disbanded force.

The bulk of enlisted ranks reflected the usual educational level prevalent in other branches and units of the Legion, i.e. from semi-literacy to 4th elementary. The educational level of senior NCOs however ranged from 4th elementary to 1st secondary. The vast majority of officers did not have any higher formal educational qualifications.

With the phenomenal growth of Amman and other towns in 1949–1956, the best tradesmen tended, by that time, to leave the Legion for more remunerative civilian employment. Yet, in the absence of complex industries—in fact, so long as the army remained the largest single industry in the country—the attraction and retention of technically skilled personnel has not been critically difficult.

The preceding illustrations of the organisation and structure of certain units suggest that, until 1956 at least, the Legion was still trying to retain its original morphology and character of a highly trained, mobile *corps d'élite*. The rapid expansion prompted by the Arab–Israeli War and the armed truce that has obtained between Israel and Jordan since that time introduced two new and major departures in the Legion's composition and development. In the first place, the urgent need to form, train, and develop its own technical branches, additional arms such as Artillery, Armour, and Engineers, meant the recruitment of greater numbers of townsmen, many of whom have increasingly come from the West Bank. Yet until 1956 recruitment of such settled tradesmen and other personnel with technical skills was harnessed and controlled so to speak by basic military training for all the enlistees. The practice of direct commissions, even on temporary contract terms, for graduate mechanical and other engineers, for example, was never considered by the Legion, let alone followed. In fact, General Glubb was categorically and vehemently opposed to such procedure for cogent reasons referred to earlier.

While the bulk of recruits for Legion units continued to come from the Amman Training Centre, especially from the Boys' School and Cadet School, further training was carried on within the units and arms of the service themselves. Specialised training was provided locally by the Training Wing of the Centre, and advanced training was by exceptionally tight selection from the *Qiyada* (GHQ)—actually, by General Glubb himself—for courses in the UK. Promotion, whether to NCO ranks or officer grades, remained a traditional Legion procedure, characterised by a series of examinations, performance ratings by unit commanders, and other military qualifications, and conduct criteria.

The ratio of officers to the total strength of the Legion in 1956 (1,500 : 25,000) remained relatively low for an Arab army. 2–3,000 : 25,000 would have been a more common, albeit an inflated, officer ratio. Moreover, trained staff officers (among Arab personnel, i.e.) remained scarce—one of the alleged political bones of contention, as we shall see later, between Glubb and the King.

One of the most significant aspects of the patterns of training and recruitment remained that of the overwhelming beduin-tribal and peasant composition of Infantry and Armour units on the one hand, and the 80 per cent over 20 per cent predomination of *hadarī* personnel in the technical branches (Maintenance, Signals, Medical Corps) and Engineer arm on the other. The only *hadarī* officers and NCOs in the beduin Infantry and Armour regiments until 1956 manned few administrative, interpreter, clerical, and educational sections of the headquarters establishment in a regiment or a brigade. Technical maintenance squadrons attached to units were also *hadarī*. But these were in a minority, and normally had no troop or line command in the units.

Regimental and other commanders did observe a certain antipathy between beduin-tribal and *hadarī* elements in units. The beduin was, if not inimical, at least scornfully indifferent to the *hadarī* officer or NCO. Occasionally a *hadarī* officer or NCO had to be transferred out of a unit because of this feeling which frequently engendered a tense atmosphere. Moreover, given the wide and varied tribal distribution of beduin personnel, competition and conflict extended to personal identification with one or another tribal group. So that this inter-tribal friction within regiments constituted another level, or dimension, of unit disciplinary problems for the commanding officers. It should be noted, however, that if a *hadarī* officer was militarily *efficient* and did not affect an intellectual superiority or appear otherwise snooty, he was invariably well received by the beduins.

The sense of collective responsibility and security (the "sacred collectivity") so central to a beduin, or tribal, society carried over to the Legion. Though disciplined and loyal—especially to their CO, to the Pasha (General Glubb) and to the monarch—beduins of the same tribal group tended to stick together against all outsiders. Even though with the passage of time the identification of the beduin officer and NCO after long military service with the tribe was somewhat eroded, whenever their interests, careers, or security were threatened they invariably resorted to the assistance offered by their somewhat transformed tribal collectivity. Whereas earlier the Legion had to discipline the individualistic attitude of the beduin, in the context of a confrontation of interests with non-beduin personnel in the Legion, the beduin sought refuge in the collective sense of the tribe. It seems that tribal societies—in this case beduin—exhibit in their lives simultaneously a pattern of both fission and fusion. One or the other is provoked by different contexts. Thus, even though most of the tribes in Transjordan had been, by 1930, effectively pacified, the use of beduin units in the new Desert Patrol Force commanded by Glubb to effectively control inter-tribal conflict in the 1930s was in great measure based on the foreknowledge of these tribal peculiarities.

# PART III

CHAPTER VI

# Politics and the Legion 1948–1957

GENERALLY, one can say that for the period under discussion the attitude of the officers and NCOs was clearly of two kinds. On the one hand, the tribesman-beduin in the Legion (overwhelmingly in Infantry and Armour) understood loyalty in personal terms, not on any higher institutional level. He was loyal to the Pasha, *Abuna Abu Faris* ("Our Father, Father of Faris"), General Glubb, to Sayyidna ("Our Master"), the King, and to the commanding officer of his regiment. The latter embodied and personified the *Jeish*—the army—for the beduin. This despite the fact that as a recruit the beduin, when inducted, took an oath to serve "king and country". As was shown in the political disturbances of the period October 1954–January 1956, the beduin's attitude clearly was one which assumed that only the *hadarī*—the town slicker—officer could be involved in politics. To some extent this may have been a rationalisation—or another way of expression—of the constant, underlying friction (a result of the antipathy referred to earlier) between beduin and *hadarī* elements in the Legion.[1]

The attitude of *hadarī* officers and NCOs, on the other hand, is both more complex and difficult to deal with, as well as more crucial to any political involvement of the military. First, one must bear in mind that before 1949–50 the townsman officers and NCOs in the Legion came mainly from the few sparsely populated towns of Transjordan: al-Salṭ, Irbid, Amman, Kerak, Madeba and Tafileh. Very few of these had anything approximating higher education; a

---

[1] On these disturbances see below. Obviously this formulation of *beduin-hadari* relations is not based on any rigorous survey of actual personnel on my part. This I did not undertake; and I doubt if it can be undertaken with any measure of success for some time yet. On the other hand, it is based on the measured opinion and qualified judgment of senior British officers who held key command positions in the Legion during this period. It should be noted that this dichotomy of beduin versus settled (in this case urban) can, in the case of Jordan, be misleading. In 1945, for instance, 10 per cent of the population in Transjordan was nomadic and 30 per cent semi-nomadic. Even though settled in towns, cities, and villages, the remaining 60 per cent consisted largely of descendants of tribal groups that had settled in various localities, especially during the time of vast tribal migrations in the last 300 to 500 years.

H

few of them had completed secondary school. In this sense, they did not represent a highly sophisticated group of urbanites. Moreover, they rarely received direct commissions,[2] since this practice was unknown—and unacceptable—to the Legion. The long process of promotion and strict GHQ and British-commanded unit supervision imposed a certain discipline which even the more ambitious and devious among them would have found too difficult to circumvent. Meanwhile, staff experience until the early 1950s remained limited. Their training when in Cadet School, or within the unit, for promotion from the ranks was more practical-military, i.e. an applied soldier's education. It did not entail the kind of academic-theoretical training common in military academies and staff colleges.[3]

Only with rapid expansion of the Legion did systematic staff training of a greater number of Arab officers begin. During this period also the largest intake of townsmen—including those to be trained for commissions—especially from the West Bank (ex-Palestinians)—occurred. And these came mainly into the technical branches of the army: a potentially significant political group. Until the Palestine war, however, there was no overriding political consideration that would have influenced the political attitudes of *hadarī* Jordanian officers, or affected their loyalty to the monarchy.

Nevertheless, the two instances of the political involvement of officers in Jordan that I propose to discuss for illustrative purposes were led by Transjordanians, and especially officers who had been commissioned in part on the strength of their secondary school education. These have been, so far, the only two known overt attempts by army officers to challenge the monarch's authority and to overthrow his regime. There have been of course repeated occasions on which the resources of the military have been called upon by the monarch in order to cope with civil-political disturbances and to retain firm political control over the country. The two most critical such occasions were in the period October 1954–January 1956, and in April 1957. On both occasions the predominantly tribal-beduin *ground* operational units (i.e. mechanised infantry and armour) were clearly the crucial upholders of the *status quo*, never hesitating to use force against civilian political groups.

The bulk of the conspirators, but not all the leaders, on both occasions were officers in the administrative and technical branches

[2] The original officers engaged by Peake in the 1920s were an exception, since they were almost all ex-officers of the Ottoman army.

[3] A Military Academy and Staff College, each offering a two-year course, were opened in the last three years. One must wait and see what social and political impact these will have on the Jordanian officer corps in the future.

of the Legion. In fact, British regimental commanders suspected as early as 1953 the informal existence of what they called an "administrative network" of politically orientated officers inimical to both the Chief of the General Staff and to the regime. General Glubb, however, tended to consider any political interest, or involvement, of Legion officers as strictly the result of external influences, or infiltration—in these instances, mainly Egyptian influence. There was truth in the charges of Egyptian exploitation of the unstable political situation in Jordan in the 1950s, yet a categorical rejection of any other motives for the political involvement of Legion officers was clearly not justified. To some extent, it reflected the impact of political influences—both external and internal—upon the more sophisticated and ambitious officers in the Legion.

Before looking at the role of the Legion in supporting the regime against civil disturbances, it is useful to illustrate the political involvement of army officers in conspiracies against the regime by a brief account of the Abdullah al-Tel incident in 1948. The matter of the abortive coup allegedly led by General Ali Abu Nuwar in April 1957 will be discussed in conjunction with the political situation in Jordan in the period 1954–1956, and that immediately following the dismissal of General Glubb.

Colonel Abdullah al-Tel was born in 1918 in the town of Irbid in Transjordan. Before the rapid growth of Amman, Irbid was the most populous town in the country. After graduating from the local secondary school, he was employed briefly as a Customs Officer on the Palestine–Transjordan frontier. Early in the Second World War he enlisted in the Legion, and was assigned orderly room clerk to one of the companies. He then went quickly through the usual Legion promotion channels and obtained what was practically a direct commission. When the Arab-Israeli war broke out in May 1948, Tel had just been promoted from captain to major that March. He was commanding one of the garrison companies which came to man the walls of the Old City. During these operations three of these infantry garrison companies were improvised into a battalion (a Jordanian regiment, that is) and Tel was made CO of the regiment, but still with the rank of Major.

According to the account of General Glubb, it seems that, while on one of his inspection tours of units, the late King Abdullah was impressed by Tel's briefing on operations while the unit was under mortar fire. In recognition of such courage the King promoted Tel to the rank of Lieutenant-Colonel on the spot. Glubb makes no secret of his putting through the promotion papers only because of the royal command; nor of his having expressed his disapproval to the King on the grounds that Tel had no seniority in rank.[4] In any event, Tel came to command 6 Infantry Regiment in the Jerusalem sector. At that time Jerusalem was the centre of political agitation and opposition against Abdullah of Jordan. The articulate members of the public in general and its leaders in particular were embittered by what in the summer of 1948 looked like a losing Arab cause in Palestine at large.

In his own account, Tel stated that he had contemplated a coup against the regime as early as December 1948.[5] He further stated that he had broached the idea with a number of "sincere" or "loyal" officers, on the grounds that there was need for change in the country. He explained that he never approached any number of officers as a group but always individually; so that strict secrecy could be better observed. He referred to these officers as "Free Officers".[6]

---

[4] See *op. cit.*, 255–256.

[5] See *Kārithat Filastin, mudhakkirāt abdullah al-tel* (vol. I), (Cairo, 1st and 2nd printings, 1959). (*The Catastrophe of Palestine, Memoirs of Abdullah al-Tel.*) A second volume, as promised by the author, never appeared. It seems Tel is now back in Jordan.

[6] No source on the Legion, or Jordan, is clear on the question of the "Free Officers". Tel in his memoirs says nothing about them, pleading that to do so would jeopardise their safety in Jordan. He does however claim Ali Abu Nuwar and a Major Mahmud Musa as members. Glubb, on the other hand, refers to them only once, and then to describe the fraudulent character of their pamphlets.

"In 1952, an Arab Legion officer in the Supply and Transport Corps [obviously a townsman] had been dismissed from the service for financial dishonesty. Intent on revenge, he went to Beirut, where he printed a number of pamphlets directed against myself, and signed them 'Free Officers'. We obtained information of the activities of this ex-officer through the Lebanese police. He was warned and no further pamphlets appeared."

In 1955 pamphlets began once more to appear with the signature "Free Officers" (*op. cit.*, 412). Glubb goes on to explain that the 1955 ones were drafted, printed, and posted from Egypt. The implication, however, is that there were such pamphlets about as early as 1952. Brigadier Young in his book *Bedouin Command* (London, 1956) implied that the Free Officers may have been a more ominous organisation than the CGS thought. All the same, one must bear in mind the popularity of such appellation for all and sundry conspirators among army officers in the Middle East.

In relating the events of the civil disturbances of January 1956 Young makes various references to the Free Officers [he calls them "The Liberal Officers Rally"] as well as to specific officers who, he believed, had been politically involved. His account centres upon the involvement of his own 9 Regiment in dealing with the disturbances in the area between Zerqa and al-Salṭ. He emphasises the refugee problem and the West Bank political restlessness, but asserts: "In this storm the beduin were our sheet-anchor." He reports conversations with Arab officers in which the strong view was expressed by the latter that arabisation of the officer corps was slow since "Arab officers were already perfectly capable of commanding brigades". He also reports their sympathy for and approval of

The last suggested point was crucial in Tel's political campaign. Not only had Abdullah been identified in the minds of Palestinian Arabs for a generation as the trusted friend of the British, but also as the arch-enemy of their traditional political leaders, the Husaynis. Some among the latter had led the Palestinian Arab armed resistance against the Jews before the Arab armies entered the conflict. But in this instance Tel had in his possession extensive blackmail material

---

demonstrations especially among those officers who were townsmen (i.e. from Irbid and al-Salt). He also reproduces a translated text of one of the Free Officer pamphlets, and states that he had known of the movement's existence since the summer of 1954. His view is that its members came primarily from "among the intelligentsia—the artillery and the engineers". (Recently, he informed me that he was first warned of this development by Lieut.-Colonel Constant of Engineers.) He identifies such officers as Colonel Sādiq Shara'a who became Chief of Staff after March 1956 when Ali Abu Nuwar had been appointed CGS; Ali Hiyari who for a while was GOC 1st Division; and Muhammad Ma'āyiṭa who commanded Artillery, as possible members of this movement. Moreover, he mentions extensive discharges and transfers from the Legion of as many as 1,000 beduin troops to the National Guard once Glubb had been dismissed.

One gets the distinct impression, from reading Brigadier Young's account, that he was aware of some political movement within the Arab officer corps. Perhaps his long command in Jerusalem and close watch over affairs there gave him this vantage observation point. What is interesting is that he considered this movement far more ominous and credible than General Glubb did at any time. See *Bedouin Command*, pp. 137–189 (Recently he informed me that all British officers in the Legion at that time credited General Glubb with so much inside knowledge of all that went on in the Legion and the country that they rarely reported to him their suspicions on evidence they had of such goings on. Equally, it seems, towards the end of 1955 General Glubb ceased to keep British officers—at least unit commanders—informed of what he thought was the situation, or at least his appraisal of it. Here one senses a dangerous proclivity—a naïve readiness—on the part of British officers to attribute omniscience to their CGS). The difficulty of course cannot be blamed wholly on the CGS. The Legion had expanded so much and so rapidly since 1951 that it was difficult—if not impossible—for the CGS to have personal knowledge of every officer and NCO in it.

Young reports an interesting incident in Zerqa cantonment six days after the departure of Glubb from Jordan. At that time Ali Hiyari was Chief of Staff, General Radi Ennab had been made CGS, and Abu Nuwar CO of the Brigade posted on the West Bank. Along with other British officers, Young was getting ready to leave the country. Brigadier Mitford was still OC of the Armoured Brigade. It seems that 1 Armoured Car Regiment and 2 Field Artillery Regiment had been ordered by Abu Nuwar to surround Zerqa cantonment. These orders from the CO Jerusalem Brigade were unknown to the CO Zerqa Brigade. Young explains this manoeuvre as an attempt by Abu Nuwar to intimidate recalcitrant fellow Arab officers in the Young Officer movement; and opines that the headquarters of the movement was in the West Bank headed by Abu Nuwar, with a branch in Zerqa. (See esp. pp. 180–183.)

With the exception of Radi Ennab, all these officers Young mentions were then in their early thirties.

in the form of photostatic copies of the secret correspondence between Abdullah and the Israelis, who had been negotiating to reach some agreement—and peace—since the UN Partition Resolution in 1947. Tel, moreover, had been present in some of the meetings between the Israeli delegates and the King at his winter palace in Shuna.

In addition, then, to his convenient location in embattled and embittered Jerusalem as CO 6 Regiment, Tel had been singled out by royal favour as special courier and secret emissary of the King in his delicate negotiations with the Israelis in 1948. As commander of 6 Regiment, deployed within the walls, Tel was in constant communication with an international brigade of journalists as well as Israeli military personnel from the other side. Journalists swarmed into the Holy City, since its fate had attracted world concern. Tel spoke for the Legion within the walls. The other regiment fighting outside the walls did not naturally attract as much attention. Moreover, it was commanded by a British officer.

When in February–April 1949 the Jordanians negotiated and signed an Armistice Agreement with the Israelis in Rhodes under UN auspices, Tel was appointed Governor of Jerusalem, relinquishing his regimental command. This removed him from GHQ control and placed him under civilian administrative authority. It was from this position that Tel began to explore his coup possibilities with two kinds of political allies. First, he approached civilian anti-Hashemite leaders in Jerusalem, Ramallah, Nablus, Tul Karem and Hebron. In Ramallah especially, the Baath party (originally founded by Michel Aflaq and Salah el din al-Bitar in Syria) had a large following. It was led by Abdullah al-Rimawi—at that time in the political wilderness. Through its press, a steady campaign against the regime was conducted with the active encouragement of Governor Tel.

Second, it was public knowledge that the Egyptians were unhappy about Abdullah's acquisition of Central Palestine; so were the Syrians. Tel therefore tried to combine an alliance of Palestinian malcontents with assistance from anti-Jordanian Arab states. For both arrangements he had incriminating evidence insofar as the Arab definition of treason in those days was concerned. It did not occur to Tel that first, Abdullah made no real secret of his view that a negotiated peace with Israel was the best Jordan could bargain for under the circumstances prevailing after the Armistice Agreement; it was also the best the Arabs could hope for after the failure of their joint military campaign to destroy the incipient Israeli State.[7] Nor

---

[7] See text of an interesting letter from Abdullah to ʿAbd al-Hamīd Saʿīd, President

did it occur to him that even if his plan had been successfully implemented his role as courier and emissary for Abdullah with the Jews both as CO of 6 Regiment and as Governor of the City in 1948-1949 could be used against him to discredit him politically.

In any event, Tel sought, in visits to Syria and Egypt in the spring and summer of 1949 while still Governor of Jerusalem, the help of the new ruler of Syria, Colonel Husni al-Zaim, and of the authorities in Egypt. In both instances, he claims, he was encouraged and promised material help. In the case of Syria, however, he states that the rapid succession of coups (Hinnawi-Shishakli) within a few months militated against his plans. Yet with such encouragement, Tel became more outspoken in his criticism of conditions and official Jordanian policy. These received extensive coverage in the Arab press. Meantime, Central Palestine secured by the Legion was incorporated (annexed) in the kingdom by a resolution of the Jericho Congress in December 1948 and ratified by the Transjordanian Parliament the same month. The annexation of Arab Palestine by Abdullah was now a fact, and a clear and challenging answer to the All-Arab Gaza Congress of October after which, with the support of Egypt, an Arab government of all Palestine was formed there, headed largely by elements antagonistic to King Abdullah.

In these circumstances it was clear that Tel was attempting a political movement which would rely for its success upon outside assistance and an alliance with anti-Abdullah elements among the Palestine population. Here perhaps lay the seeds of Tel's failure. One seeks in vain for any evidence of extensive infiltration among the officer corps. It is quite likely that Ali Abu Nuwar (then a captain) and Colonel Muhammad al-Maʿāyiṭa, a tribesman officer from the south of Transjordan, were involved to the extent of tacit approval of Tel's moves. Both these officers had been military members of the delegation that went to Rhodes for the Armistice talks in February 1949. But there is no evidence of any extensive conspiracy within the army. This moreover would have been difficult for Tel to achieve, for until the end of September 1948 he was no more than a regimental commander. And the other regiment in the Jerusalem sector was

---

of the Young Muslim Men's Association (YMMA) in Cairo, dated 5 June 1938, in response to the latter's approach to Abdullah about the Palestine Question. In it Abdullah bluntly deplores the uncompromising attitudes of Palestinian Arab leaders; their sale of land to the Jews under the Mandate; and makes clear his solution to save Palestine for the Arabs by uniting it with Transjordan. *Mudhakkirat* . . . , pp. 266-268.

commanded by a British officer. From October 1948 until June 1949 he had been Governor of the city, and his contacts with army officers had consequently become even more infrequent.

One must conclude that Tel gambled upon the incriminating evidence he possessed regarding the Abdullah–Israeli negotiations. To this extent his conspiracy did not aim at a purely military coup, but rather at a political uprising fomented by the evidence of treason on the part of the King. One could argue that Tel might have contemplated separating Central Palestine from Jordan with outside Arab support. This was impossible at the time, however; for apart from his relative remoteness from military command, the Israelis would not have stood for it.

His departure from Jordan to live in exile in Egypt is still a garbled story. Tel claims that he left the country on the advice of political allies at home, and that of the Syrian and Egyptian governments. The idea was that he could best work for the Arab cause from outside Jordan. So at the end of 1949 he slipped out quietly. In Egypt he apparently received a stipend from the Egyptian Government for some years, until his political usefulness was considered ended. Glubb, on the other hand, alleges that the Egyptians initially offered him a salary to go to Egypt.

The question remains why, in addition to the propitious political conditions of the Arab world, did Tel ever attempt such a movement, especially when he had slim hope of infiltrating the officer corps adequately to implement his plan? The reason (or psychological reasons) becomes clear if one reads carefully his own explanation of why he decided upon this course of action when he did.

"My most cogent argument in convincing them [other officers] was the attitude of the Jordan army towards the Egyptian army in the battle of the Negev; the liaison between top authority in Amman with the Jews officially after the receipt of Sassoon's first letter on 8.12.1949, [meaning 11.12.1948] . . . I began to prepare the people in Palestine to accept the idea of a coup, with the help of selected loyal young leaders from Jerusalem, Nablus, Ramallah and Hebron. We used the columns of the *Baath* newspapers edited by Rimawi for this purpose, and we were successful in apprising the people of the truth of the situation until they were willing to act against the government, the king, and the British. We succeeded in making the people lose all confidence in all three of them. Then came the coup of Husni al-Zaim in Syria on 30.3.1949, which moved us to think actively about implementing our scheme. We assessed the situation, including the alienation of Prince Talal from his father and political conditions at home, the position of the British in Jordan, the British subsidy to the Legion,[8] and the enemy on the frontiers. After careful consideration of all eventualities we laid our plan."[9]

Tel was claiming to have disapproved of and opposed King Abdullah's policy of a negotiated peace with Israel. It is possible that he was motivated by genuine patriotic Arab sentiments. From the same quoted excerpt one also infers that he was encouraged by the Zaim coup in Syria, understanding from that that army officers were now ready to overthrow older leaders who had not handled the Palestine situation properly.[10] The urge to imitate a Zaim was therefore strong. His political tactics for those days (1948–1949) were also reasonable: the pursuit of alliances and alignments with opposition leaders within the country and Arab detractors of King Abdullah outside Jordan. His strategy, on the other hand, was mistaken. Its ultimate failure shows that without a strong conspiratorial group within the officer corps, particularly among officers with troop command, a coup cannot be effectively carried out simply with the assistance of politicians.

Between May and September 1948 Tel commanded the 6th Battalion (Regt.) (not the 7th, as Abidi, *Jordan, a Political Study 1948–1957* (London, 1965), states, p. 27n.). He was appointed Military Governor of Jerusalem on 28 September 1948, and Governor of the Old City on 6 March 1949. Upon his appointment as Military Governor, GHQ immediately issued an order to 6 Regiment stating that the duties of Colonel Tel were limited to those of Military Governor and that he had no command over the Regiment. The latter was turned over to Lieut.-Colonel Muhammad al-Ma'āyiṭa.[11]

With this order, GHQ cleverly and properly severed any formal military relationship between Colonel Tel and his old regiment. But the order also had the effect of pushing Tel towards further political involvement with opposition leaders. In fact, after his appointment as Governor of the Old City under a civilian administration, Tel became totally involved in the preparation of a political movement

[8] It cannot be emphasised enough that the defence of Jordan from 1945 to 1956 was *wholly* borne by the British taxpayer. Financially it cost the Jordanian population literally nothing.
[9] *Op. cit.*, 587–588. The reference to the Sassoon letter concerns the difficult and unsuccessful negotiations between Abdullah and the Israelis. (These are discussed by Tel on pp. 437–544).
[10] A condition perhaps true of Syria and Egypt, but not Jordan.
[11] Date of order 2 October 1948. Note that Ma'āyiṭa was a member of the Jordan Armistice Delegation to Rhodes, and a friend of Abu Nuwar. In the April 1957 attempted coup against the regime Ma'āyiṭa joined Abu Nuwar in the ultimatum to King Husayn to form a nationalist coalition government of which they could approve. It is possible that Ma'āyiṭa's conspiratorial activities began in Jerusalem as a result of his close association with Tel.

against the monarchy. Interestingly enough the Baath leader Abdullah al-Rimawi and other Palestinian opposition politicians (Anwar al-Khaṭīb and others)[12] later served the regime as cabinet members. It is certain that at no time did any of these politicians have complete confidence in Tel's ability to deliver a sizeable portion of the Legion in the case of a coup. It is also certain that, early in 1949, Tel himself sensed the growing ire of the King and that of Legion GHQ, especially General Glubb, over his political activities. Without extensive support from his fellow officers—particularly now that he was no longer on the active commissioned list of officers—he felt that time was running out on him.

Tel tried one other avenue for his activities, namely, a liaison with Crown Prince Talal. The latter had been popularly identified with the cause of Arab nationalism. As a matter of fact, Talal never got along with his father, King Abdullah, suffered from mental illness from a young age, and may have therefore viewed all opposition activity against his father as proper and deserving. Tel claims in his *Memoirs* that in April 1949 Talal had agreed to a coup which would depose the King and detain Glubb and all British officers of the Legion in Amman camp. Then he, Talal, would have taken over the kingdom in co-operation with loyal officers whose names would have been presented by Tel on the day of the coup.[13] According to Tel, everyone seemed to encourage him in his work, that is, Talal, fellow officers, Syrian and Egyptian leaders. Yet it became clear by spring 1949 that the annexation of Palestine and the presence of Legion forces in firm military control precluded the success of any conspiracy short of the use of force or direct outside interference.

[12] The Transjordanian 'Ākif al-Fāyiz, a leading member of the Bani Sakhr, is mentioned by Tel as one of those who sympathised with his political aims. Ironically, al-Fāyiz in 1956–1957 was the person who kept the Palace informed about conspiracies within the officer corps, using his extensive contacts with tribal officers in the army. See *op. cit.*, pp. 581–582, where Tel claims that in March 1949 he visited opposition leaders in Jordan such as Sulayman al-Nabulsi, Shafiq al-Rusheydat and 'Ākif al-Fāyiz. The latter, incidentally a Deputy in the 1956–1957 Chamber [under the Nabulsi nationalist coalition government: elections of 21 October 1956] representing *Badu al-shamāl* (The Bedouins of the North), received in April 1957 communications from tribal officers in the Legion indicating the possible existence of a military conspiracy against the regime. These he immediately communicated to the King. Moreover, he had a beduin captain [Ṭalab Fahad] a Company CO in 1 Regiment Armoured Cars, report in person on developments in the army. See account in Māḍi and Mūsā, *op. cit.*, 669–671. Incidentally, Rimawi, al-Khaṭīb, and Rusheydat became members of the Nabulsi Cabinet of 29 October 1956 as Minister of State for Foreign Affairs, Minister of Public Works, and Minister of Justice and Public Instruction respectively. 'Ākif al-Fāyiz is currently one of the most influential deputies in Jordan.
[13] See *op. cit.*, 592.

Considering Glubb's evidence that Tel came to see him in the summer of 1949 for advice, certain inferences can be drawn.[14] Either Tel decided that only by return to active duty in the Legion could he hope to establish a wider, stronger network of conspiracy among the officer corps; or he had realised that his political future was uncertain under the circumstances. In any event, he resigned early in June 1949, retired to his home town Irbid and, according to him, continued to maintain his liaison with political allies both within and outside Jordan. He left for Egypt in October 1949. It is, on the other hand, quite possible that Tel had decided that he would be able to organise a coup from that distance. As a matter of fact, he was sentenced to death *in absentia* for his alleged part in the conspiracy which led to the assassination of King Abdullah in 1951.

The case of Tel is interesting for many reasons. Tel was born in 1918, so that at thirty he was Governor of a city whose fate in 1948–1949 was of international concern. His native town, Irbid, as we saw in the earlier historical sections of this study, had been an initial opposition stronghold against Abdullah's recently formed Principality. Within six years of enlistment (1942) he had risen to the rank of Major, and a few months thereafter to the rank of Colonel. Like Abu Nuwar later, he was the recipient of special royal favour. Whereas Abu Nuwar had been involved in official representational capacities for the Armistice Agreement, Tel dealt with the most secret and delicate negotiations between an Arab king and the Israelis. The fact that he took copies of *all* the documents and correspondence relating to this matter with him indicates that he intended to use them for political blackmail. By his own admission, Tel used to brief opposition politicians of their contents even while the negotiations were in progress.

At thirty Tel was, as Governor of the Holy City, very much in the political limelight. He may have sincerely considered Abdullah's policy one of treason against the Arab cause. What is certain is that he used it to advance his own political ambition. He perhaps misjudged the determination of other Arab states, particularly Egypt, effectively to oppose Abdullah's annexation of Arab Palestine. Yet, inter-Arab politics at that time were easily misleading. A settlement between Jordan and Israel never came to pass, partly as a result of Arab pressure and partly as a result of Israeli intransigence over the conditions of a settlement. Moreover, what Tel perhaps did not realise was that Abdullah's negotiations with Israel were widely

---

[14] Tel, it seems, suggested to Glubb that he would resign his Civil Governorship of Jerusalem and return to the Legion if he were given the rank of Brigadier (see *op. cit.*, 256).

known, in fact they were common Arab knowledge; only their exact nature and content were secret.

In the final analysis, Tel was unable to get very far because of (1) his inability to infiltrate the officer corps to any meaningful extent; (2) his identification with the town of Irbid and lack of close relations with any great number of tribal officers. His brief command of 6 Infantry Regiment during actual operations could have worked in his favour. His mistake, though, was to relinquish troop command for the governorship. For all one knows the King's pushing him up so quickly and his appointing him to the civilian governorship of the Old City may have been cleverly deliberate.[15] As it turned out, he gave Tel enough rope until the only way he could escape the noose was to leave the country. It is also possible that the way in which he went about his political activities so soon after his brief army career did not endear him to either the officers or men of the Legion.

Until the incorporation of Central Palestine into the Hashemite Kingdom of Jordan, political party activity in the country was limited in aims and scope. We saw that as early as 1928 parties were permitted by Abdullah to organise and operate under licence. The same pattern was followed after the war in 1947. Yet leaders of parties usually represented sectional interests of tribal chiefs, notables, and generally the very small upper propertied classes. Most of them aimed at extracting a greater share of power by demanding the curtailment of the monarch's prerogatives.

Only after the union of the two Banks did mass party activity characterised by certain ideological overtones against the *status quo* emerge. Moreover, some of these parties were Jordanian branches, or renditions, of wider organisations cutting across Arab state boundaries. Such was the Arab Baath party in 1952 (later renamed in 1954 the Arab Baath Socialist party) which, along with leftist elements and a few communists, organised a National Front. Many of its leaders and members were new Jordanians, that is Palestinians, especially from the Ramallah–Jerusalem and Nablus areas.

It is not necessary here to discuss parties in detail, but only to characterise their nature and activity insofar as they affected the political stability of the Legion. Generally before union, parties especially in the 1920s and 1930s, were agreed on the existence of the Principality and were not in any way seeking the overthrow of the ruling house. Even if some among them harboured such aspirations,

---

[15] General Glubb does not agree with this explanation, for he is convinced that the King was deceived by Tel.

the mandate relationship with Britain until 1946 would have rendered their fulfilment a near impossibility. After union, and particularly soon after the assassination of King Abdullah in July 1951, the country entered upon a most precarious political transition.

The brief interlude of King Talal's accession to the throne (July 1951–August 1952), followed by his quick abdication,[16] gave a wide opening to anti-Hashemite political elements. Major support and inspiration for the latter came from the West Bank. The Palestinians —or at least their political leaders and city-dwellers generally among them—considered their incorporation into the Kingdom of Jordan the unilateral act of an ambitious Arab ruler, and against their real wishes. They did not consider their continued existence in an Arab enclave of Palestine the consequence of a saving action by an Arab army—the Legion. Rather they viewed the latter as the willing instrument of this ambitious ruler in acquiring territory. They now constituted over 65 per cent of the total population of the kingdom. In contrast to the Transjordanians they considered themselves economically, socially, and politically more sophisticated. Moreover, they tended to be attracted to the more Pan-Arab, and Arab nationalist, views of groups and parties active elsewhere in the Arab world. This was particularly the trend after they had lost what they considered to be Arab territory—their country.

Thus, parties which were organised between 1952 and 1956 reflected three political trends in the country. First, the local Transjordanian groupings, generally loyal to the monarch and anxious to retain their political ascendancy and privileged status in an expanded realm that now included a more advanced but alienated and embittered population, continued to exist and function. Second, a number of groups and parties reflecting ideological tendencies which ranged from the mild socialist and the Pan-Arab nationalist to the communist appeared on the scene, heavily populated by Palestinians. Third, groups and parties with as strong, but conservative, ideological coloration, particularly a militant Islamic one, became active.

Until his assassination, King Abdullah managed to curtail, and frequently suppress, ideological groups at both ends of the political spectrum. He was opposed to both the extreme Right and the extreme Left. Only in the traditional local-parochial Transjordanian groups did he continue to see a useful adjunct to his essentially tribal-autocratic rule. The accession to the throne of his young grandson in April 1953 unavoidably heralded the risky inauguration

---

[16] King Talal was deposed on medical grounds: he was declared mentally unfit, after he was found to suffer from acute schizophrenia.

of a new era. King Husayn, for instance, embarked upon a deliberate policy of political liberalisation. This meant principally the extension of free political association to parallel certain fundamental reforms in government and its institutions.

In May 1953 the new prime minister, Fawzi Pasha al-Mulqi, "a king's man", gave sway to this innovation. The political parties that emerged on the scene reflected the changes that had occurred in the political morphology of the country, especially as a result of the Palestinian situation. It became apparent that by 1956 at least two or three of these parties had a relatively large following; that such groups as the National Socialists and the Baath claimed the allegiance of townsmen and some villagers, petty bourgeoisie and intelligentsia, especially in the West Bank. It was also clear that they had a small following among officers, particularly those in the administrative and technical branches of the Legion. What was more dangerous was that the Baathists, for instance, and, in 1956, the Arab Nationalists, were concerned with the fundamental question of whether Jordan should exist as a nation-state at all, or whether it should be part of a larger Arab sovereign entity. To this extent these new parties reflected not simply the alienation and frustration of ex-Palestinians, who until that time saw no reason why they should be loyal to a monarchy which many of them considered traitorous to the so-called Arab cause, but also the effects of the gusty winds of a new Arabism preached from Cairo and Damascus. To this extent also, these were not Jordanian parties in the real sense of national groups. There was no fundamental agreement between them and among their members that the Jordanian entity was viable or even desirable.[17]

It is against this background that one must assess the political influences on the Legion which partly led to the abortive coup of April 1957. An important step which opened a political Pandora's box in the Legion was its integration with the National Guard in 1956. Another was the separation of the police and gendarmerie security forces from the Legion in July 1956. Until then, the National Guard was a separate body and organisation, trained and controlled by Legion GHQ. The merging of these two institutions into a total force of about 55,000 officers and men meant bringing into closer proximity Legion officers with National Guardsmen, who were largely Palestinian border villagers.

To the unsuspecting observer the integration of these two forces

---

[17] See on parties at this time, Jean-Pierre Alem, "En Jordanie, l'Agonie d'un Royaume", *Orient*, No. 2 (April 1957), pp. 100–113. See also, W.Z.L., "Communism in Jordan", *The World Today*, vol. 12, No. 3 (1956), pp. 109–119. See also Abidi, *op. cit.*, pp. 191–212.

appeared as a deliberate act of the government to associate west Jordanians with the armed forces of the country, and to make defence particularly against Israel a common and more widely shared national responsibility. In short, this act appeared as an attempt to merge an essentially élite regular force of beduin, tribesmen and Transjordanian peasants with a territorial frontier force wholly consisting of settled Palestinian agricultural peasants and a few townsmen. It must be noted, however, that this consideration was already in the mind of General Glubb when he first organised the National Guard in the face of great opposition from politicians on both sides of the Jordan. What was less readily apparent was the likely objective of the new nationalist government in 1956 to use the merger for political purposes: perhaps in order to infiltrate the Legion with certain political currents.

The King instinctively perhaps sensed that the opposition which had appeared since the union of the two Banks differed in nature from the opposition that arose occasionally under his grandfather's rule. The only practical riposte to a supra-Jordanian nationalism (Arab, Pan-Arab, and the like) appeared to him to be the political integration of the leaders of this opposition into the élite of the state both in its civil institutions and, more guardedly, in the army. In retrospect, this seems to be a partial explanation of Husayn's so to speak rolling with the nationalist punch in 1956–1957. He chose perhaps a most difficult and dangerous balancing act. He sought to straddle the gap between the old parochial and always promonarchical, old-fashioned Transjordanian leadership, on the one hand, and the new emerging leadership on the other. The latter came mainly from the West Bank. It was initially orientated towards Arab nationalism. But by 1956–1957 certain elements in it were beginning to lean more towards Jordanian national interests. They were still, however, less conservative and more ambitious than the established East Jordanians. The King thus sought at the same time to bridge the gap separating these two groups.

Simultaneously, he was under great pressure to render the Legion into a national army in the sense of making its officer corps exclusively Arab. At the moment, the core ground force remains heavily tribal and thus conservative Transjordanian, whereas the technical branch, including the rapidly expanding Royal Air Force, is creating a new group of better educated, more sophisticated townsmen officers and NCOs. The King had even risked as early as 1954 entrusting the portfolio of Defence to a Palestinian. The position of Chief of the General Staff, however, continues to be a prerogative of Transjordanians. But even this may go to an ex-Palestinian in the future, as surely as the premiership of the country may go that way soon.

It is therefore this phenomenal, patient and stubbornly institutional and legal process of integration which is perhaps the young King's greatest achievement so far. When at one time parochial nationalism in Jordan united behind the throne only the old conservative Transjordanians, while at the same time dividing the alienated Palestinians from them, today the latter's nationalism does not appear as vehemently committed against the *status quo*. Rather the latter are interested in becoming the major, if not sole, recruiting ground from which the élite with whose aid the monarch shall rule, will come. It is not fair to argue that such a trend and development reflects no more than the temporary, or passing, failure of Arabism—as preached by Cairo and Damascus—to realise its aims. That this failure had a sobering and felicitous effect upon ex-Palestinian Jordanians there is no doubt. But there is a more positive and independent reason for the change in the attitude of Palestinians towards both the King and what they now consider their country—Jordan. The nature and context of Palestinian Arab politics have changed since 1949. The Arab loss of Palestine unavoidably discredited the anti-Hashemite leaders of Arab political organisation there, namely, the Husaynis. These are no more. The present generation of leaders that has emerged—men in their thirties, forties, and some even in their fifties—is a new one in the sense that it is well educated and professionally trained; the intellectuals in its ranks have barely a connection with the familial and religious traditionalism, or conservatism, of the earlier generation of leaders. Some of them are already in the Legion officer corps.

A very intelligent and knowledgeable senior British officer who had raised and trained his own regiment in both Jordan and the Federation of South-west Arabia commented once: ". . . in Arab armies the officers are the only people who matter." Thinking back over his experiences with the Arab Legion from 1952 to 1955, he reported that he was convinced "that much of the discontent among Arab officers had stemmed from a feeling that they were not being given sufficient responsibility".

Obviously, then, a straightforward source and area of political conflict within the Legion until 1956 was the control of the establishment by alien—foreign—senior officers. Resentment was not necessarily mixed with hatred, or even coloured by political considerations at the outset. Yet such resentment has been easily exploited since 1954 by both opposition political leaders and groups within Jordan and by external elements. Among the latter, Cairo

Radio was prominent. One suspects that much of this resentment at the outset was not based on any widespread anti-British feeling. It was still on the level of personal ambition on the part of Arab officers who aspired to—and anticipated—promotion to senior positions. From that level, it was not difficult, given the reception of internal and external political influences, to articulate the resentment in political terms. This despite the fact that until 1956 the bulk of Legion officers distrusted politicians. When it came to promotions, security of position and related career matters they probably trusted more their British senior commanders for fairness and impartiality than they did one another. They felt, as Lunt put it, that "... under Arab control promotion would depend more on favouritism, or tribal affinities than on military efficiency...".

Yet it is this kind of resentment General Glubb knew about but could not easily counter or cater to; for he was primarily responsible for the defence and security of the country. This was an especially heavy responsibility when the armed truce on the border with Israel was so precarious. His first and foremost duty therefore consisted of ensuring the maintenance of a highly efficient striking force that could and would fight. He considered this to be the best deterrent against attack. He had to maintain this posture in the best interests of Jordan irrespective of political considerations and pressures. The intuitive response of the King to this situation seems in retrospect to have been near perfect. He managed to exploit this situation to his advantage in protecting the integrity—the very survival—of his kingdom, but not without sacrificing General Glubb, the man clearly most responsible for the defence of the country until 1956. Later it turned out that Glubb's conception of both the Legion and the National Guard was most realistic in the context of the conditions prevailing in Jordan. Eventually the National Guard was separated from the Legion but kept under the control of the latter.

When General Sir Gerald Templer visited Jordan in December 1955, plans were drawn up for the further expansion of the Legion. In General Glubb's view, arabisation of the officer corps could not be realised before 1965 at the earliest. His own account stated that Britain (as per the Templer Mission) was willing to raise the 1955 Legion subsidy of £10,000,000 to £16,500,000 for the first year of the expansion scheme, and then to £12,500,000 for each subsequent year. This would have allowed the formation of a fourth infantry brigade, representing a 25 per cent increase in strength. Two Brigades would be available for operational deployment and two for training and reserve. A new tank regiment and one of medium artillery would have been organised, in addition to an increase in strength for support units (transport, workshops, signals, administration). General Glubb considered the King's demand for three infantry divisions and an armoured division unrealistic, since he argued that the Legion could not provide adequately trained officers and NCOs so quickly. He argued, for instance, that the 1955 ratio of 1,500 officers to 23–25,000 strength would, in order to satisfy the King's demand, have to increase by 3,000 to make up a 4,500 officers to 65–70,000 overall strength. Since the output of the Cadet School at the time was 100 per year, it would require thirty years to produce the 3,000 additional officers needed. Assuming the output were doubled, it would still have taken until 1975.[18] It should be noted, in this connection, that the possibility of opening a Military Academy or a Staff College of limited scope was not entertained by General Glubb. These two institutions might conceivably have improved the officer-training situation.

It is only fair, however, to emphasise the two most serious limitations upon expansion in those days, particularly as regards the question of officer strength. One was the major problem of finding suitable officers. This in turn was closely linked with the level of literacy among personnel and the fact that until 1956 the rate of illiteracy among recruits was fairly high—about 50–75 per cent. The other limitation consisted of a more subtle and complex difficulty, namely, the fact that the administration, operational and other command functions were articulated and set on record in English. This problem was not peculiar to Jordan. Other Arab armies faced it twice over: a shift from the Turkish military terminological legacy to English and then to Arabic. In the absence of military manuals and texts in Arabic, extensive and tricky translation programmes had to be devised, particularly in Iraq in the 1930s and 1940s. Thus, whereas Arab officers, especially those with troop command on the company level and a few of them on the regimental level, proved their capacity in acquiring high-level tactical ability, their record in administration was on the whole inadequate. Another reason for this shortcoming was the level of education, and the widespread use of English for administration[19] in the presence of a British CGS and senior commanders.

One can thus identify three general areas of conflict in the Legion. First, there was the conflict between political leaders on the one hand and GHQ on the other over defence plans (see below) and officer promotions. There was no open, or other, conflict as such between General Glubb and the government at any time. I am using the term

[18] See Glubb, *op. cit.*, pp. 393–394.
[19] All of General Glubb's office work was in Arabic

"conflict" only to depict the recurrent unwillingness of government leaders to openly express to Glubb any disagreement with, disapproval of, or misgivings about the performance of his duties as CGS. I am also using it to underline the ambivalent—though quite common—attitude of government leaders in privately agreeing to a certain defence policy while publicly refusing to support, defend, or justify it for political reasons. Finally, I am using the term "conflict" to refer to the propaganda attacks by Palestinian political leaders, especially upon the Legion, and the implied references to its CGS without suggesting that there was an actual conflict between them and the CGS. Second, there was the matter of aspiring junior officers who felt that the promotion pattern in the Legion was too rigid and slow. Third, there was the question of Legion expansion, already referred to, which came to a head in 1956.

It is of course true that seconded British regimental commanders were professional regular army officers, all of them with World War II command experience.[20] It is also true that the average Arab politician's view of an army was more heroic-romantic than it was practical-scientific. They thought about armies more in terms of dash and numbers than in terms of efficient organisation, training, and fire-power.

A shift was also occurring in the view of opposition political leaders—and especially of those from the West Bank—regarding the composition and nature of the Legion. They felt that the Legion had to be a "national" army, and not merely a picked corps of regulars. By a "national" army these leaders meant, first, an army staffed exclusively by Arab officers, and second, one staffed more and more by formally educated officers. The latter would automatically have been more politically oriented too. From his writings it is clear that General Glubb continued to consider the beduin, the tribesman, and the peasant as the most felicitous recruiting grounds for the Legion. With military efficiency in mind (and after all Glubb was responsible for defence organisation), he had to ignore the fact that socio-economic change in Jordan was favouring the townsman, especially after the massive infusion of Palestinians into the body politic. So that while the monarch was anxious, for sound political reasons, gradually to integrate the two banks of the country, Glubb was faced with the task—given general security conditions then—of retaining the Legion as an efficient élite fighting force.

As for the defence plan proposed by General Glubb in 1955 and

---

[20] Field grade officers like Peter Young, Galletly and Griffiths of Infantry; Wormwald and Lunt of Armoured Cars; Leakey of Tanks and Hutton of Tanks and GHQ; Tyrrell and Elliott of Artillery, were all officers of great experience.

rejected by the King and the cabinet, I do not propose to discuss its military soundness for I am not qualified to do so. Suffice it to say that the plan was devised to provide the best defence of the country in case of an Israeli attack on Central Palestine, given the financial and other resources of Jordan at that time. It was also based on an appreciation of Israeli mobility and military tactics. It was briefly predicated upon preventing the rapid cutting off of the Jordan valley salient by the highly mobile Israeli forces. It therefore concentrated on making it possible for the Legion to move quickly into the centre from either the north or the south of this valley and so prevent either an encirclement of their positions in Central Palestine or a cutting of their line of communications to their supply and logistical rear in Transjordan. To the militarily not too knowledgeable opposition politicians, all the plan meant was that it did not call for the concentration of crack forces of the Legion along the length of the actual frontier line with Israel. Yet to have opted for the latter strategy the Israelis would have been able to descend easily from the northern plain directly into the valley, thus cutting off the forward Legion positions with hardly having to engage any of them seriously. On the whole, the objection to the plan was purely political, because it was not based on grounds of military appreciation. In fact, it was rejected without discussion of any relevant military points.

General Glubb was fundamentally correct in wishing to retain the Legion as a mobile, long-enlistment volunteer regular force. Its mobility was crucial to a long and wide frontier. By virtue of these purely military considerations he was, on the other hand, laying himself open to political attack. This became more severe when the scheme for the further expansion and gradual arabisation of the Legion was considered at about the same time as the Defence Plan. To the politicians the target date of 1965 for the last British officer to leave the Legion appeared a long time hence.[21] They argued that an army consisting largely of martial elements was no longer appropriate for the Jordan of 1955. What they were really aiming for was the hasty, if not immediate, removal of all British officers

---

[21] See Glubb, *op. cit.*, pp. 387–388 and 393–394, where he argued that the retention of British officers was essential to the Legion's efficiency in case of an Israeli attack. "However, although we unwittingly decided that, for the present, the British officers were necessary to ensure efficiency, we prepared extremely detailed plans for their replacement. As a result of my personal intervention we secured two entries a year at the British Staff College, Camberley. Calculating in considerable detail the ages of all officers, their qualifications and the output of the Staff College, we produced a plan according to which the last British officer would leave in 1965" (pp. 387–388).

from the Legion. This, in turn, was related to their identification of the CGS with the monarch. And with the latter, so-called nationalist politicians were at that time engaged in serious political conflict. It is unlikely that they would have accepted or even understood the explanation that crack, regular mobile armies with the necessary equipment and fire-power can, under certain conditions, be far superior to mass conscript ones.

The contention of General Glubb that the Legion was everywhere popular with the rural and tribal population on both sides of the river is well founded. First, these were the elements largely comprising the Legion. Second, via the National Guard the rural population came into more direct working contact with Legion units. Third, the Legion was responsible for defence and security—two most important aspects of a villager's existence and survival. The townsman and city dweller, especially west of the river, resented and even disliked the Legion, even though this was the force which retained Central Palestine for him. The townsman had suffered humiliation at the loss of the remainder of Palestine to the Israelis. The humiliation among the more intelligent townsmen must have been compounded with a sense of shame that they did too little and too late to defend themselves. From this, it was an easy step to accuse the Legion for not being a national army and to demand its transformation into a real one by the simple act of removing all British officers in it.

Given this generally tense political atmosphere in 1955–1956 underlying which was really a mounting conflict between the monarchy and a new group of opposition leaders who in turn were affected by wider Arab political currents, resentment and political unrest were bound to infiltrate members of the Legion officer corps. Thus, the alienation of politically oriented officers from the CGS and British officers in the Legion was by the beginning of 1956 complete. On the one hand, the King and his government expected Glubb to carry on with his responsibilities and duties for defence and security, while on the other certain Arab officers, taking their cue from politicians in the country, were determined that the Legion should become a strictly Arab-officered army. The King, who was exposed to immense and constant pressure both from his new ADC Ali Abu Nuwar and like-minded officers at home and from the "nationalist" camp of Arab states to terminate the alliance with Britain and not to accede to the Baghdad Pact, must have been in a very difficult position. In retrospect, it appears that perhaps instinctively he followed the Arab nationalist line and possibly forestalled serious trouble in the army. He could not do this without sacrificing General

Glubb in a most abrupt manner which was followed shortly afterwards by the departure of the remaining British officers in the Legion.

Glubb's suggestion that in dismissing him the King was first under the influence of young nationalist Arab officers—particularly his ADC Ali Abu Nuwar and his clique—and second, that he resented having to take the advice of an older man in command of his army, may reflect accurately the feelings of a young monarch struggling under immense and inimical pressure to establish his political primacy over an unstable and precarious realm. Even though he had twice rejected Glubb's resignation and at no time questioned the latter's loyalty, it is possible that the King suddenly decided that he could not afford his CGS *politically*. As a result of the pressure brought upon him by these officers, it is also possible that he came to recognise the *political* significance of removing all British officers from the Legion. The radical Arab officers on their part anticipated that this would have given them a free hand in the army to pursue their political ends. Thus, while the King may have been convinced that even Glubb, who as CGS was fully under the orders of a civilian government and under the head of the state, was now a political liability to the throne, the nationalist officers, on the other hand, must have considered his continued presence as the strongest protection of the monarchy. The different interests of these two sides converged at the dismissal of General Glubb in March 1956. Their convergence also stopped there; for immediately thereafter they parted ways.

\* \* \*

In examining more closely the turbulent period 1954–1956, and the role of the Legion in upholding the regime, it is well to remember that the constitution of 1952 still afforded the King extensive powers in conjunction with the Executive, i.e. the Cabinet. The King continued to rule as well as reign. The deteriorating political situation in the country in 1954 could only be met by the dismissal of the liberalising prime minister and the dissolution of parliament. New Defence Regulations granting the Executive enormous powers over political parties and the press were promulgated in an effort to restore order prior to elections for a new Chamber. The new government of Tawfiq Abu'l-Huda wanted to ensure the election of progovernment or at least safe candidates. According to General Glubb, Abu'l-Huda made no secret of his willingness to "rig" part of the elections, particularly in Amman. He even suggested that the same should be done among the voters in the Legion. Glubb, who refused outright such a suggestion, compromised on the notion of presenting the soldier electors with a ballot that had government candidates clearly marked. Despite his assertion "Very few soldiers were interested in politics" (the beduin perhaps were not), General Glubb goes on to report that "as was to be expected, such units as workshops voted for rather left-wing candidates, not Tawfiq Pasha's nominees. A few soldiers voted Communist."[22]

The elections of 16 October 1954 were significant for civil-military relations in Jordan on two counts. First, there was the fact that a number of military personnel voted for opposition candidates. One suspects that voting for non-government candidates among Engineer and Artillery officers was heavier than General Glubb reports. This indicated to some extent the consequence of the influx of non-tribal personnel and recruits into the Legion, especially in the more technical branches. As one observer remarked in 1957, "with the incorporation of Palestinians, the Legion lost its homogeneity".[23] Second, the use of the Legion to quell widespread demonstrations in the country on election day further alienated the army from the civilian population. As Glubb himself stated, it was the first time in its thirty-year history that the Legion had opened fire on a group of civilians. It did so on 16 October 1954, to restore order.[24] The suppression of opposition press media and the return of loyalist members to the Chamber rendered opposition possible only in the form of demonstrations and civil disturbances.

The mounting opposition of anti-regime leaders to the Legion in the last two or three years of General Glubb's command is reflected even more clearly in the perhaps most difficult political period of the 1950s, namely, 1954–1956. The rapid expansion of the Legion, which, as I showed, unavoidably introduced new elements into its ranks, coincided partly with the acceleration of political activity in the country. Much of this activity was opposed to the regime and the *status quo*. Reports of "political talk" in their messes was common.[25] General Glubb himself reports knowledge of certain officers with political views and connections detrimental to the Legion's welfare and the country's security.

The political alienation of the Palestinian and East Jordanian radical nationalists from the Legion had increased in the years 1953–1954. It was caused partly by the spate of unusually ferocious

[22] See *op. cit.*, 348–357.   [23] See Jean-Pierre Alem, *op. cit.*, p. 108.
[24] See *op. cit.*, 356–357.
[25] Several of the British officers I interviewed, who then commanded certain infantry regiments, a light AA regiment, and artillery units, reported knowledge of political talk among Arab officers. Some reported a general atmosphere of restlessness among their officers. By November 1955 some of them felt they were sitting on top of a volcano.

border clashes with Israel in the period October 1953–March 1954. Among the latter, the Israeli army's attack on the border village of Qibya on the night of 14–15 October 1953, and on Nahalin on the night of 28–29 March 1954 were especially disturbing. Regarding the Qibya incident, the charge was made by the opposition leaders that the signal sent for reinforcements to Brigade HQ by the NCO on duty in the village National Guard post went unheeded. One has no way of determining if the charge was justified or not. In any event, a ministerial court of inquiry at the time found it necessary—or expedient—to dismiss Brigadier Ashton from the Legion.[26]

Taking advantage of the constitutional reforms affecting the liberalisation of political life in Jordan instituted by the young monarch through his new prime minister Fawzi Pasha al-Mulqi (April 1953–May 1954), opposition leaders, especially from the West Bank, organised demonstrations in the major towns and cities. These aimed their attack and invective primarily against the British composition of the command of the Legion and the Western powers generally. Palestinians at least could still resuscitate the emotional issue of the loss of Lydda and Ramle during the Palestine War operations in 1948–1949. They still adhered to their contention and belief that General Glubb was mainly responsible for an unnecessary withdrawal of the Legion from that area of operations, thus permitting further loss of Arab land to the Israelis. And this was aggravated by the immediate expulsion of the Arab inhabitants by the Israelis—one of the few times when such expulsion quite definitely took place.[27] The demonstrations, moreover, were not solely organised by radical, Arab nationalist, and leftist elements and groups; extremist rightist, religiously fanatic groups like the Muslim Brethren and the Freedom Party of Shayhk Taqi al-Din al-Nabhani were equally active against the government. For the Legion these political disturbances were ominous, for not only did they assign

---

[26] See the account by General Glubb, *op. cit.*, 308–310 and 312–316. See also Mādī and Mūsā *op. cit.*, 586–588.

[27] It should be noted that the decision not to hold Lydda and Ramle was made with the full agreement of the King and the government. In fact, during the first armistice the CGS requested permission to send forward civil police to the two towns, which had been without any government since 15 May 1948. The Prime Minister denied such permission on the basis of policy decisions taken earlier not to attempt to take or hold Lydda and Ramle. Unfortunately, when popular indignation erupted later about this matter neither the King nor his government did, for obvious political reasons, dare admit that this had been their own decision. Consequently the weight of public indignation fell upon the CGS who, as such, was in no position to defend himself. To do so would have meant denouncing the sovereign and the government.

guilt and responsibility to its CGS, but indirectly indicted an army that was viewed as a monarch's praetorian force.

Once more the opposition's attack was aimed at the British command of the Legion. When earlier in the year it was accused of being unable, or unwilling, or both, to cope with the external threat to the Arabs, namely, the border armed attacks by Israeli troops, now it was identified in the popular mind of the masses as first the suppressor of civil liberties, and second—not unrelated to the first— an upholder of British influence in the country. The King was not at that moment an object of attack. In a way, he had covered his rear; for he had inaugurated his reign with a declared policy of political liberalisation embodied in concrete legislation.[28] He had permitted party activity. It left the conservative Transjordanian political leaders who controlled the Executive allied to the Legion as the obstructionists of the nationalist cause.

The monarch also hastened to secure his political flanks to keep pace with the rapid involvement of the Arab region in the Cold War. He therefore sought to start negotiations for the revision of the Anglo-Jordanian Treaty of 1948. This appeared doubly urgent in the eyes of the government upon the heels of the Anglo-Egyptian Agreement of 10 October 1954. At the same time the West, namely, Britain and the United States, were involved in a diplomatic campaign to associate Middle Eastern states with their global cold war policy, including the negotiation of defence pacts. Given the furore over the Baghdad Pact in early 1955, pressure on Jordan was not exerted by the West alone, but also by the anti-Iraqi Arab states, namely, Egypt and Saudi Arabia. The government and the King found themselves between the Scylla of Great Power solicitation, backed up by the offer of good military hardware and economic aid and the Charybdis of Arab nationalist and Arab unity agitation. Britain, for example, proposed early in 1955 an annual grant for the maintenance of the National Guard amounting to one million dollars. She also gave Vampire aircraft to the Jordanian Air Force. The Turks, who were members of a Western-sponsored military alliance, were also offering token aid with military aircraft. A flurry of state visitors to Jordan in 1955—President Celal Bayar of Turkey, General Abdel-Hakim Amer of Egypt, and later Sir Gerald Templer, British CIGS— clearly indicated the involvement of Jordan in the periphery if not the centre of attempted alliances and alignments in the Middle East.

The position of Jordan *vis-à-vis* the Baghdad Pact, the relationship

---

[28] See regarding this legislation, Abidi, *Jordan, A Political Study, 1947–1957* (London, 1965), p. 111–118.

with Britain, and the more explosive question of Arab nationalism and unity was a difficult one throughout 1955. Political groups, especially the Baath, National Socialists, and leftist National Front groups, were active throughout this year, vociferously demanding that Jordan take an Arab nationalist course. Agitation by Egypt further implied that this course should fall in line with her policy. Moreover, the Israeli Gaza raid in February 1955 together with a proliferation of other border clashes exacerbated the political situation further. There was also popular admiration in Jordan for the rising prestige of Egypt after Bandung in April 1955, and the Czech arms deal announced in September 1955. The late Major Ṣalāḥ Sālim of Egypt visited Amman in March 1955, and General Abdel-Hakim Amer in December. The latter is reported to have made the following entry in the Visitors' Book of the Army Officers Club at Zarqa:

"My visit to the Club, which represents the youth of the Army, impressed upon me that I was in the company of young officers who wish to elevate the standards of the Army of the sister state, Jordan. My visit has strengthened my faith in the Arabs and Arabism."

Clearly, the inscription was meant to appeal to the more ambitious young officers who favoured the immediate arabisation of the officer corps; to wean them from their British officered command; to galvanise any resistance among them against a re-negotiated British connection; and finally to encourage their opposition to a Jordanian association with the Baghdad Pact.

Both press and public appeared elated with the Egyptian visitors: their response was enthusiastic. Four changes of government within the year, on the other hand, only reflected the chronic instability of the country, caused partly by these external influences, and partly by the refusal of West Bank politicians to either co-operate in the formation of a viable government, or clearly support any that excluded their numbers in it.

When Templer arrived on his mission in early December the political atmosphere was tense to say the least. The package offer he made to Jordan appealed to both the King and his cabinet. Its most attractive terms related to the strengthening of the army, payment of British subsidies, and, best of all, significant aid in the development of an operational Air Force. Where the offer presented serious and, as it turned out insurmountable, political difficulties was in its stipulation that Jordan join the Baghdad Pact and exchange the existing Anglo-Jordanian treaty for a new special agreement between the two countries within the context of the Pact.

The Templer-Jordan discussions and the airing of the issues toppled Said Al-Mufti's government, since the West Bank ministers would not co-operate with, let alone support it.[29] The King found it difficult to get any leader who could form an acceptable government. Finally he called upon Hazzā' al-Majālī (a member of the famous Majālī tribe from Kerak) to form a government. The latter was willing to stick his neck out publicly by declaring openly that his government meant to accede to the Pact. The next day, however, riotous demonstrations broke out in Amman and other towns, making it plain to the government that Majālī's policy was unpopular and would be resisted by the force of civil disturbances.

Two days of rioting brought the Legion once again into action in support of a government that could not find enough public support to rule. On 19 December Majālī's government fell and parliament was dissolved by the King. The crowds most probably felt, and perhaps were convinced, that their organised opposition had produced the crisis. The outgoing Prime Minister, on the other hand, was equally convinced that there was for the first time massive intervention by Arab state agents inimical to the regime. Glubb, for instance, has reported that both Saudi and Egyptian representatives financed some of the demonstrations.[30]

At the same time, Egypt, Syria, and Saudi Arabia came forward with an offer of financial aid to permit Jordan to forego both British aid and accession to the Baghdad Pact. Interestingly enough, while wavering in its policy under such pressure from neighbouring Arab states and the difficulties of civil disturbances at home, the caretaker government of Ibrahim Hashim stalled for time. It made credible noises on the Arab front, while it continued to consider the basic Templer proposals at least in so far as these affected the strengthening of the army. It was in retrospect a combination of a partly instinctive and partly deliberate multi-pronged policy on the part of the young King to follow such a circuitous and perilous course which eventually divided and disarmed the opposition. This, as we shall see, he was able to do in large measure because of his correct assessment of the political role of the Legion. By then he must also have come round to appreciating the importance of Glubb's conception of the Legion as the foundation of his state, even though the pressures he unwillingly permitted to bear upon him had already committed him too far in the dismissal of his CGS.

[29] See on this general question the discussion in Abidi, *op. cit.*, 109-142.
[30] See *op. cit.*, 375-415.

But early in January new demonstrations and riots of unprecedented ferocity broke out. The mobs took to burning public buildings, government offices, and private homes. Once again the Legion became directly involved in restoring order, particularly the beduin 2nd Regiment. In addition to the use of tear gas, the troops repeated the firing at the crowds which had occurred for the first time in October 1954. The alienation of the agitated public from the Legion was now complete. In their view, the King, assisted by the army, its British commanders, and the British Government, was bent upon suppressing their nationalist aspirations. The King, on the other hand, was determined, now that public order had been restored, to beat the nationalists at their own game. This involved fantastic risks. But these he took and survived. He did not accede to the Baghdad Pact; nor did he accept the financial aid offer of the three Arab governments. Instead, he restored order in his realm, divided the opposition, and embarked upon a policy of vague Arab co-operation to avoid committing himself to any binding agreements with the other Arab states.

Meantime, *the important thing was to gain complete control of the Legion, to identify it as a "national" army, i.e. an Arab-officered army, and thus hamstring opposition charges against it.* It is in this context that Glubb's dismissal in March 1956 makes sense. More important for the King was that with this single act he was able to accelerate a future understanding with Britain on terms far less obnoxious to extremist nationalist elements. His care in insisting that his dismissal of General Glubb had no bearing whatsoever upon the legal and political relations of Jordan with Britain was nothing short of ingenious. Not only did it not harm him at home, but it elicited the desired response in Britain.[31]

As for Jordan's external detractors, these now shifted their attack from the foreign command of the Legion to one upon the Anglo-Jordanian Treaty and specifically the British subsidy. In March they invited Jordan to participate in talks leading to some agreement for the co-ordination of Arab policy, mutual defence pacts, and other relevant arrangements; and they renewed their standing offer of aid. Husayn, however, responded with his own proposals for wider Arab talks, wider Arab collective pacts. His policy was not simply one of safety in numbers, but contained the shrewd realisation that the more Arab states he could involve in these deliberations the less the likelihood of their reaching agreement. And all this time he clung to the British subsidy as per the Anglo-Jordanian Treaty.

The Suez Crisis of June–October 1956 seemed to divert attention

[31] See *The Times*, 8 March 1966.

from these matters. Jordan's security became the immediate problem. The threat from Israel, even though as it turned out later only a feint, was imminent. So was the potential threat from any Arab armies that might ostensibly come to Jordan's aid. Moreover, the elections held on 21 October 1956 reflected primarily the issue of Jordan's position in the Arab world rather than any other specific internal issue. A corollary of this problem was the matter of the disposition of the Anglo-Jordanian Treaty. The obvious alternative to the abrogation of this treaty (which would have satisfied the Nationalists) was to seek one with the Arab states. The King and his supporters clearly did not cherish such an arrangement that might be dominated by Egypt. To opt for an alliance with Iraq alone would smack too obviously of a Hashemite dynastic bloc. The King's diplomatic drive for a wider Arab collective security pact was meant as no more than a smokescreen. Ideally, he felt a new arrangement with Britain was the best course.

The election of a forty-member Chamber returned eleven National Socialists, two Baathis, three National Front (leftist, Communist), five Muslim conservatives, and eight pro-regime deputies.[32] The National Socialists led by Sulayman al-Nabulsi officially adhered to the preservation of the regime (i.e. they were at least formally committed to the continued existence of the state of Jordan). This was not the case with the Baathis and National Front deputies. The King, with impeccable constitutional style, invited Nabulsi (who failed himself to win a seat in the election!) to form a government, since his party had won a majority of the seats. Ominously, the Baathis and the National Front supported the coalition government he formed. All three parties were agreed on the issues of anti-colonialism and non-alignment, further liberalisation of political life (i.e. a curtailment of the monarch's prerogatives), and the displacement of traditional Transjordan leadership. Still more ominous was the exclusion from the Cabinet of the pro-regime Arab Constitutional party which had secured the second largest number of seats in the

[32] Election results were as follows:

| | | |
|---|---|---|
| | National Socialists | 11 |
| Usually considered promonarchists { | Constitutional Bloc | 8 |
| | Independents | 9 |
| | Baathis | 2 |
| | National Front | 3 |
| | Muslim Conservatives | 5 |
| | Palestine Arab Bloc | 2 |
| | | 40 |

Chamber. Meantime, the King, just before the formation of the elected coalition cabinet, had concluded a Tripartite Military Pact with Egypt and Syria.

The Nabulsi government is crucial to an understanding of civil-military relations in Jordan, because during its tenure of office a split between the King and the Cabinet over matters of national and international policy developed into an open mutual defiance. It is unlikely that the monarchy would have survived this estrangement between King and an elected, popular, nationalist government without the decisive role of the Legion. Thus it seems that the King at first went along with the new Cabinet's reorientation of Jordanian foreign policy towards closer co-operation with Egyptian–Syrian–Saudi Arabian inspired Arab unity and against the British relationship. This government was moreover willing to sign the Arab Solidarity Agreement (it did so on 19 January 1957) by which Arabia and Egypt pledged to pay Jordan an annual subsidy of £12½ million. This virtually, though not formally, terminated the effectiveness of the Anglo-Jordanian Treaty. In practice it accelerated negotiations with Britain for its formal termination, which occurred on 13 March 1957. Six months later, British troops evacuated their bases in Mafraq and Aqaba.

In the meantime, the announcement of the Eisenhower Doctrine on 5 January 1957 presented the King with the appropriate and convenient occasion to express disapproval of his government's foreign policy. While the government and members of Parliament publicly declared their disapproval of such doctrines by pleading non-alignment and indicating a desire to establish closer relations with the Soviet Union (especially after the Suez War), the King was unequivocally firm in his commendation of the Doctrine. The latter presented him with the opportunity of rejecting Arab aid, which he must have mistrusted from the beginning. Nevertheless, the Cabinet seemed to defy the monarch's wishes and not heed his warnings, for it remained implacably opposed to Western overtures. The breach between Cabinet and King was now open.

At this crucial point the King embarked upon a diplomatic offensive of his own initiative, using his Chief Royal Chamberlain. He inaugurated this by floating the idea of a meeting of Heads of Arab States to discuss not simply Western colonial aggression but also Communist subversion, implying his approval of the Eisenhower Doctrine. More important was his open defiance and ignoring of the Cabinet. On its side, the Cabinet embarked upon a diametrically opposed diplomatic offensive marked by a decision to accord formal recognition to the Soviet Union and Communist China. This the

Cabinet argued was in accordance with Soviet aid to the Arab cause over Suez and essential to its proclaimed positive neutrality. The King, however, interpreted these moves by the Cabinet as calculated to undermine his position.

Here it should be recalled that upon the dismissal of Glubb Colonel Rādī 'Innāb was promoted Major-General and temporarily appointed interim CGS. General 'Innāb was an ex-Palestinian who had served as Chief of Staff under Glubb. His training was really in police work. He was, in any case, due to retire that summer. This expectation in itself made the regular succession to Glubb uncertain. General 'Innāb however asked to be retired in May. He was then succeeded by Ali Abu Nuwar, while Ali al-Hiyarī was appointed CO Division. Ali Abu Nuwar, a high school graduate from al-Salṭ, had received training at both Sandhurst and Camberley. In his early thirties he was assigned to the post of Military Attaché in the Paris Embassy, where he was serving as late as the summer of 1954. From this post he also kept watch over Israeli arms shipments from France. It is likely that while in Paris Abu Nuwar also established close relations with his Egyptian counterparts. That summer the King paid a visit to Paris and it seems took a liking to Ali who had accompanied him on his various outings in the city. Soon after returning to Amman the King had requested Glubb, via the Prime Minister, that Abu Nuwar be posted back to Amman as his ADC. Glubb objected at first, for he argued that the normal tour of Military Attachés was from two to three years and that Ali had been at this post just under a year. Nevertheless, he acceded to the King's wishes which were communicated in the form of a veiled order. Along with Ali, other young officers in their early thirties were posted to the office of the ADC to the King.[33]

As Chief of General Staff Abu Nuwar apparently effected transfers, promotions and retirements among officer personnel. These to some

[33] It should be noted that, unlike Abu Nuwar, Tel had had no staff or advanced military training. On the other hand, Abu Nuwar was only slightly younger than Tel—i.e. of the same generation—a townsman from Salt, near Jericho. Ali al-Hiyari, a cousin of Abu Nuwar, had almost identical military training as Abu Nuwar. Glubb, moreover, reports in *op. cit.*, 294, that Abu Nuwar was reported attacking the monarchy and the British as early as the spring of 1952. "Never before had Arab Legion officers engaged in politics", stated Glubb. Yet Colonel Tel had done so as early as 1948. There is, one notes, a pattern here in addition to the similarity of background between Tel and Abu Nuwar, in so far as Abu Nuwar also tried a liaison with Crown Prince Talal, especially during the latter's very brief reign in September 1951–August 1952. All radicals at that time seemed to look to Talal as a possible ally in their political designs. It is not unlikely that Abu Nuwar was slipped off to Paris as Military Attaché soon after to keep him out of mischief.

extent paralleled the retirements effected later by the Nabulsi Cabinet in March–April 1957, especially in the Public Security office, including the Director, Commander Bahjat Ṭabbāra—an ex-Lieutenant-Colonel. Significantly, he also changed, at the end of the summer 1956, the organisation of the Legion. He abolished Division Headquarters under which infantry brigade groups had been organised and reorganised them into separate brigade group headquarters. This did not affect Armour which was already organised as a separate Brigade. Presumably, independent Brigade headquarters afforded the new Chief of Staff the opportunity of direct dealings with each Brigade commander without the intermediary of a division headquarters.

Glubb, furthermore, alleged in his account of the April 1957 coup that Abu Nuwar had been a known Baathi; that he had influenced the King towards terminating the Anglo-Jordanian Agreement (my feeling is that the King decided on the latter course with a perhaps instinctive though not clearly articulated desire to disarm the Nationalists); and that he poisoned the King's attitude towards Glubb.[34]

The significant factor is that Ali Abu Nuwar, Ali al-Hiyari, and officers with similar background and orientation were politically more involved than others. Given their proximity to the King and therefore the seat of authority and centre of power, they must have felt they could advance their political position. Moreover, there were no British officers left in the Legion with command functions.

While the breach between Cabinet and King was widened further by the former's formal protest to the latter regarding his independent diplomatic endeavours, this small group of officers (perhaps no more than fifteen) contemplated their own defiance of the monarch.[35] It seems that their first attempt was a complete fiasco. On 8 April a mysterious alert operation was conducted by 1 Armoured Car Regiment which ended in surrounding Amman completely. When questioned by the King the Prime Minister, Nabulsi, proferred that the military operation was designed to extract his own resignation. The CGS, Abu Nuwar, dismissed it as an operation to spot-check vehicular traffic entering and leaving Amman. But when on the next day the cabinet had dismissed Ṭabbārah, the Director of Public Security, and appointed General Muhammed al-Maʿāyiṭa (a known

---

[34] The monarch was then young and therefore open to certain influences.
[35] I have ascertained that among these there were at least two infantry officers from Irbid; two artillery officers; and one engineer officer. They were all high school graduates and were among officers subsequently arrested on charges of plotting against the regime.

Ali Abu Nuwar man) in his place;[36] when the Nablus Chief of Police, who was suspected of pro-Nabulsi party affiliations, was transferred to Amman, the King became suspicious. He dismissed the government the next day.[37]

The difficulty, however, was that none of the "safe" politicians whom the King had invited to form a new government were able to do so. Meantime, the Abu Nuwar cabal slowly came to the open. It appeared in collusion with the Nationalists who had submitted their minimum demands for any co-operation in the formation of a new government. Ali contacted on 13 April Said Pasha al-Mufti who was trying to form a government. Along with General Ali Hiyari (Deputy CGS) and Muhammed al-Ma'āyita (Director of Public Security designate), Abu Nuwar asked Mufti to inform the King that the situation in the army was most dangerous and could erupt unless he permitted the formation of a government headed by Abd al-Halīm Nimr (deposed Minister of Defence and Interior in the October 1956 Nabulsi government) who was of course acceptable to the recently dismissed government also. This was no less than an open ultimatum, and a clear threat to use the army against the King. The confrontation with Mufti was practically timed to coincide with the appearance of National Socialist party members at the Palace to propose that a coalition government under Nimr would be acceptable. The King agreed to this arrangement as it was to include Independents.

[36] It will be recalled that Ma'āyita, although a tribesman from the south of Transjordan, had been a close associate and colleague of Abu Nuwar as far back as the Armistice Delegation in 1949–50. He had been, however, senior in rank to Abu Nuwar as a Lieutenant-Colonel in 1949, and CO 6 Infantry Regiment in Jerusalem since October 1948 when he succeeded Tel to that command. In 1956 he came to command artillery.

[37] Sir Alec Kirkbride has suggested to me that in my analysis of the critical 1954–1957 period I "give too much credit to King Hussein in the sense that I do not believe that the policy which he adopted was the result of careful forethought. Looking back, I agree that his actions were almost perfect in meeting and overcoming the difficulties and dangers with which he was faced. For his age and inexperience he undoubtedly showed wisdom; he also possessed to a marked degree the family courage, but I also believe that good luck (some might call it providence) played a large part when it came to his deciding what to do. My recollection of Hussein was that his decisions were impulsive, like those of his grandfather, King Abdullah. Hussein was also blessed with flashes of shrewd intuition, a gift which Abdullah also enjoyed" (Private communication, 9 May 1965). Perhaps luck is an element that is always present in politics; yet in retrospect Husayn's actions appear deliberate and, often, in sequence. Possibly one can say that he *reacted* to situations rather than thought out his moves well ahead of time. Nonetheless, his *reactions*, whether with forethought or not, impress one as the right ones from his point of view. Moreover, it is quite possible he gauged correctly the inability of other Arab states (e.g. Syria and Egypt) to act in the crisis.

K

It is perhaps at this point that Abu Nuwar miscalculated. The government which he and his fellow officers wanted was about to be formed. Yet again mysteriously his cousin Ma'n Abu Nuwar, CO of the Amīra Aliya Brigade, ordered all its regiments—many of which were Beduin in composition—to move forty miles east of Zerqa for an all-night celebration. He also instructed that all weapons should be left behind. The Brigade incidentally comprised all-Beduin armoured car and infantry regiments, as well as a regiment of artillery which was perhaps the centre of the conspiracy. Ali had recently appointed his cousin to command this Brigade as a calculated measure in the plot, for he could not have hoped to otherwise infiltrate the Beduin company commanders.

The King was not unaware of the conspiracy afoot among artillery officers. After the incident of 8 April he made a point of having his own contacts with loyal beduin officers, who kept him abreast of events. As it turned out one of these, Captain Țalab al-Fahad, a company commander in the 1 Regiment Armoured Cars, allegedly through the intermediary of Deputy 'Akif al-Fāyiz came round on the 13th to apprise the King of the movements of the Aliya Brigade. Suspecting a trap the regiments ordered east of Zerqa refused to obey Colonel Ma'n's order, mutinied and clashed with the artillery regiment in Zerqa. Some casualties were reported. A few loyal troops, however, managed to speed off towards Amman to ensure the safety of the King.

The King took along the CGS, Ali Abu Nuwar, and sped off towards Zerqa to investigate the situation himself. Meeting troops coming towards Amman, the King was barely able to save his CGS from them, and sent him packing to Amman. It was obvious by then that the whole coup had aborted.

What is interesting is that neither the CGS and his group of conspirators, nor the Nabulsi cabinet, had been able to gain control over the Legion in terms of capturing to their side officers with troop command. While artillery, engineer, and other officers and personnel in the technical branches were sympathetic to the conspirators, it is certain that: (1) the core mobile ground forces were tribal-beduin and therefore loyal to the King, (2) as east Jordanian elements, these viewed with acute distrust political machinations largely led by both West Bank politicians and officers who were socially townsmen even though they were also East Jordanians. It is also certain that (3) the arabisation of the Legion by an act of the King had diminished the potential of a conspiracy aimed against him by officers on the grounds of Arab nationalism. Here the various diplomatic manoeuvres he had assiduously conducted in the preceding two years also paid dividends. He made it appear, that is, that there was no alternative to him in the country.

More practically, in terms of the Legion officer corps itself, and aside from any such political considerations as pro-Egyptian, pro-regime, Arab nationalist or other, there were substantial reasons for the inability of the radical officers led by Ali Abu Nuwar to successfully challenge the monarch's authority. The removal of Glubb and other British officers from the Legion left command key posts open to Arab officers. A scramble for them was likely. The subsequent retirements, appointments, and transfers of officers effected by Ali Abu Nuwar as the new Chief of Staff activated all the latent sources of rivalry within the Legion. This rivalry existed on many levels. There was, for instance, a kind of regional rivalry between officers from the more populous towns in the Balqā' and 'Ajlūn districts, the western and north-western parts of east Jordan on one hand and the tribal areas in the north-east and south of east Jordan, e.g. Banu Sakhr, on the other. There was also the wider rivalry that derived from both a social and occupational distribution in the Legion between beduin on one hand and the east and west Jordanian townsman on the other. Finally, there was a latent source of conflict in the Legion based on the religious rivalry between Muslim and Christian officers. Several of the latter, for example, were dismissed from the Legion in the summer of 1956. This led to serious rioting in Madaba, a heavily Christian town south of Amman.

Given all these sources of fission within the officer corps, it is certain that the resentment created by the policy of the new Chief of Staff, Abu Nuwar, was real and serious enough to undermine any conspiracy led by him.

There were certain similarities between the Abu Nuwar attempted coup and the Abdullah al-Tel defection in 1949. Both were Transjordanian officers and townsmen. Both came to the Legion with a high school education. Both received what amounted to direct commissions. Both experienced very fast promotion. The similarity, though, ends there. Al-Tel had been a Customs officer before he joined the Legion. He had not had as extensive and professional military training as Abu Nuwar. The latter had been to Sandhurst and had received some staff training, but had had no regimental service. Yet both entertained subversive political schemes after having ingratiated themselves with the ruler—the monarch. Tel, for instance, was rapidly promoted from Captain to Colonel at the insistence of King Abdullah. Moreover, he soon became a confidant and military courier of the King, as well as a go-between in Abdullah's secret negotiations with the Israelis. Abu Nuwar got very close to the new King in 1954 in Paris and became his ADC and adviser soon thereafter. One may view this pattern as one of infiltrating the highest echelons of authority and power. While firmly entrenched there, both proceeded to build their own political network among opposition politicians. In the case of Tel, his network was confined mainly to embittered Palestinian political groups in Jerusalem, Ramallah and Nablus. It barely extended into the Transjordan part of the country. As for allies in the officer corps, Tel hardly had any. To this extent, his attempted conspiracy was not only ineffectual but perhaps stupid. It was doomed to failure from the start.

It should be noted that all of Tel's machinations were conducted from Jerusalem. He misjudged the strength and ability of his Palestinian fellow conspirators and allies to pull a coup from the West Bank. Moreover, at that time, not many Palestinians had been brought into ministerial positions, or the government service in general. He also banked heavily upon the promises of assistance and support of Egyptian and Syrian leaders. In fact, the whole Tel operation strikes one as politically naïve.[38] Abu Nuwar, on the other hand, as the King's ADC and, after the dismissal of Glubb, as Chief of the General Staff, was in a position to recruit allies within the officer corps. Abu Nuwar also may have been in contact with Egyptian and Syrian elements—at least the fact that he went to Syria after his little mischief was found out indicates that this must have been the case. Yet his difficulty was even more complex.

Palestinian political leaders who in 1948–1949 may have been anti-regime and alienated from the government were, by April 1957, more closely associated with the state of Jordan. The young King had gone a long way towards meeting their nationalist demands, while the split in the Arab world was widening. Moreover, Abu Nuwar was in too much of a hurry, as his frantic transfers and retirements of military personnel indicated. He had barely enough time to foster a core of revolutionaries in the officer corps. Finally, he was absolutely unable to crack the tribal edifice of operational hard-core ground troops.

General Glubb in his account described Abu Nuwar as a Baathi. This may have been so since Tel in his account intimates much the same. Yet the Baath in Jordan even under the best of political circumstances could muster only three members in Parliament. It is not clear, on the other hand, that Abu Nuwar had established firm relations with civilian politicians in 1956–1957, especially those in

---

[38] The optimistic way in which Tel reports the promises of Syrian and Egyptian assistance for his plans strikes one as eminently naïve. See *Mudhakkirāt ʿabdullah al-tel*.

and out of government, let alone that he had extracted any commitments from them. The sands of such conspiratorial alignments shift normally anywhere in the world, but perilously so in Jordan. Nor was Abu Nuwar identified closely in the minds of operational army units as a commander of some military standing. He had not had any unit command; he had been overseas as a military attaché since 1953–1954.

Tel, on the other hand, had had command of 6 Regiment in the Palestine War. And soon after he had been appointed Military Governor of Jerusalem. It was from this position that he proceeded to develop his conspiracy. Significantly, he did this in two ways. First, he began the systematic discrediting of the Legion by projecting its betrayal of the Palestine Arabs. This obviously referred to one and one matter only: the betrayal was both possible and deliberate because of the Legion's British CGS and command. Second, he decided to use the top secret information (including documents) he had acquired in his role as courier between King Abdullah and the Israelis to discredit the regime and the monarchy. It is almost certain that Tel anticipated—in fact, expected—this two-pronged attack to elicit a mass uprising. Yet in characteristic fashion he continued throughout this time (1948–1949) to seek, by pressure and cajolement, veiled threats and other methods, his own advancement within the Legion.[39]

It is not strange, nor is it difficult to explain the failure of Tel in 1949. After all, the Legion was still predominantly beduin-tribal. Townsmen recruits, especially West Bankers, had not yet come into the Legion in large numbers. What is strange, however, is that Abu Nuwar had not been able to muster a larger number of conspirators in the Legion by 1957, when the number of townsmen personnel in the technical branches of the army and artillery had risen sharply.[40]

One explanation is that if one had a way of identifying the detailed background of each of the thirty or forty alleged conspirators in the Abu Nuwar abortive coup, one would find that with few exceptions most of these officers were in the administrative, engineer, artillery and technical maintenance branches of the Legion. Until 1957 all of these were still no more than support units to the operational ground forces. The latter were completely mobile. Above

---

[39] At least on the basis of General Glubb's report that Tel tried to bargain with him for a return to the Legion with the rank of brigadier. See *supra*.

[40] Townsmen were generally in artillery, and West Bankers were particularly so in engineers, signals and maintenance units. See section on "Rapid Expansion of the Legion", *supra*.

all, unit officers with troop command in the operational ground forces were far removed from the conspiracy.

It is, I think, clear that the preponderance of tribal-beduin personnel in at least seven operational units (five infantry regiments and two armoured cars) served to balance the predominantly *hadarī* units in the army, and thwart the success of conspiracies hatched and conducted largely by townsmen officers or simply by officers in the support, technical, and administrative echelons of the Legion. It is also clear that the general assumption on the part of the tribesmen that political conspiracies are the exclusive malaise of townsmen helped to maintain the breach between them. Also the obvious association of West Bank opposition leaders with such conspiracies further alienated the tribal element in the Legion.

But there were also positive obstacles to the success of conspiracies. King Husayn had managed within three to four years to capture the role of father and chief of the army, enjoyed previously by General Glubb and the late King Abdullah. He was also able to project an acceptable image of the nationalist as a result of his diplomatic activity regarding the Anglo-Jordanian Treaty, the Baghdad Pact, and the Arab Collective Pact. Meantime he had also incorporated a larger number of Palestinian politicians into the departments of government, the Chamber, and the Cabinet. To the tribal elements in the Legion he had by 1957 succeeded to his grandfather's position of *military chief*. As far as the tribesmen were concerned, he was not only Commander-in-Chief but also their Chief Shaykh, that is, their Chief Tribal Ruler.

On a more material level, it should be noted that the army in Jordan is a relatively privileged group of society. Its welfare services are extensive and, for the tribesmen, most advantageous. Education, housing, medical care, pay and allowances that are not otherwise easily attainable in Jordan all contribute to a sense and feeling of security. King Husayn himself has consistently taken a direct and immediate interest in these matters affecting the army. Of course this is not a practice peculiar to Jordan. Especially in Middle Eastern countries where military regimes have come to power, the material-economic and social welfare benefits for the armed forces receive immediate and continuous attention from the rulers. It is not an exaggeration to assert that housing projects, pay and allowances in the Iraqi army have placed the army officer in an enviable position *vis-à-vis* his civilian counterpart in that country. Similar situations prevail in Egypt. Hence conspirators find it even more difficult to persuade larger numbers of officers to indulge in subversive activities. So long as the Legion in Jordan remains a privileged group in this material-economic sense, the possibility of coups is not eradicated but lessened.

Nevertheless, one must assume in any future projection that the further integration of West Bankers into the army, whether as recruits, NCOs, or officers, will have certain political repercussions for the army in particular and for the country in general. These repercussions may not be dangerous so long as operational ground forces and officers with troop command remain predominantly tribal-beduin and Transjordanian in composition. It is conceivable, though, that the technical units will expand to the point of becoming a potent political force within the army's command structure. If, on the other hand, the political—i.e., institutional-legal—integration of the new generation of West Bank leaders inaugurated by King Husayn continues in its present pace, it is likely that the transformation of the Legion from a *corps d'élite* into a larger military establishment will occur smoothly and without political upheaval.

The present evidence indicates that the King intends to retain a *corps d'élite* within an expanded, or even a rapidly developing, national army. Ironically, this policy regarding the military and the defence of the country is a belated vindication of General Glubb's work. Thus, the operational mobile forces—infantry and armour—will continue to be predominantly tribal-beduin and generally Transjordanian. The more technical branches and support units will probably increase in strength and they will continue to be predominantly townsman in composition, and increasingly come from the West Bank. So far, however, there has been no conscription law in Jordan; that is, there has been no provision for a national service system as exists, say, in Egypt.

Border clashes—not merely Israeli attacks against Jordan—and villager infiltration across the lines have been, and remain, a serious political problem in Jordan; and one that could perilously undermine the stability of the regime. It is for this reason that the government and the Legion have been, and continue to be, vigilant in preventing such border infiltration by Arab villagers. First, infiltration can bring at any time massive Israeli military retaliation. The over-extended resources of the Legion along a 400-mile border do not present a comfortable military situation from the Jordanian point of view. Second, any inadequate counter-measure to Israeli retaliation by the army because of its limited resources inevitably brings forth political disturbances, ostensibly in protest against military incompetence but actually against the regime.

So far the Jordan army and government have managed to maintain the stability of the country as well as the precarious truce on the border with Israel—two issues that are inexorably related to one another. This, as I just said, has been accomplished partly by a firm and strict prohibition of armed, or other, infiltrations by Arabs across the border. Similarly, the government is obliged actively to oppose and prevent any para-military or military incursions by members of the PLO[41] into the Israeli border areas, since these can bring about the massive Israeli military retaliation against Jordan referred to above. It must also oppose the PLO for very good political reasons. In the absence of national conscription, the PLO may succeed in recruiting West Jordanians into its guerilla and other political units. The very fact that the PLO proposes to liberate Palestine implies the charge that the present Jordanian control of Central Palestine does not represent legitimate Arab authority at all. To this extent the PLO represents a political movement which, in order to realise its objectives, must necessarily alienate those Palestinians who are now subjects of the Jordanian kingdom from their rulers. In short, it must subvert the present regime in Jordan.

The national conscription scheme rumoured recently as a measure favoured by the government may counter and undermine the effectiveness of the PLO. It could also have the added effect of accelerating the further political integration of the two banks. On the other hand, it could very well undermine the efficiency of the army, given the extremely limited financial resources of the country. Thus, since the early summer of 1966, the government has instead moved against the PLO to counter its subversive activities in Jordan.[42] It is now therefore more likely than ever that the regime in Jordan will adhere to the notion of the army as a highly trained, long-enlistment regular force.[43]

---

[41] On the Palestine Liberation Organisation and its political implications for Jordan, see my "Nasser and the Arab World", *New Society* (London, 23 December 1965). See also *Orient*, No. 34 (1965), pp. 41–50, 181–196.

[42] This in addition to the raids mounted by *Al-'āṣifa* of *Al-fatḥ* and the PLO against Israel from Syria via Jordan.

[43] Further on this point, see the Conclusion.

# Conclusion

I HAVE tried to show that the Legion virtually created the state of Jordan. If it did not found the state, the Legion clearly served as the primary instrument of its pacification, control, and maintenance for thirty years from 1921 until 1951. As a military force the Legion was raised, trained, commanded, and financed by Britain via a legal-political mandate and treaty relationship with first Abdullah's Transjordan and Jordan, and later Husayn's Jordan. Until 1948 the Legion was practically the praetorian guard of a ruler who combined the attributes of a tribal chief, religious notable, and quasi-constitutional monarch. In great measure King Abdullah considered the Legion as the force that would some day play the crucial role of implementing his wider Arab political visions, such as the unification of a Hashemite-ruled Fertile Crescent. Before his death he witnessed its role in securing Central Palestine, and in the incorporation of its population to form the expanded Hashemite Kingdom of Jordan.

With the Palestine War and after, the Legion had outgrown its limited praetorian guard and police functions, and emerged as a highly trained military *corps d'élite*. As such it was the only Arab army that acquitted itself well in the Palestine War in 1948. Between 1951 and 1956, given the requirements of maintaining any military force, the Legion was gradually transformed into a technically more self-sufficient military establishment. But within this army (which today probably numbers 55,000) the operational core remains a long-term enlisted *corps d'élite*. Politically, the offices which affect the army most directly continue to be the prerogatives of East Bank Jordanians, so that the Chief of the General Staff and his deputy are likely to be that for some time to come.

No civil disturbances to speak of had occurred between 1925 and 1951. Yet, without any experience in dealing with them, the mobile ground forces of the Legion successfully upheld and protected the integrity of the regime in the most perilous political period of 1954–1957. So long as tribesmen from south Jordan, the north-eastern deserts of Syria and Iraq, and the eastern border areas of Saudi Arabia continue to flock to the Legion for enlistment; so long as the manual of training, pattern of promotion, and military discipline continue to follow what is essentially a British manual (one such manual had been prepared by General Glubb's GHQ); so long as the King is able to maintain his image as a foremost soldier as well as to sustain the economically-socially privileged position of the army, conspiracies within the military will either remain unlikely or, if they are hatched, will find serious obstacles in implementation.

In my preliminary formulations about the military in Jordan I postulated, among other things, that internal violence is unlikely in Jordan as a result of an army-led conspiracy against the regime. I also suggested that such an eventuality could occur only in conjunction with trouble on the border, and the general yet unresolved question of Palestine. In the course of my discussion of the rapid expansion of the Legion, however, I indicated that the massive influx of townsmen and West Bank elements into the more technical branches of the service reflect sociological changes in the country (including population shifts since 1950) and that they are apt to have some political effect upon the military. Yet the parallel integration of West Bank leaders into the Jordan political élite seems so far to have dulled the sharpness of the earlier alienation of these elements from established rule and authority. It may thus become even more difficult for ambitious army conspirators to find easy and ready response among a previously agitated pool of politicians.

The external factor, of course, cannot be overlooked. The vagaries of Arab nationalist politics showed clearly in 1954–1957 the powerful impact they can have upon the domestic political situation in Jordan. Yet, even there, the developments of the last four years (1962–1966) portray that the external factor does not have a single unified impact upon the country.

Only the new Air Force is an unknown factor in the military complex. The expansion of this arm did not begin in earnest until after 1956. Even though I have not investigated it, I can say that it is too early to assess its impact upon the political evolution and coloration of the military institution. It may, on the other hand, turn out to be the most "royal" arm of the services. But I have ascertained so far that all cadets for Flight Officer training, which is undertaken mainly in England (but some in Greece), are holders of the *Tawjīhiyya* certificate. This is roughly equivalent to the English G.C.E. with five "O" level passes. Cadets inevitably come from towns and other centres in the country where secondary schools offering work towards the *Tawjīhiyya* are available. Thus, Irbid, al-Salṭ, and Amman in the East Bank tend to predominate.

Flight Surgeons receive specialised training in England and the United States. Most of them are graduates of the American University of Beirut medical school. Some hold medical degrees from universities overseas.

It has been frequently stated that the existence of Jordan as an independent state is contingent upon the continued existence of the State of Israel—as well as upon Western aid. Such a view may be correct, but the contingency stipulation is imprecise for it is not certain that those states among the Arab countries that may look forward to its demise can agree on the manner of its disappearance.

Within Jordan civil-military relations will continue to be characterised by the following conditions:

(1) The army will remain the final arbiter of political power, to the extent that it will continue to support a monarch who, even under present constitutional arrangements, has extensive powers of rule. He does not simply reign; he also governs effectively. In these circumstances, and provided the army retains its essential *corps d'élite* of ground forces, the Legion will sustain the monarch in any serious struggle with political leaders and groups who wish to overthrow the regime.

(2) In time, the closer identification of interests between a growing West Bank group of political leaders and the monarch, supported by older, more traditional Transjordanian groups, may have the effect of further minimising the political involvement of the army. This in turn may facilitate the greater professionalisation of the military institution.

(3) There is still no evidence that tribal groups and the tribal ethos are being eroded as rapidly as in countries where the potential of economic development (including industrialisation) is greater. Jordan's economic development potential is limited. The army thus may remain the best occupationl haven for the tribesman. Its technical expansion, on the other hand, may offer the increased number of town tradesmen, also the most secure employment.

(4) If my economic assumptions about Jordan are justified, outside help—specifically Western aid—will remain a fundamental factor in the country's stability and integrity.

Whether it is possible ever to transform the Legion into a truly national army in terms of a nation-wide conscription is a difficult question to answer. I am inclined to the view that it is not. For this is closely linked to the question of whether the incorporated population of Central Palestine will ever feel totally Jordanian. The case of their present generation of political leaders indicates that this may be on the way. But can it be accomplished without a vaster national education system (a university was opened only three years ago) and national conscription? In the case of the first—education—Jordan lacks the qualified staff for schools, colleges, and a university. Even though there has been recently a high output of trained teachers in the country, these seem to prefer better-paying posts in such countries as Kuwait to employment in Jordan. In order to staff colleges and universities, Jordan must import these from neighbouring Arab countries, but imponderable dangers lurk in this eventuality. And as there are many Palestinian school teachers in other Arab countries, Jordan may have also to re-import these. In the case of the second— a truly national army—the government might run the risk of tampering with the delicate balance which the tribal *corps d'élite* provides in the army at present.

Given the fact that an originally fractious society in Transjordan was pacified and brought under the control of a central government by the use of the Legion; and given today the still lingering division between West and East Jordanians—a muted split currently, but nonetheless one that is easily prone to fanning by outside influences —one cannot contemplate a political system in Jordan that is not based on a strong ruler (in this case a Hashemite monarch), supported by an army that is steadily becoming more professional in its outlook and ethos, and one that still comprises a mobile ground force, constituting an élite within the military institution.

Many argue that there is an irresistible trend in pan-movements. Such is the appeal of Pan-Arabist sentiment with its implications of Arab unity, and that of Pan-Africanism with its aspirations to African unity.

It is not presently wise to assume the inevitability of the institutional realisation of unity if past pan-movements elsewhere are any precedent to go by. One recalls such integrative political sentiments which motivated the Pan-Slavic movement in the nineteenth century and the Pan-Islamic outcry of seventy-five years ago. The difficulty lies partly in the effectiveness and convenience of the territorial nation-state—even if it is a dynastic state—as the unit of political organisation. Inadvertently evolved and developed in Europe, it seems that even the most universalist and apocalyptic political movements have succumbed to its advantages—if Communism is an example. Another obstacle to the institutional achievement of pan-movements has been the parallel and continuous existence of nation-states even though the latter may comprise populations which share in pan-sentiments. The interests of established governments and political élites render voluntary integration into a wider sovereign unit a most unlikely eventuality. Forceful "prussianization" and Italian-style "unification" are usually held up as possible models for the fulfilment of pan-movement aspirations. This however would be a facile and anachronistic application of models that are no longer quite relevant.

While armies in the Middle East, Africa, and Asia, including the

Jordan Army, may be considered ultimate arbiters of political power, it is not always wise, or realistic, to view them as the super-nationalists in the sense that they are the best spokesmen for existing national-state aspirations. They can however be super-patriots only insofar as they uphold the legally constituted government and political authority. It is in this role that they can buttress the political leadership which articulates national-state aspirations. Some will argue that in the case of Jordan the Army might consider established government and political power as not reflecting legitimate authority. This is a fallacy, for if it raises the question "What is legitimate authority in Jordan?", it is difficult to find the answer outside the monarch. At least his authority is based on certain tangible attributes which mix religious, tribal, and constitutional dimensions of authority.

It is certain, on the other hand, that Jordanians who subscribe to Arab nationalist notions of legitimacy are not concerned with this question. They, in fact, deny that this is a proper, or relevant, question. As Arab nationalists they, theoretically at least, question the legitimacy of any authority in Jordan as a *state*, whether it is the King's or anyone else's. Again, theoretically for them legitimate authority in Jordan could spring only from a wider Arab nation-state unit, viz., United Arab State. That is, again theoretically, their conception of legitimacy as Arab nationalists, invalidates Jordan itself as a nation-state.

This, however, is a most unrealistic conception to have at present. For the Arab nationalist it may be a proper and moral conception of legitimacy to have, but not a feasible one. There is no such conception for the moment of an Arab legitimacy, or authority in any other Arab state that is legitimate because it meets the criteria of Arab nationalism. This is a point that was completely missed by the Middle East correspondent of *The Economist*, for example, in the hysterical despatches from Jordan recorded in that paper in the autumn of 1956, and spring and summer of 1957. The assertion was made then that "... there is no national loyalty on which Husayn can stand...". The "dominant national sentiment in Jordan is not Jordanian but Arab and in the state of the Arab world as it is, national loyalties are more likely to pull Jordan apart than hold it together".[1]

On the surface, no doubt the situation appeared as it was reported in *The Economist*. What one should ask here, however, is whether there was then *national* loyalty in several other Arab states. Or were

---

[1] See *The Economist*, vol. 181 (October-December 1956) pp. 336–367; vol. 183, (April-June 1957), pp. 114, 200–202, 293, 316.

these also evolving along the lines of military, non-hereditary but in effect "dynastic" states regardless of their *form*?

One of the difficulties in the Middle East, since the destruction of the Ottoman Empire, has been that of distinctly separating power from authority. The corollary to this, is the complementary task which follows the clear distinction between power and authority. That is the problem of connecting power with authority, not blurring or fusing the two. A clear principle of legitimacy to replace the old traditional one embodied in the Ottoman Padishah has yet to emerge.[2] It is also clear that the attempt to establish constitutional-parliamentary governments in the inter-war period in some of these countries failed because it could not resolve this question of the separation of power from authority. Some will argue that the revolutionary governments that have come to power in a number of these countries since the last war are legitimate by virtue of their popular representativeness—by virtue of the revolution they initiated; that especially military governments eminently qualify for this kind of legitimacy. Yet it is certain that the military have come to power because of their access to the use of force, and that all of them have so far dealt unsuccessfully with the question of establishing firm legitimate authority.

A further difficulty in this connection has been the notion held by the more forceful and lasting among the military oligarchies that they have come to lead *social* revolutions with all the diverse implications of such revolutions for economic development, modernisation, and industrialisation. It is not yet clear if any of them have embarked at all upon a political revolution, that is, one that is concerned with a formula of political organisation, a principle of authority that allows for change as well as continuity in the system.[3] On the other hand, these successful military oligarchies may not be interested in further change. Instead they may be concerned with protecting themselves against the possibility of further change; for this may entail a challenge to their authority.

It is not unfair, or unrealistic, then, to reject for the moment the proposition that the officer corps in Jordan are the best, or the foremost, nationalists. There are in Jordan, apart from the monarch, civilian political leaders who can qualify for this role just as well.

---

[2] On this question see the interesting article by Dankwart A. Rustow, "Succession in the Twentieth Century", *Journal of Internation Affairs*, vol. 18, No. 1 (1964), 104–113.

[3] See on this question my "Some Political Consequences of the 1952 Revolution in Egypt: A study of stratiotocracy", in Peter M. Holt, editor, *Political and Social Change in Modern Egypt* (London: Oxford University Press, forthcoming

What the army perhaps represents best is the forceful sanction that upholds a regime in which a monarch combines traditional attributes of authority with relevant, though by Western standards limited, constitutional arrangements. To this extent the army may comprise the best patriots in the kingdom. Since there still lingers in Jordan the division between a group—that has apparently become smaller and less significant since 1961—which doubts the legitimacy and viability of such an entity as the State of Jordan on the one hand, and a group which considers the existence of Jordan as desirable on the other, the army so far is the one institution which ultimately buttresses the latter group. And this, in turn, is an attitude which persists because of the predomination of a tribal *corps d'élite* within the army; and also because of the close and special relationship between this group and the monarch.

It would be unfair, on the other hand, not to entertain the possible socio-political consequences of changing patterns of recruitment and training in this army. After all, as discussed earlier, the demand and need for more sophisticated technical services in the army will have a long-range effect of political significance. Will this new group in the army, with its implied greater technological expertise, accept a more professional role and ethos, or will it develop a more bureaucratic attitude towards its military function? If the latter turns out to be the case, political infiltration of its ranks and its political involvement become more likely. This becomes more true if there is a parallel technological advance and economic development in civilian society. Then the interests of these two groups may be conveniently aligned against the *status quo*; for to the natural social affinity between them will be added the common link of economic interest.

But the major sociological division in Jordan between tribe and town, or between desert and settled communities (both town and country), and the initial, though presently not too sharp, political division between East and West Banks will, it seems, continue to exist for some time to come. Short of a complete de-tribalisation of the desert, it is unlikely that the sources of recruitment for the *corps d'élite* of ground forces in the army will dry up. Short of a total success of such groups as the Palestine Liberation Organisation and its external Arab supporters in alienating West Jordanians from the State and its regime, an open split and a rebellious breach between the two Banks is also unlikely.

For the moment, despite the extent of its popularity or unpopularity, there is in Jordan at least a working principle of authority and formula of legitimacy. It centres on the monarchy. The challenges thrown against it since 1951 by the West Bank community primarily have been met successfully in two ways: by the ultimate use of the Legion and a parallel, though cautious, legal-institutional integration policy on the political and economic levels of national-state existence. Moreover, given the political splits and other social divisions mentioned earlier, it is uncertain, were the present regime to be overthrown, what formula of political authority the Jordanians (both East and West) could conceivably agree upon.

Despite these divisions and difficulties, Jordan, unlike Iraq, does not face ethnic fragmentation and separatism of the Kurdish variety, or serious communal-sectarian differences of the Sunni-Shii variety. The earlier passionate political alienation of the Palestinians never erupted into an armed resistance movement. It merely confined itself to assassination and flirtation with wider external Arab political forces. It cannot conceivably separate from Jordan, for it would not be able to withstand the Israeli threat. To bank its hopes on outside assistance it would have to overthrow the total political edifice of the present Jordanian regime. But the latter possibility it cannot entertain either, exactly, because the army, as presently constituted, would not allow it. The one real alternative left would be to infiltrate this army and wean its officer corps away from their Commander-in-Chief. We have seen that in both instances of the Tel and Abu Nuwar incidents this infiltration was limited at best, and sloppily conducted at worst. As more Palestinians get to share in power and participate in the authoritative allocation of the country's resources and the formation and implementation of its political programmes, two diametrically opposed developments could follow. On one hand, potential dissidents among them could seek to infiltrate the officer corps and army ranks. This could be the case with the rise in the number of recruits and officers from West Jordan. On the other, the greater proximity of these new elements in the political élite to power may tend to tie their interests with those of the regime. In that case infiltration of the army would be both undesirable and more difficult. Moreover, so long as the monarch continues to pre-empt and portray effectively the leadership of this army, competitor candidates for this role become still more limited in number. This is not to say though that the problem of succession will not arise in all its complex and politically explosive possibilities in the future. But here, too, the composition and political loyalty of the army will be crucial.

It is possibly meaningful that until 1957 the majority of officers in the Jordan Army were lieutenants and second lieutenants, so that at least 80 per cent of the officer corps were between the ages of 23 and 30, and under the rank of captain. In 1957, General Glubb explained:

"Thus the whole officer structure was extremely precarious. There were immense numbers of lieutenants and second lieutenants, some of them of excellent quality. But good captains were scarce. Battalion commanders could be found only with great difficulty, and senior staff officers did not exist, much less brigade or divisional commanders."[4]

Obviously, after March 1956, the arabisation of the officer corps was accomplished by mass and rapid promotions. Yet the Jordan Army even then was not top-heavy in officer grade distribution in comparison with other Arab armies. Arab regimental commanders were too new in their posts in April 1957 to become wholly committed to political conspiracies. Thus the relative thinness of top officer grades, and the earlier scarcity—but since 1957, novelty—of battalion commanders may have been a blessing in disguise.

An interesting area in the study of the military might be the effect of massive purges of the officer corps, sweeping transfers, and retirements. These occurred in the period March 1956–April 1957. It is, however, one of the most difficult questions to investigate adequately at the moment. While the practice has been used primarily to remove politically intransigent and undesirable personnel, one must note that it could have the effect of sparking off defensive coups by the personnel affected. Hence the remarks made earlier in this study about the resentment aroused among officers in the Legion by the actions of the new Chief of Staff, Ali Abu Nuwar, after May 1956.

Until 1956 the Jordan Army was a long-service volunteer force; there were no conscripts in it. Regiments were about 500–900 strong. In some of the infantry and armoured car regiments over half of the men came from tribes *outside Jordan*, that is, Iraq, Saudi Arabia, and Syria. To this extent, these recruits constituted an essentially mercenary group that would have been difficult to interest in political movements aimed against the regime short of wildly lucrative material promises. This is not to say that beduin tribesmen in the Legion who came from Jordan were necessarily less mercenary. Nor should it be inferred that mercenaries are necessarily free of political ambitions. After all, the Turkish mercenaries of the Abbasid caliph in Baghdad were not free of such ambitions. Nor were the Mamluks in Egypt, even though they were originally imported as slaves. But so long as these mercenaries are relatively well paid, and the prospect of loot is very small, the likelihood of their joining a political

---

[4] *Op. cit.*, 387. It should be noted that a Cadet (*murashshaḥ*) usually served in training with a unit, or regiment, as a platoon or section commander for at least three years before becoming a second lieutenant.

L

uprising against the *status quo* is indeed small. The Legionnaires, particularly the beduin among them, are not well educated. If they helped overthrow the regime their position *vis-à-vis* any new rulers would not change significantly, as they could not run the state. Perhaps also there is not much of a state to run; whereas as long as they remain Legionnaires they are well paid from sources which could dry up if this state did not exist. The Arab Legion officer, and particularly the beduin officer, is plainly in a different category from those in an army in which officers on the whole are relatively well educated in the academic and administrative sense.

Length of service for these ranks was rarely ever under five years. More significantly, top NCOs were perhaps the most committed ranks to the *Jeish* with rarely less than ten years' service behind them. Their involvement in conspiracies was unlikely partly because they had attained high NCO rank after long and exacting service. Thus it was common for a soldier to reach lance-corporal rank only after at least four years' service. In many respects these NCOs represented perhaps the most professional element in the Legion; at least in terms of expertise, discipline and *esprit de corps*.

Nevertheless, the question of the army's political involvement remains unresolved in Jordan as in other small states. How to make the officer corps an absolutely professional body is a problem that plagues Jordan too. Jordan shares this problem with her sister Arab states. Perhaps Jordan does not face it in as great or sharp a degree as some other of these states. Rapid technological expansion in the Jordan Army, as in other armies, may very well provide one area of professionalism, namely, expertise. It may even produce the corporateness essential to this professionalism. But whether it can also produce among officers a real sense of social responsibility is difficult to say. Here I am assuming that social responsibility is directly related to the professional behaviour of an officer in a military sense. Yet from the viewpoint of the Arab nationalist and, therefore, anti-Jordanian regime, officer social responsibility may continue to mean behaviour by an officer in an *unprofessional* military way. In Jordan, even corporate ethos is problematic unless all tribal and other primary relations and loyalties, but not *values*, present in the army are completely broken down. The question may be how to break these loyalties while at the same time preserve the values.

In the final analysis such problems as the availability of suitable officers, administrative ability, illiteracy, efficiency, can all be met adequately at some point in time. But the problem of expansion in armies like the Jordanian one boils down really to the economics of defence. This in turn is related to real efficiency.

In the case of Jordan one can argue that the absence of military *coups d'état* since 1949[5] has been due to the absence of the most common accelerator of coups and violent revolts against the *status quo*: namely, defeat in a war. The Legion did acquire territory in the Palestine War, even though one could argue that it was territory allocated to Arabs in the first place by the UN Partition Resolution. Then its Palestinian and other Arab detractors soon thereafter could not oppose effectively the regime the Legion supported in a sustained manner. This was due to two fundamental reasons, closely connected with the whole question of revolution. First, the opposition could neither infiltrate the Legion in any extensive and significant way, nor produce an armed uprising against the authorities. The latter eventuality would have been tragically futile, because the military institution was far more powerful than anything they could have mustered. Second, King Husayn—and here perhaps is where his political shrewdness was manifested at its best—avoided identification with an exclusive, intransigent élite of old Transjordanians.[6] Rather he responded to new forces instinctively and therefore abruptly at first. Then gradually he attracted to his side many of the leaders of these new forces. Despite a period of civil disturbances, widespread violence was successfully avoided.

Those few officers who manifested an élitist status—the "political generals" like Abu Nuwar, Hiyari, and Ma'āyiṭa—ended outside the prevalent ethos of the officer group as a whole. To a great extent this was due to the fact that the monarch had, with the aid of his by and large loyal military institution, survived the removal in 1956–1957 of two elements from the Jordanian political scene that had heightened opposition to his regime. British officers left the Legion, and the arabisation of its officer corps had by summer 1956 become a reality. The Anglo-Jordanian Treaty of 1948 had by spring 1957 been abrogated and by that summer all British troops stationed in the country had departed.

But since much of the opposition to the regime involved groups

---

[5] Immediately the Palestine War ended there were coups in Syria. The coup of 1952 in Egypt was partly justified by its leaders in terms of the Palestine War. Coups followed in Iraq (1958, 1963), the Sudan (1958), Syria (1961–1966), the Yemen (1962), Algeria (1965).

[6] Here one should refer to Erskine B. Childers, *The Road to Suez* (London, 1962). Childers devotes an Appendix to his book (pp. 397–401) to debunk the commonly held theory of a coup led by Ali Abu Nuwar in April 1957. Childers puts forward the theory that the coup was engineered by King Husayn and the Americans. His version is based largely, if not exclusively, on his interviews with President Nasser in Egypt and General Abu Nuwar who, at that time, was in exile.

who also rejected the very notion of a Jordanian state, the opposition from the latter since that time has not been contingent upon an anti-imperialist platform. Their recurrent activity has always been a source of threat to a regime whose legitimacy they do not recognise and whose state they reject. The assimilation of a number of past leaders of these groups so far may have, on the other hand, reduced their ability effectively to challenge the regime. Nonetheless, the question of the existence of a Jordanian state, as we know it today, sharply divides its population. Radical West Jordanians who, following the so-called Arab nationalist line, wish to become part of a larger united Arab political entity, still constitute a considerable source of revolution and, therefore, potential violence.

Needless to say the position and role of the army in any political upheaval—including a revolution—is of the utmost importance. Indeed, it is decisive. The remark by Katherine Chorley in 1943 is still valid and relevant:

"Insurrections cannot be permanently won against a *professional army operating its technical resources at full strength*. They can be won only when the introduction of some extraneous factor cripples the striking power of the professional fighting forces for one reason or another. The part to be played by the army is therefore decisive in any revolution, whether social or nationalist."[7]

It is in this sense I remarked earlier that Palestinian leaders could not have organised a mass insurrection against the regime. I also tried to show that until 1957 a coup by any small group of army officers was most difficult to implement successfully. For the same reason, conspirators among civilian groups, or political élites (Baathis, Communists, or other), short of successfully infiltrating the officer corps, cannot easily lead an effective insurrection against the regime. Given the composition of NCOs and other enlisted ranks in the Jordan army, it is most unlikely that these will respond favourably to revolutionary schemes short of a disastrous defeat in a foreign war.

Thus, if one accepts the proposition that the Hashemite Kingdom of Jordan should continue to exist as a sovereign independent state, a 30–40 per cent "mercenary" element in the ground forces is absolutely essential. In a small, poor country like Jordan a conscript army is unsuitable, for it would place an oppressive burden upon its limited financial resources. Moreover, given the peculiar political problems of Jordan both at home and in relation to the wider Arab

[7] *Armies and the Art of Revolution* (London, 1943), p. 23. Italics mine.

world, a conscript army would be politically unsuitable too. Finally, in view of the armed truce with Israel and the peculiar problems that arise from it, a conscript army would be unsuitable from a military efficiency point of view.

Furthermore, this 30–40 per cent mercenary element in the sense explained above serves as a make-weight in the army and contributes to the latter's greater insulation from politics. In short, a loyal, highly mobile professional élite force is the foundation of a Hashemite—or for that matter, any independent—state of Jordan, that is, one that is not part of a larger Arab entity, or one that will not be overrun by Israel to preclude its absorption in a wider Arab arrangement.

One observes that conscript armies are no longer the rule where states wish to make the maximum (as well as the best) use of their financial and human resources. Instead, the emphasis is being placed on highly efficient and mobile smaller striking forces, equipped with the latest weapons and transport; and having access to immense concentrated fire-power.

It has been argued so far that the option by Jordan for a core professional army in preference to a conscript army is both reasonable and necessary. This is particularly so if it is assumed that stability in Jordan—but not necessarily stagnation—is essential to peaceful change.

The argument, of course, can be made that, faced with an adversary like the Israeli Army which can call upon the highly developed technological resources and know-how of Israeli society, the Jordanian Army, if anything, needs ever more officers with high academic qualifications. This is especially so in a country where similar technical resources and capabilities are not readily available in the society at large. But it is unlikely that a country the size of Jordan will ever be able to—or should—afford a sophisticated, expensive military machine. And to accept readily the phantasmagoric common Arab notion that the commissioning of academically qualified officers into the army will somehow automatically improve its fighting ability could only lead to political difficulties. The new air force perhaps now gets the best educated personnel for flight officer and engineer training and other duties. Eventually, there may arise among these a politically ambitious cabal. It is too early to tell. For the moment, therefore, the question often raised by military sociologists, to wit, what form (or forms) of military organisation is best applicable to non-Western, non-European, states, has no definitive answer. As this study attempts to show in the case of Jordan the form of military organisation which evolved in Jordan has been peculiar to specific conditions prevailing in the country. The king has been so far a military as well as a civilian monarch.

If one argues that political revolution is related to social and economic change, one could easily assume that where change is difficult because of the ruler's intransigence, conflict and violence can ensue involving the military. But it is not always theoretically or intellectually safe to assimilate and identify the military with revolution, i.e. with conflict and violence. Whereas in certain countries of Europe the military institution—at least its officer corps establishment—has opposed and resisted social and political change, one observes that in many new states of Asia and Africa the process has been reversed. Nevertheless, in the latter case the espousal of the cause of revolutionary change by the military has not always been followed by observable or noticeable institutional, i.e. structural, change. The accession to power by military groups in several of these countries has not brought about significant changes in the overall patterns of political life. Rather such occurrences and upheavals reflect the important role of force in political life in the absence of more regular institutionalised processes of change. In fact, one finds that the enthusiastic commitment—over-commitment—of such radical military leaders to over-ambitious goals of modernisation and development far outstrip the actual resources of their countries as well as the capabilities of their own leadership. Thus there is usually generated a condition of *stasis* which can lead to their eventual overthrow by a renewed military challenge from other groups.

In the case of Jordan it appears that, even though there the power of the regime does ultimately rest on the monopoly of force—as in fact is the case in all modern governments—there is some structural-institutional relationship between this power and the overall social structure in the country. The monarch has used his ultimate monopoly of force (in the military, that is) that is always in the background only in conjunction with a cautious scheme for greater political, social and economic integration of his country. So that in this sense the military has aided the monarch in a controlled, albeit slow, process of change. So long as the monarch's leadership and competence in bringing about change is recognized and respected, the likelihood of challenge from countervailing groups or forces is not too great. It is not inconceivable, on the other hand, were the monarch and his regime to become unresponsive to the requirements of normal change, for rival groups—including those that might arise in the military—to challenge the regime.

Given the crucial role of the army in any violent attack upon the *status quo*, it cannot be asserted that it always remains opposed to revolutionary change. The criterion perhaps here is the extent to which there is a disturbance of the structure of the military institution. After all, a military establishment can become just as disaffected professionally—and politically—as any other institution or structure of the social order in a particular country. It is primarily for this reason—and in order to forestall or avoid the conditions for such disaffection—that the monarch in Jordan pays especial attention to the needs and problems of the military.

In the case of Jordan there are further reasons for the difficulty—given present conditions—any revolt, coup, or other upheaval against established authority may encounter. So long as the composition of the army and the officer corps remains roughly what it has been—tribal-beduin and peasant in infantry and armour, and townsman in the technical, administrative, and support units—there is no guarantee that officer-led coups or revolutions will succeed. In the civilian sector the likelihood of the success of popular revolts and insurrections is even less. No revolutionary party or conspiratorial group possesses a civilian paramilitary organisation. The army is the only armed force in Jordan. It is here that Jordan's attitude to the new Palestine Liberation Organisation can be partially explained. The latter constitutes a potential armed force under the direction of rebellious or conspiratorial political groups.[8] It is also here that Jordan's recent consideration of separating once more the National Guard (largely composed of Palestinian villagers) from the army makes sense. (As mentioned earlier, these two organisations were merged in 1956.) The argument for separating them derives from the notion that fraternisation between personnel of the two forces could produce politically unwelcome results. Furthermore, National Guard personnel (who are not professional—and only part-time—soldiers) could be more open and receptive to anti-regime political propaganda and subversion. Their separation however, would still leave the equipping, training and discipline of the National Guardsmen under Legion Control.

On the other hand, the monarch in Jordan has minimised the anti-regime political activity of civilians, and thus their inclination to infiltrate the officer corps, by expanding his ruling élite and responding gradually but positively to some of their demands since 1954. He has in effect related them meaningfully and effectively to an evolving social and political order. By gradually changing the system that prevailed under his grandfather, King Husayn has in great

---

[8] It is rumoured that ex-General Ali al-Hiyari is currently working for the Organisation in Cairo.

measure minimised the sources of disturbance and the conditions for violent change in the system.

One must bear in mind that when Arab Palestine was annexed in 1948 there were twice as many Palestinians as there were Transjordanians (roughly 750,000 : 350,000), and over half of these were destitute refugees. Naturally one would expect that the foremost concern of the refugees—and soon the settled population in Central Palestine—at that time was for security, protection, and plain survival. All three of these needs were mitigated, if not fully met, by the Jordanian monarch's act of merging the two Banks. At the beginning the matter of representation remained unequal: a Transjordanian minority remained politically privileged and in effective control of government. Yet the gradual but wholehearted and courageous integration of an ever-increasing number of West Bankers into the echelons of government—the Cabinet, the Legislature, the Courts, the Bureaucracy—reflected real enfranchisement, and the successful erosion of any élitist intransigence on the part of Transjordanians.

The army continues to be headed in 1966 by a Chief of General Staff who is a member of the Majali tribe from Kerak and the ex-commander of the Royal Bodyguard. The Deputy Chief of General Staff is the younger maternal uncle of the King. The Director of Public Security is also an army officer and a member of one of the southern tribes. His deputy is a townsman, an ex-Artillery colonel.

Three to ten years after independence the military in many African states have overthrown their first rulers who had come to power at the successful end of their anti-colonial leadership. In Jordan the army in many ways founded the state. Subsequently—at least for the period covered by this study—it was "radical Arab nationalist" and other opposition political leaders who sought to alter the *status quo*; not the army. The weathering by the monarch of the stormy period 1954–1957 was very much due to his relation to a loyal and efficient fighting ground force. The latter's discipline and efficiency, in turn, were the result of the training it received at the hands of experienced British officers for almost a decade, headed by General Glubb.

Even though this study has been concerned with the role of the Legion in the founding of the State of Jordan, the consolidation of the ruler's power in Amman, and later the integration of the two Banks in the country, one must raise the inevitable question: is Jordan, as it exists today, a viable nation-state? Given its natural resources and present economy, it is doubtful if Jordan can sustain a population over 2·5 million. Short of converting its desert areas into productive regions, Jordan will for the foreseeable future depend ultimately for its independent existence upon foreign aid. On the other hand, Jordan could exist and possibly prosper, within some larger unit, such as a federation or confederation of states. With present political conditions in the neighbouring Arab states as they are, this is not an immediate possibility. At the same time so long as the political power confrontation between Arab states (mainly Egypt *versus* Saudi Arabia in the Peninsula; Syria and Iraq in flux) continues Jordan can only assume a watchful posture. The struggle for power between so-called revolutionaries and conservatives in the Arab world may take such a course in the coming decade as to force Jordan into different and new alliances and enmities.

Another general question that may be posed in connection with this study refers to the nature of power and rule in states like Jordan and its immediate Arab neighbours. The idea is widely held and accepted among students of Jordan that the monarch rules fairly autocratically with the assistance and support of a military establishment. This view contends further that such a condition prevails because of the traditionalist tribal element in the army. In short, the regime persists because the military exercises *de facto* control of the state. Yet, when one looks at Iraq, Syria, and even Egypt the situation does not appear to be too different. In Iraq, for instance, a monarchy that was accused of autocratic power has been replaced by a republic in which presidential—executive—power is supreme, highly personalised in a leader-ruler and supported primarily by a military establishment. The difference has been that the *coup d'état* there turned out to be the only instrument of political change. In Jordan this has not been the case. Change, on the contrary, has been effected by the regime, protected by the military.

Thus, while regime changes in Iraq and Syria may have been effected by military coups the resultant state or governmental structures have not proved to be less authoritarian, despite their popular acceptance or acclaim. Nor is there real evidence that these have been much more welfare-oriented—a precondition that seems today to be the *sine qua non* of revolutionary governments.

If the wish to modernise among these societies today manifests itself in the type of regime characterised by strong, centralised, personal rule and authority—in short, *efficient* rule—rather than in more classical forms of regimes characterised by the diffusion of power, it is difficult to exclude Jordan from this general pattern.

Rather it seems that in all these states and regimes there is a continued dependence upon the role of force—upon coercion rather than consensus—for political action and for rule. The undisputed proof of this state of affairs is the ascendancy of the military in political affairs in all of these states. Judging from the various programmes of the oil-rich and not so rich states in the Arabian Peninsula (Saudi Arabia, Kuwait, Bahrain, the Arabian Federation) either to strengthen and modernise their military institutions or to create a military force where none existed before, this condition may soon permeate these areas too.

The masses, led by articulate urban classes and usually spearheaded by the army, who either vociferously and wholeheartedly support, or even participate in, the overthrow of some "reactionary" regime, are so far invariably faced with the tragic reality that in these societies there is as yet no recognised principle of authority. They realise that traditional authority has collapsed and that the attempt of the previous generation to superimpose an imported principle of legitimating power (the parliamentary-representative system of government) lacked the socio-economic and cultural requisites for its success. Only foreign tutelage and ultimate control permitted that élite to usurp power under the guise of parliamentary institutions without the use of, or recourse to, the military. Once this relationship ended, so did the authority of these rulers, for they no longer had easy access to power. The latter was now deposited in the military, who soon legitimated it for their own rule.[9] The "men of the sword", in Islamic terminology, came once more to control the state. Thus the matter of distinguishing between power and authority remains a vexing problem.

To the extent that these "publics" feel that their revolutionary regimes are more considerate of their socio-economic welfare, to that extent they are clearly justified in clamouring for their appearance in the Arab world. Perhaps the belated infusion of mass society into Arab politics, the complex—and frequently insoluble—problems of independence and economic development preclude the emergence of other than strong, authoritarian central governments. That may be so. But the Arabs cannot justify their zeal for such regimes on the basis of the facile distinction between tyrannical, on the one hand, and liberated, free systems on the other. Nor can they make a distinction, at this time, in the nature and form of government (i.e. authoritarian versus limited) on the basis of the superficial opposition of monarchies versus republics in the Arab Middle East.

[9] Turkey is a qualified exception.

# Epilogue

ON November 13, 1966, an armoured brigade of the Israeli Army crossed the frontier in the Hebron area of Jordan. It carried out a devastating four-hour raid on the village of Samu. When it was all over, little of the village remained. Some 120 dwellings were demolished; several villagers were killed and wounded. The Jordan Army suffered an unknown number of casualties.

The political consequences of this punitive raid by the Israeli Army for the regime in Jordan were grave. Its political repercussions throughout the Arab Middle East were, as expected, dangerously unsettling. If anything, the raid emphasised the terrifying capacity which the Israel-Jordan frontier situation possesses in generating violence within Jordan. It also underlined the yet incomplete integration of West and East Jordan.

Whatever the ultimate political motives of Israel in directing its punitive raid against Jordanian territory may have been,[1] the brief clash at Samu succeeded in bringing to the surface something other than the imminent Arab threat to Israel's security. Rather such action inevitably led Israel's adversaries once more to indulge in their internecine conflict of attempted mutual elimination.

Despite the riots and demonstrations in Jerusalem, Ramallah, and Nablus against the regime which immediately followed the Israeli raid, it soon became clear that no effective insurrection was possible without massive outside interference. It became equally clear that the major Arab protagonists were not convinced that a buffer state like Jordan had outlived its usefulness. After all, the Egyptians have had their border situation with Israel neatly—if perhaps temporarily—resolved since 1956–1957 when the United Nations Emergency Force (UNEF) took up its duties there. The Iraqis in November 1966 appeared anxious not to veer from their recently found course

---

[1] The raid against Jordan has been illogical and thus incomprehensible to outsiders. After all, Jordan has been the one Arab country which for ten years now has made a serious effort to restrain its Palestinian citizens from illegal frontier activities. In one of his press conferences at the end of November 1966, King Husayn suggested that the Israelis attacked his country and not another which had actively and openly encouraged Arab guerillas against Israel, because they wished to involve the powers. The suggestion is not altogether fantastic. With foreknowledge of the consequences for the political stability of the area, the Israelis may have deliberately chosen to mount their raid against Jordan in order to attract the attention of the powers.

towards a semblance of normalcy at home. Nor was it likely that any of the Arab radical states which agitated against the "incompetent" Jordan regime relished the thought of taking over the physical confrontation with Israel along a 350-mile-long frontier. What was certain and obvious was that a convenient overthrow of the regime in Jordan would have been welcome to the anti-Hashemite regimes in Syria and Egypt, as well as to the Palestine Liberation Organisation (PLO) and its followers.

The Syrians, more than any of the other Arab radical states, had a score to settle ever since Jordan welcomed so many Syrian political refugees in the summer and early autumn 1966. Hence their frenetic campaign against the Jordan regime. An Associated Press report on December 7, 1966, quoted Syria's Chief of State, Dr. Nureddin al-Atasi, as follows:

"The elimination of the Jordanian throne which is protected by U.S.-British imperialism is the only course for progressive forces in Jordan to liberate the two Banks of the country on both sides of the Jordan river and thus clear the way to return to Palestine."

These remarks, addressed to a mass rally in Damascus, were followed by a pledge of armed support to the "rebellion" in Jordan against the "traitor Husayn".

The facile assumption is made by the average anti-Hashemite Arab that with the elimination of Husayn somehow the Arab-Israeli problem will be automatically resolved. An extremist radical Baath government currently in power in Syria helps to strengthen this assumption and give it political substance and dynamism. It moreover dexterously transforms the Arab-Israeli question into an internal radical versus conservative political confrontation in Jordan. This, in turn, is part of the wider conflict exemplified by the confrontation between Egypt and Saudi Arabia in the Yemen and, soon, elsewhere in south Arabia.

One thing is clear: the radical Arab states, particularly Syria and the United Arab Republic, now insist that only radical Arab regimes can deal with Israel; only they can help the Palestinians restore their lost homeland. Earlier the conflict was one between Arabs and Israelis. Now it is ideologically more complex: conservative Arabs cannot possibly be interested in restoring an Arab Palestine; radical Arabs have the monopoly of this righteous interest and intention.

It is also interesting to note that the Fertile Crescent has reached a high level of political agitation. This is directly related to the wider conflict between Egypt and Saudi Arabia in the Peninsula. The

Syrians, or at least their present regime, recognise the danger presented to their radicalism by Jordan and Saudi Arabia. They have watched the conversion of an old but active Palestinian opposition in the 1950s to a staunch supporter of the regime in Jordan. New Palestinian elements have been found to challenge authority in Jordan.

A change in the nature of the Palestinian opposition to the Jordanian regime has passed unnoticed. The old die-hards of 1952 and 1954–1956 were the men of the establishment in November 1966. Thus, Anwar al-Khaṭīb, Mayor of Jerusalem, to cite only one example, boldly condemned the riots in his press conference during the disturbances. Much of the articulate opposition now comes from Palestinian Arabs who have never lived in Jordan; they are settled in Beirut or Cairo.[2] Their audience and followers are Palestinians of two categories: those living in Syria, Lebanon, and Gaza, and the unemployed and underemployed refugees in Jordan itself. Although one must not denigrate by underestimating the sentiment of gainfully employed and prosperous Palestinians both inside Jordan and in other Arab countries for a restored Arab Palestine, it still would not be easy for them to risk their gains by an uncertain venture against Israel. If they suspect and mistrust the Jordan government's intention and ability to do anything about restoring Arab Palestine, they must equally doubt those of other Arab governments too.

What is really involved then on a practical and mundane level is the rise of a new opposition group among Palestinians, largely directed and led from outside Jordan, supported and financed by radical Arab states currently in conflict with more-than-ever-active conservative ones. This new opposition group qualifies in the eyes of radical Arab states to succeed, by overthrowing, the regime in Jordan. In this way, Palestinian Arabs of the radical variety at least would secure a state of sorts which they presumably would govern. If this also means that the newly acquired state will become the base from which they will evict the Israelis from Palestine remains to be seen. Ideologically, this is the basis of their claim to the right to overthrow the regime in Jordan by force: that is, in order to move against Israel. Ideology admittedly sets goals to be attained, sometimes even determines the means by which these goals will be realised. It does not however always determine policy so cavalierly even when

[2] See especially the works of the publicist Anīs Ṣāyigh, head of the PLO Research Bureau in Beirut; especially *Al-hāshimiyyūn wa al-thawra al-'arabiyya al-kubrā* (The Hashemites and the Great Arab Revolt) (Beirut 1966), and *Al-hāshimiyyūn wa qaḍiyyat filasṭīn* (The Hashemites and the Palestine Question) (Beirut 1966).

it is a major element in this process. Other factors may take precedence over ideology in policy-making.

\* \* \*

So far events and developments since November 13, 1966, have emphasised some of the suggestions about the Jordan Army made in this study. Thus, the greatest source of internal violence remains the Israel-Jordan frontier, and the so far incomplete integration of the population on either side of the river. Moreover, a successful insurrection is still difficult without massive outside interference. As for the role of the army in these circumstances, it has been typical. Its basic structure and morphology tended to sustain the regime. It is however difficult to ascertain so soon if the events of November 13 and the subsequent disturbances in the country have produced significant fissions within the military. Much of this will depend on the view that members of the officer corps have about its efficiency and high command.

I did suggest that the Jordan Army will remain essentially a regular, long-enlistment volunteer force. After the Israeli raid, the King announced a mobilisation scheme for all Jordanian males. This sort of emergency military conscription law promulgated by the Jordanian government during the crisis does not, from all indications so far, imply the introduction of national conscription as such. That is, it is not intended to produce a mass conscript army. Able-bodied males (18–40 years old) will be given military training for several months within regular army units, but they will not form part of the regular army. Moreover, the loophole of a fee paid in lieu of service (the old Ottoman *bedel-i askeri* and old Egyptian *badaliyya*) has been conveniently provided. Thus, the Jordan Army, and especially its élite units, retain their original character.

Opponents of the Jordan regime among the radical Arab states are nevertheless anxious to bring under the Arab Unified Command presided over by an Egyptian Army General either the regular Jordan Army, or, failing that, an expanded National Guard, or a newly mobilised and trained frontier force. This was also the case in the 1950s when, as a condition for contributing to the finances of the National Guard, certain Arab states were insisting that the command of that force be given to an Egyptian officer.

One thing is now certain. A new group of Palestinians, organised, trained, and financed by certain radical Arab states, is openly challenging the old, but now assimilated, Palestinian opposition in Jordan. For the King to permit this new group an active and open existence in his country, could mean risking his throne. To keep them out altogether, he would equally risk a dangerous confrontation with radical neighbour states—actually Syria. The only course open to him is to depend on the army. This, too, is not always absolutely a safe thing to do.

Be that as it may, the events of November 13 and after do not warrant any extensive reconsideration of my discussion and analysis of the role of the army in Jordan from 1921 to 1957. Nor do they affect my attempt to interpret the efforts of the regime to integrate the two Banks until that date. The main thrust of the challenge to the regime since November 1966 has come from the outside. Only if this challenge is taken up successfully by elements in the Jordanian officer corps can it realise its aims. Jordanians on the West Bank alone cannot so far take it to its successful end, so long as the regime can command the loyalty of its armed forces. Even though a dismemberment of Jordan (some might call it partition) by neighbouring Arab states (say, Syria, Iraq, and Saudi Arabia) is theoretically possible, it is practically unlikely.

What the radical states—especially Syria and the U.A.R.—realise perhaps but are, for the time being, unable to deal with is that no amount of outside support and agitation will be enough to overthrow the Jordan regime, or for that matter any other Arab regime, without the active support of the army.

Finally, the Arab-Israeli confrontation apart, both the form and context of conflict in the Arab Middle East have changed and shifted in the last five years. The further radicalisation of the regime in the U.A.R. and its most recent departure from its vaunted positive neutralism have contributed to the conditions that affect the new forms and contexts of conflict.[3] The same applies to the even more recent radicalisation of politics in Syria. The confrontation of so-called radical versus conservative Arab forces in the Yemen since September 1962 has had two serious consequences. First, it has produced the first inter-Arab war of this generation. Some might refer to it as the first Arab imperial war. Second, it has expanded the context of the political conflict in the Arab Middle East to include the Peninsula and now the more traditional area of inter-Arab conflict—the Fertile Crescent. The Arab Middle East is no longer an area for Great Power rivalry and conflict only. It is now an area for both that and inter-Arab confrontation.

---

[3] Throughout 1966, both Western correspondents in the Middle East and academic students of the area have suggested that a marked shift to the Left in the U.A.R. had been discernible.

What is tragic is that the conservative forces in the Peninsula, who have access to greater material wealth than the radical, are at least for the moment intent upon utilising much of this wealth to acquire the sophisticated modern instruments of violence. The prospect of inter-Arab relations there might be, as John Kelly suggested recently, of an Orwellian nightmare rather than the world of Pollyanna.[4]

What is also exercising the materially less fortunate Palestinian Arab and renders him easy prey to radical notions of salvation against Israel is the fact that in practically every country of the Arab Middle East the ruling groups that had "betrayed" him in 1948 have been overthrown—except for two. These are the Hashemites in Jordan and the Āl Saʻūd in Arabia. Their elimination thus easily becomes a prerequisite for salvation.

The educated, middle-class Palestinian Arab, living in Beirut, Damascus, Cairo and other Arab cities, feels great frustration. In Arab states all around him where *ancien régimes* have been overthrown he sees members of his own generation in positions of influence and power. His chances for an Arab state in Palestine in which by now he would have shared in power and perhaps governed were lost nearly twenty years ago. For this other Arabs were greatly to blame. Nor has his own generation in the radical states done very much for him. Only in the despised—some of them rich—dynastic states have thousands of his fellow-Palestinian Arabs been able to secure employment and a source of livelihood; but not eminent positions of power. The latter he now desires passionately, and these seem within his grasp only in Jordan. He cannot however fulfil his desire without violence. His elders among the Palestinians who had been in 1948 and until 1957 just as vehemently opposed to the dynastic state in Jordan eventually compromised and became reconciled to a share in power within the *status quo*. The young radical Arab now sees the possibility of attaining what his elders did without compromise—that is, by means of a violent revolution against the dynastic state in Jordan.

By way of conclusion one can merely, at this stage, emphasise what is simultaneously obvious and ominous. Inter-Arab violence has increased since November 13, 1966. Sabotage and assassination common in Aden and south Arabia for some time now have spread to Saudi Arabia and Jordan. The regimes in the United Arab Republic and Syria particularly appear to have activated a policy of confrontation with the conservative regimes—the remaining

---

[4] See J. B. Kelly, "The Future of Arabia", *International Affairs*, vol. 42, no. 4 (October 1966, pp. 619–640).

monarchies, or dynastic states, in the Arab Middle East.[5] At a time when the Palestine Liberation Organisation (PLO) went underground in Jordan, its Secretary, Ahmad Shuqayri, declared from Cairo that King Husayn would be eliminated. It is now assumed by the PLO that the physical elimination, i.e. assassination, of the Jordanian monarch will "liberate" Jordan and make way for a new radical regime that would proceed to liberate Palestine. In the meantime, reports of dissatisfaction among the ranks of PLO-supported guerilla formations with the PLO leadership and executive committee may, in turn, obfuscate the original objective, namely, to liberate Palestine. It is not therefore certain that assassinating the monarch in Jordan will lead to the vaunted salvation for Palestinian Arabs.

\* \* \*

Since going to press this Epilogue has acquired a trailer. While my study of the Jordan Army covers only the period 1921–1957, I deemed it necessary in discussing its peculiar role in the State of Jordan, to make certain remarks about inter-Arab state politics in general. These were included in the Conclusion to my study and in the first part of this Epilogue. The latter, as I made clear, was prompted by the Israeli Army retaliatory raid on Samu village in the Hebron area on 13 November 1966. Since then the six-day Arab-Israeli war which broke out on 5 June 1967 has had disastrous effects upon the Jordan Army. While paying tribute to its discipline, tenacity in defence, and general fighting quality, the Israelis also claimed to have destroyed four of its regiments. This would represent roughly under half of its combat force but not of its total strength.

The battle for Jerusalem was long and fierce. Apparently it took the Israeli forces at least 48 hours to secure the old city and its hilly approaches before it was able to push forward to other key points such as Bethlehem and Jericho and thus to extend its control to the Jordan river. With that Husayn lost the West bank of his kingdom to Israel and nearly a million West Jordanians found themselves under Israeli military occupation. An estimated 100,000 of these were reported to have fled to East Jordan, thus to become refugees for the second time in twenty years.

[5] See a series of articles by Muhammad Hasanayn Haykal, *Aṣl al-ḥikāya* (Origins of the Story) in *Al-Ahram* of Cairo (December 1966), esp. no. 6 in the series, *Al-hāshimiyyūn* (The Hashemites) (January 6, 1967).

This short, but blitzkrieg-type, war has shown that the Jordan Army is a garrison force best suited for limited combat operations. Lacking the support of an adequate airforce, this élite military force could not have offensive depth. Nor could the country's economic circumstances withstand the involvement of its armed forces in prolonged full-scale military operations beyond a very few days. King Husayn knew perfectly well the limitations of his small non-conscript army. The fact that its performance rendered it more troublesome to the Israelis than being just a mere nuisance in their all-out war on three fronts attests to its organisation, discipline, and combat quality.[6] It also indicates the good quality of line officers on the company and platoon level, a consequence of the emphasis placed on officer training since 1948.

If King Husayn had everything to lose, including a large part of his army which has been the main prop of his regime and dynasty, the question is why did he proceed to engage the Israelis in battle from the very first day of hostilities? Better still, why did he embark upon that dramatic flight to Cairo a few days before the outbreak of hostilities to sign with President Nasser a Joint Arab Defence Pact? Complete or even adequate answers to these and other related questions must await the availability of historical evidence. For the moment I wish only to entertain alternative explanations of his actions on the basis of Jordan's recent history and the history of its relations with the other Arab States in the last 10 years.

Ever since 1957 and until the Israeli Army raid on Samu, Jordan had been under fierce political attack from Egypt and Syria. King Husayn and his regime had been subjected to relentless invective from Cairo and Damascus in the name of Arab revolution, Arab nationalism and socialism. He had been vilified as the stooge of 'Anglo-American Imperialism' and the silent condoner of Israeli intrusion into the Middle East. As the grandson of the late King Abdullah, who had consistently since the late 1930's counselled moderation and a possible rapprochement with any Jewish state, he has been suspected of similar inclinations. What is worse, the Syrians attributed to Husayn the desire and intention to realise his grandfather's ambitious plan of a larger Hashemite kingdom which would include Syria.

It seems likely that young King Husayn was thrown off balance by the precipitous brinkmanship of the recognised leader of the hard Arab nationalist line. He could not have avoided considering Nasser's closing of the Straits of Tiran and the Gulf of Aqaba as being

[6] Casualty figures released by the Israeli Defence Ministry indicate that the heaviest losses to their armed forces were incurred on the Israeli–Jordan front.

directed also against Jordan. After all Aqaba is the only access Jordan has to the sea. His experience of repeated attempts by the so-called Arab revolutionaries to undermine his throne in the last ten years perhaps prompted him to seek an accommodation with Egypt in the hope that, during the crisis (before it escalated into a shooting war), President Nasser and the Syrians would desist from subverting his regime. On the other hand, it is also possible that like other Arabs he genuinely believed that Egypt's armed might was, this time, so superior to that of Israel that he could not afford to remain outside the pervue of a possible Arab victory. It is too much to assume that he either wished to meet Nasser's policy and thus strengthen his position in Jordan, or that he believed that his pact with Egypt would deter the Israelis from attacking his territory again so soon after Samu. Finally King Husayn may have simply acted by honouring the agreement which he had signed with Egypt. Whatever his considerations may have been it is now clear that the outcome of the hostilities has been militarily catastrophic for Jordan; for essentially King Husayn among all other heads of Arab states has lost heavily and significantly.

The loss of central Palestine, i.e. the West bank of Jordan (which may turn out to be temporary), has put the frontiers of the kingdom back to the pre-1948 line, that is, what used to be Transjordan. This is important territory not only because it contains one million of the country's population (total: 1·8 million), but because it has so far constituted the main source of Jordan's phenomenally thriving tourist trade (600,000 tourists in 1966 with receipts totalling £12–£15 million). It also comprises the most fertile agricultural land in the country. In any event, without air cover, the defence of that long jutting border with Israel was never feasible from the start.*

Egypt's loss of the Sinai, for instance, would not be of the same order. The Egyptian soldier can hardly be expected to consider the defence of that arid mass of desert and craggy hill territory as important as the defence of the Delta. As for Syria there was hardly a genuine gesture to relieve the pressure on the Jordanians during the first two days of the fighting.

The question has been raised what will happen to King Husayn now. While one should refrain from making predictions, I am inclined to argue that his political future will depend on political changes which may occur in the Arab countries generally. Although Jordan has suffered a crushing military defeat including the loss of perhaps its most important territory to Israel, King Husayn's honouring of his agreement with Egypt, his actions during the

* See pp. 115–116 *supra*.

conflict and the performance of his royal army have all tended to strengthen his position not only within what was left of Jordan in mid-June 1967 but even in the wider Arab world. He has shown indirectly that the Palestine Liberation Organisation and its vaunted Liberation Army were no more than political devices by the most belligerent Arab states aimed primarily against himself and his regime.

While possibilities of plots against the regime in Jordan remain it appears for the moment at least that an extremist Baathi regime in Syria may find it difficult to harrass it for some time to come. Much will depend on the outcome of any projected Arab Summit Conference to be held in Khartoum. In this instance, it would be naïve to suppose that such meetings will be free of inter-Arab recriminations. One might even envisage curious and perhaps surprising realignments between the Arab states. More specifically, however, what happens to Jordan will depend to a great extent on the attitude and behaviour of the militarily victorious Israelis.

Ever since 1954 the Jordan regime led by King Husayn had sought to prevent border incidents that could provoke an elicit Israeli armed retaliation. As a poor country, Jordan had moreover to remain economically dependent largely on Western aid and more recently partly on financial assistance from certain Arab states. For these and other reasons the King and his regime have been accused of not being interested in the liberation of Arab Palestine. Early in 1965 the PLO and its guerrilla army were created with the ostensible purpose of attacking Israel, but with the more immediate objective of embarrassing the Jordan regime to the advantage of Egypt and Syria. Yet Jordan, of all Arab countries since 1948, had made the effort to assimilate and integrate some 750,000 Palestinians as full citizens of the kingdom. Their constant exposure from the PLO's and other Arab states' propaganda forced the Jordanian government to maintain a garrison state not only *vis-à-vis* its Israeli neighbour which has again shown its devastatingly efficient organisation as a nation-in-arms but also in order to maintain security and stability within the country. This was mainly accomplished by the Jordan Army with its special relationship to the monarch. At no time, however, did this army hope to become a credible offensive military force, and as I have indicated in my study of the period 1921–1957 this development has been precluded by the limited economic, industrial and technological resources and potential of the country.

# Appendix

## THE TRANSJORDAN FRONTIER FORCE

THE TJFF was formed and trained during the first six months of its existence in Palestine. Its first recruits were selected from the Palestine Gendarmerie which had been formed in 1921 and disbanded in 1926 when it was decided to create the new TJFF. Several of the first NCOs and enlisted ranks of the new Force were thus men who already had five years of service behind them in the Palestine Gendarmerie.

The Arabs recruited and enlisted into the TJFF were mostly peasants (*fellahin*) from the villages of Palestine. Most of them were, however, literate. They made up about 70 per cent of the total of enlisted ranks in the Force. There were in addition some Sudanese ranks in the camel company of the Force before 1933, after which time this company was replaced by a new mechanised unit. There were also some Jews enlisted in the technical and administrative services of the Force, e.g. clerks, wireless operators, and electricians. Similarly town Arabs, with a better education than the *fellahin*, served in administrative duties. Circassians constituted by 1935 just under 25 per cent of the Force.

Apart from the complement of British senior commanders, the officer ranks consisted of Palestinian Arabs, Circassians, Syrian Arabs, some Sudanese and a few Jews.

Originally, in 1926–1927, the Force was composed of and organised in three squadrons of cavalry and one camel company, each about 120 strong. Each squadron comprised two companies. When in 1930 a mechanised company was added, there were altogether eight companies in the Force. By 1935 the camel company had also been replaced by a mechanised one, so that the Force still had eight companies altogether organised in three cavalry squadrons (or six companies) and two mechanised companies. The Force retained more or less this composition and organisation until it was disbanded in 1948.

The Force was commanded by a British lieutenant-colonel. At his headquarters in Zerqa, the Commanding Officer was assisted by a second-in-command, a British major, who was responsible for administration, workshops, quartermaster stores, and pay. There was in addition an Adjutant, also a British major, in charge of training and personnel. The assistant adjutant was a local Arab officer. Also at headquarters, the Senior Medical Officer was a British major, who was assisted by Arab or other local medical officers (e.g. Syrians and other). So was the Senior Veterinary Officer a British major who, in turn, was assisted by an Arab veterinary officer. Under the British Signal Officer at headquarters were local officers and NCOs responsible for the operation and maintenance of wireless stations. Many of these were Jews.

The three cavalry squadrons were commanded by British majors. So were the two mechanised companies. The normal tactical and reconnaissance unit, however, was the half-squadron or half-company, commanded usually by a local captain. Each of these consisted of two troops, thirty strong, again commanded by local lieutenants and captains.

Whereas in 1930 there were seventeen British officers in the Force, two in each of the four squadrons and companies, plus those in headquarters, in 1935 there were twenty-four. These comprised one lieutenant-colonel who was the Commanding Officer of the Force, seven majors, and sixteen captains. This complement of British officers retained more or less the same strength throughout the life of the Force.

# Index

(*Note:* The names of King Abdullah, King Husayn, and General Glubb recur throughout this monograph. I have not, therefore, made an entry for them in the Index)

Abidi, Aqil Hyder Hasan 51 n., 105, 121 n.
Abu'l Huda, Tawfiq Pasha 30 n., 118–119
Abu Nuwar, General Ali 22, 99, 103, 105 n., 107, 118, 144, 147, 149
  alleged conspiracy of 127–134
  Chief of General Staff 23, 51 n., 145
  King's ADC 23, 117
Abu Nuwar, Colonel Ma'n 130
Abu Taya, Auda 40
'Adwan 34, 47, 63–64, 65, 66 n.
'Adwan, Sultan Pasha 63
Air Force 25, 90 n., 111, 121, 122, 138, 149
Anglo-Jordanian Treaty (1946 and 1948) 11, 49, 50, 121, 123, 124–125, 126
Anglo-Transjordanian Treaty 1923 45, 47
Arab Collective Pact 134
Arab Constitutional Party 125
Arab–Israeli War (*see* Palestine War)
Arab Revolt 3, 36–37, 42
Armour 88–89, 90, 91
Armoured cars 22, 23
Artillery 22, 86–87, 90, 91
Ashton, Brigadier 120
al-'Askari, Ja'far Pasha 41 n.
al-Atasi, Nureddin 156

Baath 102, 104, 106, 108, 110, 122, 132
Baghdad Pact 117, 121, 122, 124
Banu Sakhr 34, 63
Brunton, Captain 58
budget 10–11

Cadet School 20, 24, 25, 26, 83, 87, 91, 92, 98
Childers, E. B. 147 n.

Chorley, K. 148
Churchill, Winston 43–45, 66
Circassians 70, 70–71 n., 87
civil disturbances 119–124
Constitution (1947) 49–50
Constitution (1952) 52–54, 118

*darak* 57, 58, 60–61
Desert Patrol Force 69, 72–73, 75, 76, 93

education 12–13
Eisenhower Doctrine 126
Electoral Law (1928) 48, 52
Engineers 22, 26, 84–86, 90, 91

al-Fāyiz, 'Ākif 106, 130
al-Fāyiz, Mithqal 63
Faysal, King 36, 37, 38, 40, 41 n., 42, 46, 57, 65, 67
Fertile Crescent 2, 7, 137, 156, 159
"Free Officers" 100

al-Geylani, Rashid Ali 73

Hanano, Ibrahim 67
Hashemite Kingdom of Jordan 6, 8, 49, 80, 108, 137, 148
Hejaz Railway 35, 36
Herbert, Sir Samuel 38–39, 57
al-Hiyari, General Ali 127, 127 n., 128, 129, 147, 151 n.
Huntington, S. P. 2 n., 20 n.
Husayn, Sharif of Mecca 3, 37
  King of Hejaz 41, 42, 44, 70
Husayni, al-Haj Amin 50–51

Ibn Saud, King 70
Independence party 46, 47, 61, 63, 65, 66 n., 67–68, 70 n.
Infantry 87–88
'Innab, Colonel Radi 127

Israel  15, 17, 111, 113, 136
  army of  16, 149
  border defence of  81
  raid on Jordan by  16, 120–121, 155, 158
*Istiqlal* party (*see* Independence party)

Janowitz, Morris  17, 25
Jordan Arab Party  51
Jordan University  25, 139

al-Khatib, Anwar  106, 157
al-Khulqi, Colonel Ali  59
Kirkbride, Sir Alec  14 n., 15, 38, 43 n., 50, 61 n., 66 n., 129
Kura  40, 47, 60 n., 60–61, 62

Lash, Brigadier Norman  75
Lasswell, H.  16, 16 n.
Lunt, Major-General James  113
Lawrence, T. E.  44
Lewis, B.  5 n., 77 n., 88 n.

al-Ma'āyiṭa, Colonel Muhammad  103, 105, 105 n., 128, 129 n., 147
al-Majali, Hazzaʻ  123
al-Majali, Qadr  36, 37, 69 n.
Military Academy  20, 24, 25, 98 n.
al-Mufti, Said  71 n., 123, 129
Muhammad Ali  34–35
al-Mulqi, Fawzi  110, 120
Muslim Brethren  120

al-Nabhani, Shaykh Taqi al-Din  120
Nabulsi, Sulayman  11, 51, 106 n.
  government of  81, 125, 126–130
National Assembly  50, 125
National Guard  14, 17, 79–81, 110–111, 113, 117, 120, 121, 151, 158
National Socialists  11, 110, 122, 125, 129
Nationality Law (1928)  47
Nimr, Abd al-Halīm  51, 129

Ottoman administration  34, 35–36
Ottoman empire  2

Palestine  8, 13, 15
  annexation by Jordan of  71, 77, 80, 90, 152, 157, 161
  Arab Rebellion in  73

Palestine Gendarmerie  71
Palestine Government in Gaza  103
Palestine Liberation Organisation (PLO)  30, 54, 136, 136 n., 143, 151, 156, 157 n., 161
Palestine Question  50–51, 81, 138
Palestine refugees  9–10, 16, 25, 26, 54, 84, 85
Palestine refugees in Legion  25–27, 28–29, 48, 52–53, 85–86, 90–91, 101, 119–120, 144, 157, 160
Palestine War  7, 22, 49, 51, 52, 74, 78, 84, 91, 120, 137, 147
Palestinians  9, 10, 13, 139, 144, 147, 156
  in Jordanian government  53–54
  political opposition of  157–161
Peake, F. G.  4–5 n., 14, 41, 46, 46 n., 47, 57, 58, 66, 89 n.
  Inspector-General of *darak*  59–60
  Legion Commander  68–69, 76
  organisation of Reserve Force by  62–70
Philby, H. St. John  39 n., 44, 45 n., 60 n.
political parties  48, 50–51

Quartermaster  21, 22

Rapoport, David C.  17 n.
Reserve Mobile Force  46 n., 57–58, 61, 62–64, 67, 69
Rhodes Armistice 1949  102, 103
Rifā'ī, Samir Pasha  30 n.
al-Rikabi, General Riḍā Pasha  41 n.
al-Rimawi, Abdullah  102, 104, 106
Royal Air Force (RAF)  47, 63, 64, 65
  assistance to Legion of  4, 68, 72
Rustow, D. A.  24 n., 76 n., 142 n.

San Remo Conference  37
*shurṭa*  57
Signals  22, 26
Staff College  98 n.
Suez Crisis 1956  124–125
Syrian Congress 1920  37, 42

Ṭabbara, Bahjat  128
Talal, King  52, 104, 106, 109
Ṭaliʻ, Rashid Bey  59, 61
Technical Services  89–91

al-Tel, Colonel Abdullah  99
  conspiracy of  99–108, 131, 132, 133 n., 144
  Governor of Jerusalem  22–23
Templer, Sir Gerald  121
  mission to Jordan of  113–114, 122–123
Training Centre  20 n., 26, 83–84, 87, 89, 92
Training School  69

Transjordan Frontier Force (TJFF)  70–72, 162–163

de Vigny, Alfred  2 n.

Wahhabis  34, 63, 68, 70

Young, Brigadier Peter  14 n., 15, 100–101 n.